E-PUBLISHING

Concept and Practical Approaches

E-PUBLISHING

Concept and Practical Approaches

Edited by

P.P. SINGH

SANDHIR SHARMA

DEEP & DEEP PUBLICATIONS PVT. LTD.

F-159, Rajouri Garden, New Delhi - 110 027

E-PUBLISHING

ISBN 81-7629-614-7

Printed in India at ELEGANT PRINTERS,
A-38/2, Mayapuri Industrial Area, Phase-I, New Delhi-110 064.

Published by DEEP & DEEP PUBLICATIONS PVT. LTD.,
F-159, Rajouri Garden, New Delhi - 110 027 • Ph. : 25435369, 25440916
E-mail : deep98@del3.vsnl.net.in • ddpbooks@yahoo.co.in
Showroom :
2/13, Ansari Road, Daryaganj, New Delhi - 110 002 • Telefax : 23245122

CONTENTS

Preface

E-Publishing has always been harder than it looks. Not that it's ever really tried to pawn itself off as an easy way to make a living. Long hours, low pay, less time for lunch than most people spend doing their laundry. Granted, there's a kind of shabby glamour attached to the fourth estate, a sort of folk hero profile evoking rumpled cotton shirts, smoky bars, frayed nervous systems, and dedicated cynicism. Both on the street and in the newsroom, archetypal images of the press corps seem to capture the quintessential traits of our culture. Wise and kindly editors, brave, rumptious, and robust reporters. Rugged. Tough. Independent. Savvy. Incorruptible. Exhausted.

And everybody hates them. Since the hate is based on fear – fear of what they will say, to whom they'll say it, what they will print, what they will find out that sources didn't tell them, and what that will eventually cost – hostility is usually expressed as a twisted type of courtship.

The title of this book has several parts, and promises many things. Mostly, it promises to raise questions about the scenario just described; not to trash the use of on-line media by the nation's reporters, but, rather, to explore some of the secondary and tertiary impacts that usage may exert on how e-publishing is framed in the cultural sphere, not just conducted in the professional one. It is, intentionally, a mix of material, looking at how it feels to do on-line publishing, how it affects those who consume it, different ways that media scholars might go about trying to understand it better, and the likely social and cultural impact of Internet-like technologies on the recipient world – that is to say, on the public at whom all this electronic information is eventually aimed.

Drawing from the emerging scholarly work in this field, and from the real-life experiences of working journalists who often watch their professional world being transformed one e-mail message at a time, we examine why publishers use the Internet, what changes it makes in how they approach doing their jobs, and what differences they see in conducting their daily newsgathering via this medium than any other. We also look at why and when they don't use on-line media, and what the impact of the decisions to use or not use the 'Net may mean for the outer world whose perceptions of itself are so often shaped by journalistic portrait.

We are highly thankful to Dr. K.N.S. Kang, Director, Punjab College of Technical Education for providing us the motivation to work on this project. We are grateful to all others who have contributed for the preparation of this book. We acknowledge with thanks the help of various librarians and authors of various books from whom we have heavily drawn upon the material of several publications. We would also like to thank the publishers for taking up this book for publication and bringing it out in time.

P.P. SINGH
SANDHIR SHARMA

1

Publishing in a Distributed Communication Architecture

Introduction

The architectures of information technologies reflect the societal power relationships they embody. This observation is most poignant at moments of convergence, when old social systems struggle to maintain their integrity within the context of the architecture defined by the new technology. Journalism, we contend, now finds itself at such a juncture, as it reflects on a set of mature norms and canons established during the reign of mass circulation newspapers, and as it looks ahead to computer-based information network technologies.

Newspaper and television production can be imagined as having an hour-glass shape: Large amounts of information flow in linear fashion from many sources through a narrow, journalistic "neck" and on to a mass of readers or viewers. The ability to control this linear flow rests almost exclusively with the journalist. The result is an asymmetry in *social* power, with the scales clearly tipped toward the journalist. Indeed, this inequality of power helps define the way society regards news work and gives rise to public and professional concerns about such concepts as credibility and objectivity. Thus, for example, one key component of objectivity, *balance* in news content, becomes an issue for journalism because of the perceived *imbalance* in power between journalists and their clients.

The convergence of linear mass media technologies with nonlinear computer technologies, depicted in Figure 1.1 , raises the issue of what the social relationships between information providers and receivers will look like in any hybrid technology.

At such moments of convergence, the meaning of basic concepts, which might have seemed obvious to an earlier generation, demand re-examination and explication. In that vein, we first examine the essential product of journalistic endeavor-news-and consider it as a special category of survival-enhancing information. Then, we discuss the process of news creation in the context of mass media technology. Finally, we speculate about the durability of the journalistic institution in the age of network-based information technologies.

News and Survival

Journalists report, edit, and distribute a special category of information called news. The unique character of news has to do with a basic need common to all living things for information about novel or threatening events in their surroundings. Imagine the moment when some prehistoric ancestor out on a hunt encountered a sudden rustling in the jungle bush. From an information-processing perspective, the challenge for this unkempt wag is to pay attention to the novel event, classify it based on limited information, and reach a behavioral decision about how to respond, all in real time. This evolutionary imperative, manifested by the question, "Will I be its dinner, or will it be mine?" is driven by the ability to process limited information under time pressure efficiently.

Across the millennia, civilization arguably has advanced, but the information processing problem (i.e., understanding novel events in a complex environment with limited time and resources) has remained remarkably constant. If anything, the problem has become more complex because our information needs have far exceeded the range of direct sensory observation. Information-processing technologies thus perform the critical task of locating survival-specific events at distant locations, collecting raw data about them, and packaging them into messages called news. True, sometimes novel information not directly related to survival is created by those mediating technologies. A story about a frog with two heads, for example, might make the newspaper, but it is not, in the sense used here, strictly defined as news.

If news can be thought of as survival-relevant information about novel events, then the process of news work becomes an important phenomenon for study. In what follows, we offer some preliminary thoughts about the relationship of news to the technologies that are used in its creation.

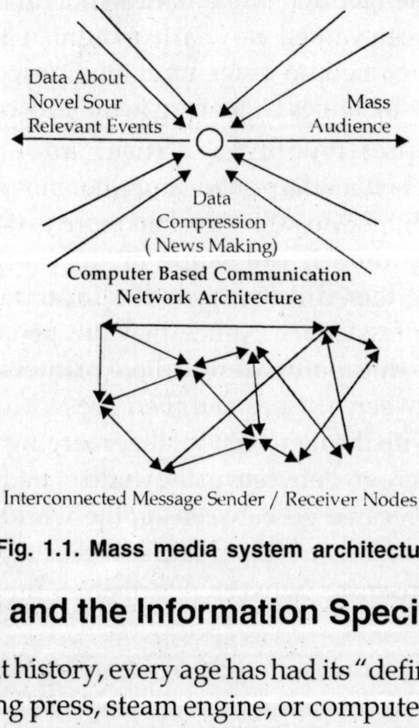

Fig. 1.1. Mass media system architecture

Technology and the Information Specialist

Throughout history, every age has had its "defining technology" (e.g., the printing press, steam engine, or computer) and, in each of those arbitrarily delineated "ages," certain prominent characteristics or anthropomorphic qualities of the defining technologies are commonly adopted as positive societal and individual traits. As we show later in this chapter, the social role of the information specialist is always negotiated within the context of the dominant or defining media technology at any historical moment.

In thinking about technology, we are less interested in its physical implementation and more concerned, to borrow a phrase from computer science, with its system architecture. Specifically, technology is process, with its architecture manifested in any number of physical implementations. War drums and newspapers are both manifestations of a technology where message senders encode information into abstract symbols whose meaning is understood by their receivers. In one case, the technology, language, is implemented by using hollow logs, and in the other, printing presses are used. It is important to understand that while the messages sent by drum might contain novel survival-relevant information, they are not news unless they are the product of a mass medium system. This is illustrated by the fact that while information about novel events seems to have been valued very early in human history, the word "news" did not come into usage until the European invention of movable type by Johannes Gutenberg in the 15th century.

While unquestionably a critical advance in human communication, neither the printing press nor movable type enabled a true mass medium. Movable type had more to do with regularity and uniformity than it did scope or, to use today's jargon, penetration. Neither did it trigger the formation of a class of information professionals. Notice that the people who created newspapers at this point were called printers, reflecting the relationship between artisans and their press. Moreover, printers stood as peers with the merchants of the emerging middle class. As the merchants were go-betweens in the world of trade and commerce, so the printers became go-betweens in the world of information. These two observations are important, because they imply there was considerable consensus between information provider and client about content.

The word "journalism" did not come into usage until 1833. That almost exactly coincides with the emergence of mass circulation newspapers in the eastern United States, a feat made possible by high-speed rotary steam presses. Those presses were able to take one message and very rapidly produce enormous numbers of exact replicas at extremely low cost. This added the important characteristic of scope to newspapers, and represents the implementation of a truly mass medium.

The production and consumption of a mass circulation newspaper might be likened to that of a Hershey bar. The first step in the production of the taste treat is to collect and to dry large quantities of chocolate beans at some remote tropical location, then ship them to a central production facility. At this point the raw material is concentrated into a powerful extract or essence. Only a small amount of that extract is then added to a vat of other ingredients, from which huge numbers of perfectly identical candy bars are produced and distributed.

Similarly, in news work, vast amounts of data are gathered from around the world and collected at some central production facility. A similar process of concentration or compression then takes place, where data are reduced to a potent extract or essence called stories, and then combined to create huge numbers of replicas called newspapers.

Mass media architectures are sufficiently complex as to require a great deal of specialization and differentiation. The collectors have power in the process to the degree they control raw material. Their title, "reporter," suggests a relationship between them and the events they cover. Editors, by contrast, derive a great deal of power based largely on their position in the message concentration process. Notice that their title (editor) refers to their relationship to the product (data/news), not to the replication technology, as was the case with the printer. Editors reside in the production facility, the newsroom, at exactly the narrowest point of information flow, where compression or condensation of the raw data takes place. Editors work at the task of data compression, creating uniform story units that enable the printing or broadcasting technology to infinitely replicate them. This power is manifested in all their editorial functions. For instance, the role of assignment editor constitutes a form of filtering Beniger calls preprocessing. This filtering role is most evident at the moment of story selection, and has been conceptualized as gate keeping and agenda setting. Copy editors, too, exert an enormous amount of power based on their ability to look within stories and actually manipulate the raw data provided by the reporters, giving it meaning by imposing structure. Given the amount of real power they have in the creation of "meaning" in the news, it's ironic that the copy editing function is depicted as one of the most tedious and least glamorous of all jobs in journalism.

Regardless of their specific function, editorial power derives from the fact that very small expenditures of energy are amplified to have enormous reach into the mass population of message receivers.

In turn, the reader receives only a diluted "dose" of the concentrated data in the form of their exact replica copy. This is important to understand because, unlike earlier days of printing, in the era of mass media, message producers, particularly for the elite media, are no longer the peers of the message receivers. Editors now control content; it is precisely their job to embed meaning or structure in the raw data. This is stated in the agenda-setting dictum that editors do not tell their readers what to think, but they do tell them what to think about.

The obvious need for professionalization at this stage of development can be seen by imagining what happens when a batch of chocolate extract goes bad at the candy plant. Of course, the gravity of mistake is amplified by the process of concentration, and the market ends up being flooded by bitter tasting candy bars. To avoid that catastrophe the concentration process must become highly standardized, and controlled by skilled technicians.

Likewise, with the advent of mass circulation newspapers, the standard production of news became the job of a professional elite largely due to a concern with quality control. For instance, if journalists wrote each story out by hand, a factual error might be confined to just one copy of the newspaper. However, when a journalist commits an error within the architecture of a mass replication information system such as a newspaper, it will be faithfully reproduced thousands, or even millions of times. (This line of reasoning can be extended to television news production because, while it differs from newspapers in important ways, broadcast journalism is obviously still a mass media system.)

Thus, standardization and canonization help motivate the generation of "good" information. The discussion of what "good" means within the normative language of the professional revolves around the central theme of truth. The practice of techniques to insure accuracy, balance, and fairness are all deemed important to the degree they help achieve truth.

While those norms lay out a practical proscriptive agenda on how to achieve the goal of objective truth, they do not really say why that goal is important. It is at this point that conceptualizing news as novel, survival-dependent information becomes valuable. Evolution has endowed the species with a set of psychological heuristics to help insure the organism attends to and processes "good" information from the proximate environment. The visual system, for instance, is designed to attend to rapid or novel motion. Humans employ sophisticated heuristics in the assessment of risk, with outcome probabilities over weighted to emphasize events taking place nearby. Stocking and Gross discuss the role these cognitive processes play in journalistic reporting.

However, humans living in complex societies have come to need information well beyond the range of their senses. Journalistic norms, then, take on the job of psychological heuristics in generating "good" information, only at a societal level. That means an account of an event is "good" to the degree that such an account will help in making important decisions about it. This can really be seen as a leap across levels of analysis, where the idea of "true" at a social level corresponds to "real" at a psychological level. Norms such as accuracy and balance are, then, heuristic responses specific to mass media. They are intended to insure that the media system generates messages that are "true" accounts about events to the degree that they can be processed by readers or viewers as if they were directly experienced and "real." The question now has to do with the kinds of psychological and social heuristics appropriate to the next generation of information systems.

The Shape of The Net

While it is true that the Internet (or Net) may represent as significant an innovation as movable type, it is equally true that the idea of a "multimedia" personal computer system has come to be accepted with only limited understanding of its true meaning or potential long-term impact as a way to communicate. Touting "multimedia" as a feature might sell computers, but it also overlooks the important defining character of the computer as a communication technology; that is, its distributed architecture. Even within communication research, the topic has come to be identified as "computer mediated communication," which describes the technology's physical implementation, and not its architecture. Similarly, if newspapers were typified by the physical implementation of the technology rather than their system architecture, we would study them as "printing press-mediated communication," rather than mass media.

However, the true power of the Internet resides in the way it is hooked up, that is, in its architecture. The flow of information through a network is nonlinear, and distributed across a vast number of sender-receiver nodes. Because message production can take place at any node in the network, information distribution is a diffuse, parallel process, unlike the compressed, serial process of mass media. This can be seen in the transmission of the simplest e-mail message. A message may become fragmented during transmission due to the packet switching protocol employed by the TCP/IP standard employed by the Internet. Thus, different parts of the message may take an entirely different route across the Net before reuniting at their destination.

McLuhan argued that technologies are extensions of human processes, and the information technologies are extensions of the central nervous system. That logic makes the idea of a computer network based on a parallel distributed-processing architecture compelling. Rumelhart and McClelland describe the architecture of human learning and memory in precisely those terms. Since their watershed work first appeared, the body of evidence supporting the idea that the brain is wired into such networks has grown steadily. Computer designers have even come to borrow from this psycho-physiological model, constructing "neural net" programs that have the capacity to learn, and link super-computers together in "massively parallel, distributed" architectures. Neither is the similarity between the architecture of the brain and the Net lost on the so-called cyberpunk genre of science fiction, in which computer hackers "jack in" to make a seamless connection between their nervous system and the Net.

Durability of Journalistic Practice on the Internet

Data concentration is unnatural in distributed network architectures that facilitate dispersed message production. Thus, the application of canons or standards produced to deal with mass media systems may be unnatural, unrealistic, and practically impossible to apply in a setting where any participant is equally likely to be a message producer as a message receiver. Members of such a system are more likely to be true peers, further eroding social codes borne out of the need to protect against the amplification of error fostered by power imbalances. First, the reportorial act of data collection is dispersed, with data collection potentially taking place at any node on the Net. Second, and most importantly, editors may lose control of the agenda.

Movable type brought standardization and regularity to symbolic human communication. The rotary steam press added scope. Networked computers now add resolution to information technology, manifested in the inherent interactivity of the architecture. Now, journalists have to examine what their role will be in the context of such parallel distributed communication architectures. An initial investigation might begin by re-examining some of the essential functions performed by journalists in a mass media system.

Data Collection and Verification

Collecting information and certifying its factual accuracy is central to journalism. Thinking back to the role of news as the presentation of survival-specific information, the demand for factual accuracy is obvious. The importance journalism places on verification can be seen in the practice of double checking sources or getting more than one source for a "story." Verification gives journalistic communication credibility and believability, characteristics which are critical if information is to be useful in survival-dependent decision making.

In practice, editors may play a part in creating story facticity, but this is usually only in a backstop or quality control mode and is facilitated by their position at the narrowest part of the hourglass architecture, where vast amounts of data are reduced for transmission as a single message to a mass audience.

By contrast, it is difficult to imagine how this verification function might work in a distributed architecture and, in its absence, the burden of verification may thus shift back to the audience. Interactive information searches will call on the users to employ a set of highly effortful cognitive skills they may not now possess.

Newspaper journalism is elegant in its ability to provide guideposts for readers. The newspaper's nameplate, a story's location in the newspaper, and the elemental writing style all aid readers in their information assessment task. Those signposts, however, will largely be absent on the Net. Judgments about credibility will have to be even more contextual and site specific. For instance, the user of a computer discussion group focusing on Italian cars might judge it to be a highly credible site for information about rebuilding an Alfa Romeo engine, but not think much of it as a source of information about race relations.

The natural response to the absence of the finely tuned societal level heuristics offered by mass media is to revert to the primitive psychological heuristics. That course, however, is fraught with danger. For instance, a key reason television consistently scores higher than newspapers as a credible source for news has to do with the idea that seeing is believing. However, postmodern media critics such as Baudrillard detail how advanced media technology simulates events in such a way as to make them "hyper-real," that is, better than real. The idea of virtual reality suggests stimuli that may be "real" or plausible, from the point of view of the user's perceptual systems, but have no foundation in the physical world. The computer-generated images of human forms "morphing" into insects is but one example.

In short, what may be needed in the age of distributed communication architectures is an even more ambitious effort at teaching "news literacy." While humans require no training in the use of the visual cortex, they may, however, need a new set of skills to evaluate the images and text available on a computer network. Notice that making the computer "user friendly" has mainly to do with making the interface more psychologically intuitive, and does not generally address issues of information evaluation or assessment. Furthermore, journalism is simply not "up to" instructing the mass audience in how to read the paper or watch TV news. To do so would require the application of journalistic norms to each and every information package. The analog of such a process in a mass media system would be to have an editor hand deliver individual copies of the newspaper to subscribers' doorsteps, and then to sit down over coffee with them as they go over the morning's news.

Data Compression

Controlling the amount and content of news on the Information Superhighway (a.k.a. data compression) is a current hot button for journalists, and the function to which editors cling with the most tenacity. Journalists increasingly reassure themselves that even cyber-journalism on the Net will still need editors to tell "audiences" what is important.

However, information compression is not particularly well-suited as a data reduction technique in a distributed architecture such as the Net. Computer science and engineering are focusing on more efficient forms of filtering than compression for this architecture. That implies complex and potentially egalitarian power relationships between information managers and end users. This might be manifest in the role of a pathfinder rather than agenda setter, with this latter function falling back to the user, whether editors like it or not. Editors derive their power from being able to say, "Because of my position in the architecture you have to pass through me to find out what's important." On the Net the pathfinder might tell the user, "Tell me what you need and I will guide you through this complex environment."

How this editor-pathfinder role might develop is, of course, unpredictable. What professional and ethical norms might be associated with this emergent role? Will pathfinders be more like social workers or more like insurance brokers? Whose interests will be served by the pathfinders' work – the pathfinders themselves, their corporate or public service governors, the established economic formation?

Moreover, some part of path finding, perhaps even a very substantial share, may exist one day as a "job" for a computer program and not for a human editor at all. This development would represent an embodiment of the Turing test and would raise metaphysically profound questions about human agency and computers. For instance, the concept of "newsworthiness" can be represented as a mathematical algorithm. The computer program, based on records of the user's previous information-seeking behavior, searches the Net, and pre-selects, or filters information for presentation. This interactive data resolution process does not exist in a mass media architecture. Such search engines raise obvious questions, including who is doing the programming, will citizens lose the opportunity for shared cultural experiences, and who will have access to details about the users' interest and behaviors?

The Net probably will not kill the mass media, but it will most certainly reshape them. It is, therefore, professionally dangerous and more than a little shortsighted for news workers to deny this broad-gauge certainty. It is also equally imprudent for communication scholars, policymakers, and the public to ignore these trends. Who knows? One day soon perhaps the term *information specialist* will sound every bit as romantic and every byte as nourishing as the title "foreign correspondent" did a century ago.

2

Public Opinion: Gleaning Points of View Electronically

Introduction

As journalists have increasingly colonized video tax and e-mail systems ranging from CompuServe to the Internet, and as public relations and public information specialists have increasingly turned to electronic means to disseminate their materials, the old rules by which information is evaluated are increasingly hard to apply, sometimes to the point of seeming irrelevant. Sometimes the "news gatherers" aren't journalists, which means they may or may not be familiar with the old canons of professional practice to begin with, and "town hall" discussions and electronic "polls" may be conducted by computer specialists rather than community leaders or social scientists. In the current rapid evolution to electronic news, are electronic opinions — regardless of who gathers them — any different from information taken from books or periodicals or press releases, or gleaned from the journalist's traditional staple, the interview, or summarized from more standard kinds of surveys?

As Elizabeth Eisenstein pointed out, the print revolution was accompanied by a number of taken-for-granted but profound changes in our concept of information sourcing. For the first time, title pages specified dates and places of publication and identified individual authors by name. In the electronic era, these powerful anchors are often not available for data gathered electronically. As a result, the reputation of the publisher and the credentials of the author — perhaps even the quality of the printing and binding — may no longer "cue" our reactions. The tradition of book publishing fixed the fluid form of manuscripts, hand-copied for centuries, adding the presence of title pages along with the ability to make an indefinite number of identical copies. Again, on-line differences are dramatic. Electronic texts can be copied indefinitely with high fidelity to the original, but they can also be altered undetectably. And what editor is responsible for the errors in electronic material?

In at least some of her work, Eisenstein is a technological determinist. She argues that the development of print was inseparable from the emergence of the Renaissance in science and the religious reformation, although she generally stops short of attributing these grand historical transformations directly to the influence of paper and ink. We needn't share her quasi-determinist philosophy, though, to argue that electronically transmitted texts are fundamentally different from texts published in more traditional ways.

In this chapter, I discuss the issue of the special but often illusionary status of information gathered through the new electronic media by considering two specialized cases: electronic opinion "polling" and the electronic gathering of opinions from scientific experts. In both cases, the ability to "tap into" cyberspace seems to enhance substantially an illusion of consensus experienced in the information-gathering process. While these problems of distinguishing between real and superficial consensus did not begin with new communication technologies, their appearance in these novel media may make it harder for us to recognize them.

Public's Opinion

Once upon a time, newspaper journalists relied on "man on the street" interviews to tap into the opinions of ordinary citizens. One of the successes of journalism education has been to teach young, would-be journalists about the perils that are described by terms such as sample bias, sampling error, and response bias — that is, the danger of assuming that John Q. Public actually speaks for his or her peers. But newspapers still publish the results of call-in surveys of their own readers as if these revealed deep truths and generalizable opinions about contemporary social conditions. And to take us from bad to worse, just as we thought we were making at least some progress here, along comes the electronic poll.

Electronic opinion polls are not only severely biased in the way of all nonrandom samples, but, at their very best, they can only hope to reflect the opinions of the technologically elite, only one of the "publics" that modern democracy is supposed to serve. For a call-in or mail-in "survey," only those who most care – and, in all probability, whose views are most extreme – will respond. For electronic polls, only those who most care AND who happen to have computers with modems AND are reached by the poll inquiry will respond. The result is a profoundly biased research sample, built right into the electronic polling process. Electronic polling might be harmless under some conditions. But the phenomenon of being able to generate swift replies from a broad range of locations and lifestyles creates a strong illusion of representativeness, which is not harmless at all.

Suspect polls are one thing. But what's wrong with the electronic town hall concept? Isn't this one of the important ways in which these new technologies will make democracy work more smoothly? Alas, only a "democracy" of the technologically elite is possible, and even this is a bit shaky. The great majority of U.S. citizens still don't own a computer, let alone a modem or a connection to the Internet highway, and this is greatly skewed by income. U.S. Census Bureau data for 1993 reported that 65% of households with incomes over $75,000 had computers, but only 6.5% of those with incomes under $10,000 and about one third of those in the upper middle range ($35,000-$55,000) did. Electronic discussions typically capture only a tiny minority of these; many users habitually "lurk" on the electronic sidelines, watching and listening from a virtual distance, while other, more assertive ones shape "public" discussions to their own agendas.

Of course, this is not too different from what happens in the non-virtual world, and it needn't be all bad. If a school board calls a meeting to approve new health textbooks, chances are only a vocal minority with an ax to grind will actually speak. Self-government depends on distinguishing between the protestations of those few and the ground swell of community sentiment, but should – and does -respond to the strength of peoples' convictions as well as the numbers who hold particular opinions. It seems reasonable, many times, to argue that those who choose to attend public meetings, who have taken the time to educate themselves and form a reasoned opinion, who are members of a particular "public" with a clear stake in a particular issue, *should* have the power and the right to dictate the outcome of that issue disproportionate to their own numbers. Everyone is given the same opportunity to speak out; there's a case to be made for listening most carefully to those who have made an active effort to exercise that right.

But electronic discussions are not, and probably never will be, equally available to everyone. Public terminals in libraries will hardly solve the accessibility problem, any more than public availability of encyclopedias has solved the problem of public education. Indeed, assuring truly equal access to information – that is, ensuring the emergence of an informed citizenry – in an increasingly complex information environment is one of the unsolved problems of modern democracies. Public education itself is not a sufficient solution; witness the breakdown of the public school system in the United States and the current "science literacy" debate. Sociologists – perhaps most prominently Daniel Bell have speculated that technologically complex societies will call into existence new forms of governance. The emergence and common use of technologically sophisticated communication systems raise parallel challenges.

Electronic Scientist

Because the Internet was, for many years, primarily an academic researcher's system, developed with National Science Foundation and Department of Defense sponsorship for the purpose of linking researchers with similar interests who were geographically remote from one another, it's not surprising that this remains one of the system's most important, if not always most visible, uses. And as the flexibility and "reach" of Internet-based systems has expanded, science-oriented networking has exploded at least as much as any other kind. But the case of scientific consensus remains unique within the more general subject of the emergence of electronic communities. First of all, there's considerable divergence within the scientific community itself as to when, whether and to what extent scientific findings – especially preliminary scientific findings – should be publicized at all. Scientific popularizers, for a variety of reasons, risk losing status among their colleagues. According to the dominant view, popularization invites public misinterpretation and can veer dangerously close to self-promotion.

The prominent *New England Journal of Medicine (NEJM)* insists that research published within its pages not have been the subject of previous discussion in the popular press. This prevents the distribution of findings that have not yet been subject to the scrutiny of the peer review process, protecting the public from untested information being accepted as scientific or medical fact by the unwary press. But it also maintains *NEJM*'s national prominence as a source of the latest and greatest "breakthrough" medical research. The first set of arguments may explain why research reports would not be publicized until they have been accepted for publication, but not why discussion should be suppressed until findings actually appear in print. Under circumstances like these, it is little wonder that only a minority of scientific researchers habitually appear in the media, a phenomenon Goodell tried to capture by her use of the term "visible scientist" to describe these media-friendly few.

This is a serious issue. Popularization that is too swift and insufficiently accurate has been blamed for legitimizing the preliminary claims of "cold fusion" researchers in Utah and for fueling the uninformed public fears of an earthquake predicted for New Madrid, Missouri. Popular "misrepresentations" of fact are said to be the source of public outcries over pesticide use (alar on apples), agricultural biotechnology (bovine somatotropin), and other food safety issues ("Jack In the Box" hamburgers).

Overlooked in all of these explanations, however, is the political character of science. Scientists are engaged in intense competition for recognition, prestige, and funding, and maintaining elite control over scientific accounts of truth can serve to limit public access to information needed to make good decisions about what risks people should and should not be willing to undergo. How much authoritarian control over scientific information is actually benign, whose interests are most clearly at stake here, and what role does (or should) popularization through the media play?

These controversies spill over into the electronic world. On the one hand, prominent scientific institutions have gleefully jumped on the electronic bandwagon, using various electronic services to make their expertise available to journalists and the general public – and to make their own in-house experts more visible in the news. On the other, dialogue among scientists, increasingly, takes place in virtual communities, a phenomenon that should be taken seriously as a factor in shaping the tone, direction, and outcome of scientific debate and the ultimate emergence of scientific consensus. But virtual communities are not exactly the same as traditional ones, and electronic debate is not exactly the same as the dialogue that has shaped science to date. The ramifications of this shift have yet to be fully explored or understood.

Scientific journals emerged from written correspondence among members of the early scientific societies. This tradition of "writing in" to these societies, to share one's own experimental results with one's colleagues, remains a vitally important part of science today. The motives behind this exchange of expert letters provided the foundation of today's scientific publishing. A key component of the scientific worldview is the belief that this kind of open sharing of information and public dialogue on its interpretation will, eventually, distill "truth." Electronic scientific dialogue seems to have emerged as a natural extension of these earlier traditions.

Less obvious is the fact that this dialogue traditionally took place within closed circles, among "gentlemen" (almost exclusively, that is among Caucasian males of upper class European origins). Opening scientific dialogue to the unqualified and uninitiated – first through popularization efforts, now through the Internet - challenges the traditional social structure of science. In the long run, this promises to extend the debate over the truth status of scientific data by opening up scientific discussions to anyone computer literate enough to figure out how to access them, scientific credentials notwithstanding. Is this a good thing, or not? Democratic access to scientific information appears to be a good thing. But this doesn't necessarily mean that anyone can "do science" nor are all scientific experts equal.

Electronic discussions have nurtured a new form of visible scientist. Even though scientists were "early adopters" of Internet as an everyday communications medium, that doesn't mean that the scientists who appear in cyberspace are a representative sample of the scientific community, any more than those who respond to an electronic poll are a representative sample of the population as a whole – or even a representative sample of the population of computer uses. And expert consensus is not the same thing as majority rule; not all opinions have equal weight, and here highly issue-specific expert qualifications must become an important criterion for the value of opinion, to be considered alongside (as for public opinion) degree of conviction and willingness to speak out on the one hand, and representativeness on the other.

Just as "public" opinion among the Internet users and lurkers ought not to be mistaken for public opinion in general, participation in Internet-based scientific discussion is highly likely to be skewed, and should not be taken as representative. Most modern-day scientists know how to send e-mail. Most of them are usually too busy to spend a lot of time chatting, however, whether electronically or in person. Therefore, it is likely that electronic discussions of scientific issues contain proportionately fewer active scientific researchers and more interested bystanders

than would be found, say, at a scientific meeting. The "brakes" provided by the review and editorial procedures followed at good scientific journals, however imperfect, are almost entirely missing in the electronic world. This has a lot of potential for accelerating the rumor-formation process about scientific topics. Add to these difficulties the new opportunities for information subsidy presented to the public relations departments at universities and research centers, who are anxious to promote their experts as THE experts in a given specialty area through new on-line services, such as Profnet, that are designed to link journalists with scientific sources, and it becomes clear that the value of Internet-based scientific opinion is at least as problematic as the value of Internet-based "opinion polls."

At the same time, mainstream science has been accused, with considerable justification, of being sexist, racist, and elitist, an "old boys'" dialogue in which some explanations are arbitarily privileged over others and in which social group membership and institutional prestige may be as significant as the soundness of scientific conclusions. Scientific progress is sometimes accomplished, as Thomas Kuhn pointed out, in great leaps rather than incremental steps. But in between these great leaps (or "paradigm shifts," in Kuhn's terms), information that doesn't fit the dominant paradigm is largely ignored, especially if it is generated by people outside the traditional scientific "in-group." So to compound the problem, it is rarely safe to assume that truth is always the province of the best credentialed scientist at the most prestigious university.

Could electronic information dissemination increase the odds that a "maverick" scientific opinion that indeed turned out to explain some phenomenon better than the mainstream one would be recognized early on? Perhaps, or perhaps not. Perhaps electronic systems, which require a certain minimal level of technological expertise and equipment, might even be further biased against maverick views. No one, journalist or scientist, can reliably predict which scientific explanations will prove useful, and which will ultimately be dismissed as dead ends. And, of course, in the end the issue of absolute truth or falsity is, philosophically, extremely slippery in its own right.

What To Do?

Nobody – at least no thoughtful person working within the legal tradition of the United States – is about to propose "accuracy watchdogs" for the electronic information world, any more than we would tolerate the notions of governmental press councils or journalistic licensing. Basic First Amendment freedoms are at stake. But the survival of democracy itself would at least appear to depend on maintaining the integrity of our information system as the lifeblood of an informed citizenry. An educated – as well as informed – citizenry and the professionalism of individual journalists are probably still among our most important safeguards against the erosion of these traditions. Educated, informed, and professional about what? About where information comes from, whose interests it serves, what its history has been, and the extent, given all these things, to which it can be relied upon.

Just as we have striven to encourage "media literacy," we need to start recognizing that "computer literacy" (along with "science literacy") means more than the ability to punch buttons in the appropriate order. Perhaps, in all three cases, we should be talking about "information literacy" instead. All information comes from sources. In the case of poll data, the sources are individual respondents speaking on behalf of a larger population. Are they representative? If not, what, if anything, gives them the right to speak for those others? In case of scientific data, the sources are generally representing points of view within a broader scientific community. What gives them the right to speak for others? Do they represent a consensual point of view, or is the jury still out on what "consensus" on a particular issue will really turnout to be? Do the scientific opinions available represent only the mainstream view, or are there competing analyses available? All these issues are relevant to more traditional news as well, but may yet be more compelling in the world of electronic news.

Eisenstein was probably wrong in one sense. Information technologies don't need to determine our futures – unless we let them. All technologies represent opportunities and choices. The nature of these choices is sometimes apparent in retrospect; only now, for example, can we clearly see how the cult of the individual automobile in the United States might have prevented us from developing more viable means of public mass transportation. Over time, we will inevitably make choices about how our new information systems will be structured and whether they will serve the interests of democracy or oppression. Some of my more unrelentingly Marxist colleagues would be likely to respond that since it is the powerful elite who develop new technologies, it is the powerful elite whose interests will be served by them. This is an important point. But I am less fatalistic than they and would argue, in turn, that all of us will in the end contribute to these decisions in one way or another. Whether our contributions occur actively or passively is largely up to us.

3

Publishing in Online Environment

Introduction

It is quite possible that in the next 30 years, as society moves more and more information processing onto computers, we will witness the death of objectivity as an ethical standard for the press in America. In its place, we could get a fragmented advocacy press of countless splinter publishers, representing not only political and ideological groups but also commercial interests to an unprecedented degree.

And in this new, bewildering babel of voices, it is likely that the traditional firewall between advertising and news will come tumbling down. The wall will be crushed under the weight of competition between journalists and other types of information providers; erosion will occur in the journalistic standards of objectivity, one consequence of which will be a parallel erosion in the public's ability to trust it. Opinion, marketing, advertising, information, and news will weave together so seamlessly, in the online environment, that the public will no longer be able to distinguish objective reporting from promotional messages.

The public already may scoff at the idea of objective journalism, as if the phrase itself were an oxymoron, but there is a special quality to news as it is produced today, at the end of the 20th century. Particularly in newspapers, but also in radio and television, the standard articulated in style guides and industry-accepted ethics codes is that news should be fair, objective, and balanced. While reporters and editors often fail to meet that standard, and public cynicism on this point runs deep, the public trust is that news should be objective.

For most journalists, one of the strongest ethical lines – critical to maintaining objective coverage – is that separating advertising from news. Reporters rarely "back off" stories that would upset advertisers, unless ordered to by their editors or publishers. Even then, some haven't, and it sometimes costs them their jobs. This is a "church/state" issue for journalists trained in the tradition of the newsroom, and yet there is no reason to assume these distinctions will exist in the online environment, particularly as objective news mixes more and more with opinion, advertising, and public relations material.

Despite this traditional separation between advertising and news, advertisers have a long and rich history of trying to influence media editorial content to their corporate advantage, both by blocking bad coverage and by trying to plant favorable stories. While most reporters and editors have strong ethical motivation to resist advertiser pressure, research has shown that publishers often allow advertisers to influence coverage in cases where there are financial pressures on the newspaper – either during times of recession, in cases of extreme competition between two newspapers, or when the newspaper is losing advertising linage because there are other outlets for advertising available within the market.

Many groups of local advertisers – real estate, auto, and entertainment advertisers in particular – have had so many problems with what they consider negative coverage of their industry in newspapers that they could very well abandon the traditional partnership between newspapers and local advertisers if there were an alternative advertising outlet that would reach as many people. Interestingly, there is no reason to assume that this partnership will automatically continue in the online environment. According to the Small Business Administration (SBA), the cost of newspaper advertising jumped 75% between 1985 and 1993, more than any other kind of advertising, including TV spots during sporting events, which rose 60%. When advertisers can find a cheaper advertising venue than newspapers, they will take it – especially if they can direct the content.

There is every reason to expect advertisers to try to continue influencing the content of news in the on-line environment. If the digital press goes through a competitive shake-out among information providers, as will probably happen at some point in its development, advertisers are likely to gain more control over content.

To understand how this will happen, however, we need to understand how both news and advertising are changing right now. The trends that have emerged in the late 20th century will shape what happens in the 21st, even if we cannot fully envision the landscape of tomorrow.

First, news itself is changing dramatically. Newspapers have suffered a serious and continuing erosion of readership in the past two decades, despite considerable efforts within the industry to be more colorful, community-sensitive and timely. Television news, as well, has undergone significant changes, brought about by commercial pressure, particularly in local coverage. While it is difficult to say what news will be like in the future, several important trends have emerged that will shape its future.

News has become extremely time-sensitive and dynamic. The night in 1991 when Bernard Shaw, reporting for CNN, stuck a microphone out the window of a hotel in Baghdad to record a U.S. bombing raid during the Persian Gulf War, changed forever the way breaking events are covered. No longer do correspondents wait to get all the facts and put them in context, neatly written. Now they phone home while they scramble and let the news anchor in Washington "interview" them about what is happening. Journalists are reporting raw and sometimes pre-verified events, which have tremendous dramatic appeal because anything can happen at any minute, as it did during the siege of the Branch Davidian complex in Waco, Texas, in 1993. Viewers now expect this type of coverage, and while they still want to read the in-depth analysis in the paper the next morning, they are less tolerant of time delays. *Time Magazine* now publishes an on-line version of itself, with daily updates of key stories, because it realizes that it will lose its readership if it cannot appear more timely. As news becomes more time-sensitive, it also becomes dynamic, changing constantly to stay current. As it becomes more dynamic, accuracy may suffer. Nonetheless, newspapers that only publish once a day may also, in this ever-changing world, ultimately prove to be too static.

News is also becoming more fragmented, partially pushed by advertisers seeking more targeted audiences, and in the on-line environment it will be able to fragment beyond imagination. Most large metropolitan dailies have gone to zoned editions so they can target news and advertising to specific neighborhoods. While large dailies are still mass media vehicles, they are under continuing pressure to fragment and localize coverage, even if that means printing several different editions of "the paper." In fact, the vast majority of daily newspapers in this country may best be regarded as specialty publications, concentrating on local coverage. A smattering of national and international news, usually provided by the wires, is thrown in as a public service. People read these papers for the coverage of local sports and local/regional political developments. At the same time, consumers continue to feed a proliferation of print and on-line special interest magazines, bulletin boards and discussion groups. More and more, "community" refers to people with shared interests. Sometimes that will be the person across the street, and sometimes that will be a stranger in a city on the other coast.

In the on-line environment, news is cheap to disseminate, while it is getting more expensive when printed on paper or produced by broadcast. In the past, the sheer cost of publishing a newspaper, or owning and operating a television station, kept news production in the hands of a relatively small number of companies and journalists. As information moves on line, many more people, groups and companies will be able to afford to tell their own version of events. Right now anyone with Internet access, a personal computer and the right software can set up his or her own "homepage" on the World Wide Web to advertise — whatever. When it is cheap enough for college students to publish their photographs and dating preferences on line, then it is time to reconsider the now truly democratic nature of the First Amendment.

In a world where everyone can be a publisher, journalists are vulnerable to losing their franchise as gatekeepers of the news. In its place, analysts predict that journalists will develop more of a guiding role, helping people find and make links among the different kinds of information they are seeking. "The more news sources you get, the more you need an editing intelligence to sort through and help you figure out what's useful," says Rob Pegoraro of *The Washington*

Post "Smart media will just become more valuable as the Net expands in size and diversity. If they show they know what they're doing."

Ironically, while news is fragmenting, those fragments are better able to link to other fragments in the on-line environment. In effect, news will be more connected in the future. A piece about an earthquake in Japan will link to a piece about the effects the earthquake will have on stock prices in London, as well as articles about an array of related coverage from around the world. Journalists will build the framework of links, and readers will be able to pick a trail to follow. The news is more in the layers of a story or issue, perhaps, than in breadth of coverage. Journalists may have to learn to think like librarians.

News is becoming less limited by production space. The on-line environment is endless, and television — with the advent of cable and fiber optics — virtually so. The printed newspaper's limitations of space, and linear story format, restrict the journalist's options for conveying information, compared to on-line resources.

As the technology of electronic publishing and multimedia improves, the different media used by news — text, sound, and video — are likely to become mixed together. The story of a suspected arson fire might include live video of the dramatic effort to put out the flames, a voice-text (like radio) that weaves together the basic story with live quotations, a text box analyzing the incidence of arson in the community, and a map of the damaged area and street closings. The medium used is the one best able to capture and convey the specific content. News also may become much more interactive, allowing readers a greater voice in shaping the information that is included in coverage.

The selection of news is also becoming more driven by commercial interests -not just under pressure from advertisers, but also by the companies that own the media. While not always directly influenced by specific advertising interests, competitive commercial pressures are squeezing news companies and threaten traditional journalistic standards. In his case study of several California television news stations, John H. McManus found that efforts to increase profits by expanding audience and reducing reporting costs had produced a new set of rules for the TV journalists that undermined accepted standards of newsgathering. He summed up the new rules the journalists operated under as: seeking images over ideas; seeking emotion over analysis, including avoiding complexity and dramatizing wherever possible; exaggerating to add appeal; and avoiding extensive newsgathering because it wastes time and effort, and may prove that information that makes the story attractive is actually false. Efforts to stem the hemorrhage of readership at newspapers has many papers struggling to make changes in format, presentation, content, and coverage.

As part of the trend to make news more attractive as a product, many journalists say the line between entertainment and news has become blurred – particularly in television, with the advent of tabloid news programs such as *A Current Affair*, but also in newspaper newsrooms, where reporters say they are admonished to "spin a tale" – or drop the story all together. Some analysts say that the coverage of the O.J. Simpson trial shows how journalists are even blurring the line between covering fact and fiction, giving equal weight to both tested truths and speculation. In the process, the public may forget which is which.

Simultaneously, the line between news and opinion has become blurred. Hard news itself often veers closer to opinion as reporters try to capture the essence of an event and interpret it for the public, particularly in on-the-spot television interviewing of far-flung reporters. More insidiously, journalists are now regularly interviewed as "experts" on trials and events they have covered, in effect giving them the option of writing both traditional coverage in the newspaper and then later, on television or a radio talk show, giving their opinions about the issues at hand. Not surprisingly, it is becoming more and more difficult for the public to distinguish the difference between news and opinion and the role of journalists – or to believe that journalists can operate in an objective manner.

Advertising is also changing as media technology changes. Along with news, advertising is becoming more fragmented and better targeted to individual buyers. Advertisers have progressed from targeting small communities of people with shared interests and buying habits, to collecting information about individual consumers. Some grocery chains keep a record of everything an individual buys so that they can target market particular products to them through direct mail and coupons.

Advertising is also becoming more connected with other, traditionally non-marketing, vehicles. Movies are made not just to entertain, but are designed, from the outset, to produce a flurry of commercial tie-ins, such as children's clothing, stuffed animals and toys. There is also a trend toward more subtle advertising, with the development of identifiable product placements in television shows, such as prominent use of Adidas shoes and Speedo swimsuits in the syndicated television show Baywatch.

At the same time, advertising in traditional venues, such as mass market television, has become easier for consumers to avoid. "Channel surfing," which evolved out of the myriad program choices on cable, allows viewers to click past commercials. On-line viewers can click past ads just as easily, yet research shows they will browse a commercial website if there is useful information. Advertisers see that their marketing of products will do better if it is well padded with information.

Advertisers also try to mimic news, essentially giving the presentation of their product the patina of objectivity, playing off the public's belief that news is balanced and fair. Some companies make commercials designed specifically to look like news, such as using a former news anchor seated at a news desk reading a "news bulletin" about the product. If you watch closely you know it's an ad, but if you are distracted while watching (by children shrieking or by dinner boiling over on the stove) the impression left by the ad is that an independent study has found one product better than another.

And in the on-line environment, advertising, like news, can become interactive. Ads may evolve less as something readers stumble over while looking for information and more as a deliberate site consumers visit when they are shopping for a plane ticket or dinner reservations.

So why do these trends add up to a threat to the wall between advertising and news? Because the established models – the traditional ways of thinking about news, what it is and who is a journalist; the commercial models for financing news production and dissemination; and the legal framework that ensures a protected space for news – these models don't always apply in this new digital landscape.

In fact, the legal distinction between noncommercial (protected speech) and commercial speech (which the government has limited rights to regulate,) is grey at best. Commercial speech is defined as speech that proposes a commercial transaction, speech that entices you to buy a particular product. Information on the label of a can is clearly commercial because it is read as part of a purchasing decision. But what about a press release extolling the virtues of an oil company's commitment to the environment? If it is not directly linked to a purchase, it probably is not considered commercial speech and therefore the government may have little latitude to regulate it. The government can act against commercial speech that is misleading, but again, that speech is only commercial if linked to a specific purchase. Not everything that promotes a product or cause is commercial speech.

In terms of the protections of libel law, courts differentiate between news and opinion on the basis of whether statements assert facts that can be proven true or false. If they do, then it is news and can be tested for defamation. If the statements can't be proven false, then they are deemed "fair comment and criticism," and enjoy the full protection of the law. In reality, most opinion is a mix of fact and commentary. At the same time, there is no federal requirement that opinion or advertising be so labeled in newspapers. What distinctions do exist lie only in the standards held in newsrooms and in the public perception. The tiny print at the top of an "advertorial" in the newspaper that says "this is a paid advertisement" is there only because the newspaper is trying to protect the integrity of the news in the paper. The tinier the print, and the more the advertising looks like news, the better advertisers like it.

Most newspapers in America, in fact, allow their advertising departments to actually produce some sections, notoriously the real estate news section and other "special" sections designed solely to tap specific advertising dollars, such as a once-a-year section on pets and pet care. The only difference between the look of such sections and the rest of the newspaper, however, is often just a slight change in typeface. Whether the public realizes that it has moved from objective reporting to promotional material is unclear. Editors of business pages in newspapers polled by the Society of Business Editors and Writers recently said they consider special advertising sections "misleading" to the public. Particularly in the area of consumer coverage – news about new products, housing, cars, fashion, furnishings, travel, and food – objective news standards and promotional interests often mix together to produce soft news. Hard-hitting stories, such as federal reports about auto safety, are kept away from special advertising sections in the vast majority of newspapers so as not to offend advertisers. Most journalists tolerate these chinks in the firewall, but these weaknesses threaten the integrity of all news because the distinctions are easily lost on the public.

Some journalists, in fact, are beginning to notice that the meaning of the word "news" has already eroded into something different in cyberspace than in the world of print. In a recent column in *The Wall Street Journal*, Walter S. Mossberg lectured on-line readers to beware of material labeled as "news" that is instead, discussion, gossip, rumor, or uninformed speculation. "(News) isn't claims or conspiracy theories passed around by people who've done no research or reporting," says Mossberg. "And it isn't merely news releases issued by companies, government agencies, interest groups and others." Mossberg defines "real news" as the reporting of events and trends by professional journalists who aren't involved in them directly, but who have either witnessed them or interviewed the people involved.

But if a government agency, such as the U.S. Census Bureau, gives an accurate, independent account of a new population trend in a press release, why should the public eschew that in favor of the reporter's account of the Census Bureau report? In the on-line environment, readers can get both – and they may be able to get the Census Bureau report for free. The public may also trust the Census Bureau report as the more accurate account. If it is readable, why not go straight to the horse's mouth? Who is to say that won't be regarded as news by the public? And where does that leave the journalist?

Similarly, if a commercial vendor can mix subtle advertising with "information" about a problem, such as medical information about childhood ear infections, and present the package in a news like format, at what point does the public forget that it is watching an ad? Some companies are already producing CD-ROMs that meld information with product promotion, such as Proctor & Gamble, which is experimenting with a CD-ROM ad for its Cover Girl cosmetics.

These trends already are having some remarkably stunning effects. Microsoft, the software monolith, is building a "newsroom" in Redmond, Washington, where it will produce free news that will pull in readers for the company's fee-based information services. Essentially, news becomes the bait for a company trolling for information customers. In such a climate, how will decisions be made about selection of news? Will articles be assigned – or purchased from other news vendors and repackaged – according to how well they attract specific readers? Will the company cover all the news that is fit to print? Will it cover news in only highly selected areas? Will that coverage be pro-business or independent in its coverage of commercial interests? Will it, in any traditional sense, be news? Can it advertise itself as news? And, will it link advertising or promotional material to specific "news stories?"

Pegoraro, at *The Washington Post,* says that current Net users are "culturally hostile to big business," and that Microsoft's venture will fail if it is too obviously promotional. That may be true given the population using the Internet today, but policymakers and journalists need to envision an audience far broader in background, technological capability, education and economic status than that using the Net now if they are going to develop new legal, ethical and economic models for the on-line world. The people using the Net now will be only a small portion of those using the Net in 10 years. Advertising will seek new niches in this digital world, and it will probably become even more targeted, more subtle, more informational – and more directly linked with news.

As intelligent on-line searching agents develop, most journalists fully expect readers to have a greater role in selecting the news they read in the morning. It would be simple for advertising agencies to collect that data (they would legally need the user's permission, but that is easily obtainable if linked to a cut in fees or some other commercial benefit) and then use it to target market individuals for specific types of niche advertising. If a consumer, for example, regularly selects articles about parenting, advertisers might send him a special "newsletter" about educational and health-conscious products for children, with special coupons attached to "news stories" about kids' health and development.

If a commercial vendor is producing and publishing news as a hook for consumers, it could easily link stories with ads. This is not unlike positioning an ad next to a story on a news page, but is arguably more audacious. In an effort to provide consumers with the best possible service, should a journalist writing a story about competitive airfares provide a link through to ticket-selling web sites for every airline mentioned in the story? Most journalists would howl "no," but should a reporter covering the release of a new study on alcoholism by the federal government provide a link to an on-line copy of the full report? How about links through to nonprofit groups quoted in the article? Fewer reporters would howl, but is it really any different?

If journalists become guides in this hypertext world, they can frame an issue by whom they choose to include in the road map. They will be able to link readers to other organizations, government sites, think tanks . . . and commercial interests. At some point the reader stops "reading the newspaper" and moves into reading promotional material, but that point may pass in a flash and barely register. The act of reading news, no longer tied to picking up the physical newspaper or turning on the television, becomes just one step in an informational quest by the consumer, one that may become harder and harder to distinguish as different from other types of information seeking.

Perhaps it is time to call in the federal government – to ask it to write a definition for the word "news," as various federal agencies have official terms for low-fat and other dietary attributes, and to ask the Federal Trade Commission to monitor misleading claims. Maybe it is time for independent news organizations to set up a national journalism licensing board. A reporter or company couldn't use the licensing trademark unless they and their journalism met certain standards. These may seem like extreme suggestions for journalists to consider, but 20 years from now they may appear more reasonable. Although, in 20 years, it may be too late.

The problem for journalists of the future may be that, in this new, fragmented world, where advertising will piggyback on news and information in ways we can only begin to imagine, there won't be a clear place for constructing a new firewall. The intriguing technological capabilities of a fully electronic world of information and news production and delivery offer us many creative possibilities. But the problem remains that the legal framework, the ethical models and the commercial methods of paying for news in the past do not translate easily into this new, multifaceted world. Advertisers have traditionally influenced news more in the deselection of things covered than in blatant unbalanced coverage in a single article or newspaper. There is every reason to be concerned about the mix and balance of coverage over time in the electronic world, particularly if news continues to fragment further to follow specific groups of readers. How overall coverage ultimately shapes public discussion, and whether that discussion will take place in a large arena with many voices or hundreds of private discussion groups of like-minded people, is at least partially the responsibility of journalists.

Overshadowing this entire discussion, as well, is the still unanswered question of who shall pay for the information highway. In a capitalist system, journalists cannot do their job if they are friendly to business anymore than if they are friendly to public officials, yet that becomes difficult when journalists are too closely linked with the commercial interests that butter their bread. The ethical standards that prop up the firewall in today's newsrooms may not get picked up by new "news providers" with other commercial agendas, and they may very well erode under competitive pressure as the world of electronic information publishing shakes out. Every act that weakens the public's belief in an objective journalistic ethic and every concession to advertisers or corporate interests poisons the ground for the new journalistic order.

4

Online News

A number of separate but related factors impose upon the daily journalist's ability to fulfill either instrumental or institutional goals. News people are constrained by economic imperatives, social perspectives, institutional restrictions, and a narrative form that organizes orally received data and makes it suitable for public dissemination. Electronic database technologies are not a panacea that will seamlessly or magically transform the news into a reasonably objective social service. But it is a new technology, and to the extent that news is structural and systemic, to alter a part is to affect the whole. This chapter attempts to show what online information systems can and, to some extent, have done. Because the use of these systems in contemporary newsrooms is so new and so tenuous, the analysis of their benefits must, to some extent, be speculative. The general argument is that these technologies will free journalists from a total reliance on the individual and thus, by definition, from limited views voiced by specific experts and officials. This freedom will allow reporters and editors themselves to define the context of a news story, thus regaining control of their own agenda and, perhaps, better approximate the profession's instrumental goals.

This advance is crucial, if limited. It is limited to the extent that it directly affects only one of the many social, cultural, and economic factors that shape the news. It is important because journalists cannot function as even minimally objective chroniclers unless they have sufficient information to question their subjects intelligently. To interview critically a physician, city engineer, corporate lawyer, or U.S. president or senator, reporters require independent access to information equal to the subject's on the event being discussed. But at present, unless a competitor or outside agency of legitimacy equal to the subject's offers a dissenting view, journalists are forced to rely on their subjects for data on the topic that the expert or official wishes to speak about.

Objectivity thus becomes a tautology in which contemporary reporters— constrained by ignorance— ask officials about events for which those officials are, in fact, responsible. To gain access to this information they have to be, if not welcomed, at least acknowledged and accepted by the police official, mayoral staff, presidential adviser, corporation chairman, or senator's aide, and this toleration is paid for in the coin of legitimizing copy. The story is defined narrowly and to the subject's benefit as what the CEO, hospital administrator, "Presidential Drug Czar William Bennett," or "chief of police" said at a specific moment. The cost of the whole is a story that puts forward as fact the subject's point of view, even though it may be inaccurate, biased, and self-serving.

The only way to break this impasse and thus to create a potential for critical and objective reportage is to free the newsperson from absolute dependence on information provided by sanctioned experts and officials. That will not remove the economic and social constraints supporting the editorial status quo or necessarily change the natural conservatism of many news managers. But for those who seek to understand and accurately describe current events, the ability rapidly to place an official datum into a broader context of information would and does change the relations between journalistic writer and editorial subject. It is this task that online technologies are able to perform, and the empowerment, when utilized, can be revolutionary.

Online Technologies

Online technologies— usually called "databases" or, less frequently, "online libraries"— efficiently place an enormous amount of information at the command of the reporter or writer.

Further, they do so with incredible specificity. Data available from online sources are so vast that it would take an expert months or years to search through them manually for the pertinent fact or the seminal article. But because these databases can be searched using specific key words and carefully crafted search phrases, the mass of accumulated literature in almost any field can be narrowed to the appropriate and crucial information within minutes by a competent data searcher. "The ability to search millions of pages of information in seconds to find a single mention of, say, a person's name, illustrates the awesome specificity of computerized information retrieval."

Online libraries currently exist that are made up of the past editions of a variety of newspapers and magazines. These databases for the first time place at the individual journalist's disposal the work of colleagues from across North America and, increasingly, the world. A reporter in Honolulu, Hawaii, can rapidly and efficiently search through the news files of over 60 U.S. newspapers, more than 150 magazines, Japan's Kyodo News Agency, England's *Manchester Guardian,* and (in translation) the Soviet agency Tass for information on any single issue or event. A reporter writing on nosocomial illness in Portland, Oregon, can seek pertinent data, quickly and efficiently, not only through a selection of international medical journals and U.S. court records, but through the published work of newspaper and magazine colleagues around the world.

So empowered, the reporter or public affairs writer can critically question the hospital spokesman, coroner, pathologist, or judge with information equal to or, at times, greater than the official's. "You say this was a unique death, a' freak occurrence,' but thirty others were reported in 1987," the reporter states. "Why didn't you know about this, and isn't it your job to make sure that equipment is safe in your facility?" When the official says no, it is not his responsibility, the reporter can say, with authority, "But the courts have found time and again that hospitals and their physicians are liable in this type of situation. The principle of law is *resipsa loquitor.*" If a hospital official dismisses a patient's death at an official inquest as "unfortunate, a one-in-a-million accident," reporters need not accept this statistical judgment on faith. In an hour or less online, that newsperson can check the available medical literature, court records, or the libraries of scores of newspapers to determine if, indeed, that death was a "freak" event or one of scores occurring under similar conditions in any given year.

Such aggressiveness will not win the journalist powerful friends. Corporate officials may not seek out those journalists as confidants worthy of leaked information, but the loss of some contacts is more than offset by the ability to question critically when events occur. The specificity of online information searching allows a reporter to draw from the widest range of public information and to focus the results of those searches on a narrowly defined problem.

Print, Electronic

Perhaps the best way to describe the potential of this electronic information system to journalism is to suggest that online information databases will bring the benefits of the eighteenth-century print revolution to late twenty-first century journalism. The system will allow daily and weekly periodical writers not only to base their reports on "what was said today by 'X'" but as well to put that statement in the broad context of a deep stream of previous work and research. One can state with some assurance that this development will occur because it happened before when, in the eighteenth century, printing technologies gave rise to a mass-market publication system. To understand the diffusion and potential of electronic information today, it is helpful to review briefly the transformations that occurred during the first printing revolution. As a number of writers have been at pains to demonstrate, the very idea of "objective fact" owes its existence in great part to the eighteenth century revolution in printing technology and the resulting growth in commercial, mass publication.

Alvin Kernan, for example, shows that a result of the acceptance of these technologies was "the textual authenticity that is probably the absolute mark of a print culture, a generally accepted view that what is printed is true, or at least truer than any other type of record." By fixing a fact, idea, word, or dialogue onto a page that can be read, reread, and considered by many people over time, print allowed individuals for the first time to see and consider an occurrence or idea as stable and discrete. This ability is, in Kernan's words, the "power of print to fix and objectify." Marshall McLuhan defines it as the "interiorization of technology," the process by which knowledge was transformed through the diffusion of printed materials from open, oral data to closed, abstract, fixed, and isolated information.

Further, by allowing for the relatively inexpensive, mass production of multiple volumes and editions of books, newsletters, and pamphlets, print as a system of knowledge created, for the first time, an intellectual context in which the views or findings of many different people on a single topic could be dispassionately— "objectively"— compared. "Print, with its logic of systemization orders information, thus making it useful by placing it firmly in a structure of knowledge." The development of this structure and its potential for objective reflection was the essence of the print revolution, which resulted in, among other benefits, a "scientific" system of knowledge placing individual statements or data within a context.

That "X" says "y" at a certain time and place is not information. It is an essentially trivial datum because there is no way to evaluate X's assertion, no context for its objective consideration. Before print, the royalty and clergy had the power to pronounce, and except in a narrow circle of the landed and wealthy, those statements were accepted as fact because the general population had no context other than the crown or church's claim of legitimacy in which to evaluate their pronouncements. Print, which allowed for the rapid diffusion of an enormous amount of information at minimal cost, created not only the periodical report but such a wealth of written material that vast libraries had to be created to be created. Over time, these libraries became a public resource whose information was, at least in theory, available to everyone and thus promised, through the creation of an educated and informed electorate, an inherent check against the unbridled excesses of the ruling class. An electorate so armed with information and an independent perspective was feared, at one point, by the small class of intelligentsia (essentially large landowners, clergy, and royalty), but the transformation to literacy— and its resulting democratization of knowledge— was unstoppable.

Before the eighteenth century, to be literate was to know a small body of classical literature, to have read perhaps (in Chaucer's day) twenty books and certainly no more than two hundred. But in the eighteenth century libraries with thousands of works came into being, and in the late nineteenth century the popular library movement gained momentum. With the increasing production and accumulation of printed materials, new ways of reading developed in which the works of one person, or information contained in one edition of a text, were critically compared with the writings of other individuals or editions of a single text. Kernan defines this fundamental change as the development of the "Gutenberg reader," an individual who reads and compares the information found in various texts, weighing the various statements against the accumulation of available information.

This transformation of society's information base was profoundly democratic. Before print, the power of information was solely in the hands of society's clear rulers— the clergy and the crown— but in the eighteenth century the commercial press gave rise, first in Britain and, soon after, in the colonies, to a print-based, information system increasingly controlled not by the crown alone but by independent publishers and individual writers who maintained the commercial information machine. Printing technology became an indispensable part of both the official posture— government printing offices, for example— and a dissenting position marked by pamphlets, polemics, editorials, and a populist press.

News and Print

Because this book is not a historical analysis of the relation of news to technology, it is unnecessary to discuss at length the reasons that periodicals retained a fundamentally oral system of information in the print era. But it is perhaps pertinent to note in passing how rare and precious libraries and print resources were before this century. "Journalists" had little access to the work of other writers, and the technology that extended their geographic reach— first the telegraph, then the telephone, and now the satellite— emphasized not critical evaluation but simple transmission of what was said at a distant place. Even if a reporter in New York wanted to consider, to question what President Theodore Roosevelt said on the campaign trail, that reporter lacked ready access to the work of other daily news professionals writing in Chicago, Boston, Buffalo, or San Francisco. Technological advances facilitated the journalist's means of transmission while creating economies of scale for the media investor, but left the process of information gathering relatively unchanged.

The growth of daily newspapers as a business extended the need for copy at the same time that technology (the boat, train, automobile, and, finally, the airplane) extended the range of society as a whole. In this rush to cover increasing areas of the globe where national interests lay, the time and resources for placing the accumulated statements into a broader context were minimal. The custom of news became set, and reporters were defined by the increasingly specialized ability to translate rapidly what someone said into so many column inches of print for the next day. There could be nothing more and, as Walter Lippmann said in 1920, one of necessity accepted, in the main, the statements of officials because "the books and papers are in their offices."

Even when public libraries became a nearly ubiquitous fixture of the North American city in this century, daily hacks were seldom given the time required for their use. Even if they had the time, the expertise required to search legal, financial, or medical literature was rarely a part of the journalists' kit bag, and the work of colleagues at geographically distant publications was rarely available for their perusal. Nor, of course, was the lack of such research tools perceived as a liability by the vast majority of editors and reporters. Few news professionals had the requisite skills to be a "Gutenberg reader," even had they been granted the time to use the library as a professional resource and seek through legal, medical or general texts to fashion a context for their stories. Reporters wrote and editors printed what people said. Lacking the crucial "books and papers," which remained on the desks of officials and officially designated experts—or the time to utilize and reflect on those which were available—reportage became by default a public address system in which the narrative form of the news lacked any critical structure. The best one could hope for was contradiction by dissenting, but still official actors participating in a specific event. The way to break a story was to quote what some other, "real" investigator said. To a great extent, the situation remains the same today.

In the absence of any foolproof criterion for choosing sources who are likely to provide valid information, journalists are uncertain about whom to believe. They cope with uncertainty by continuing to rely on authoritative sources. The presumption of hierarchy, that those at the top of any organization are the people in charge and that those in subordinate positions do what their superiors tell them tounderlies the journalist's criterion for selected sources even though journalists themselves recognize that this presumption is often of doubtful validity.

Database Technologies

Electronic information databases provide the potential for the typical journalist to develop, story by story and issue by issue, criteria for evaluating the statements of their sources. These databases take the "books and papers" from the offices of officials and place them in the hands of journalists and other public information writers who can use them to question critically a subject's statements. An example of exactly how this process works at its best may provide a better understanding of the degree to which online information technologies can transform the reportorial function and, by extension, that of any writer or advocate interested in a specific issue. To evaluate this and other examples used in this book, the reader will find it helpful to distinguish between three different levels of story, each level defined by the type of information it carries. These definitions are tentative guidelines, but will serve not only to demonstrate how the use of electronic databases can affect news content but to distinguish later among various databases themselves:

1. **Trivial or Ephemeral Story:** This is the commonplace, contemporary news report that describes "what" was said by "who" (an official or expert), "where" (here), and "when" (today). It is in the main composed of isolated and discrete data, whose accuracy is unevaluated by the newsperson, reflecting or repeating narrowly prescribed statements of one or more participants in some event. The individual data have no greater context and are of limited interest. As Tim Miller said, "Not only does the print newspaper [story] have the life span of the May fly, it also has about the same migratory range." The ephemeral story, as a category, presents an

isolated datum that, the day after publication, is quickly forgotten.

2. **Contextual Story:** This narrative takes the individual datum and places it within one or more contexts in which its importance can be evaluated. The context is typically one of a recurring class of events for which information has been accumulated and causes assigned. In the conventional news paradigm, this story would focus on the broad "what" happened or "how" an event is to be understood. It thus places a single event— a death, fire, medical condition, government regulation, or political occurrence— within a broader context, much as legal precedents serve to define issues of responsibility within the civil court system.
3. **Structural Story**: To the extent that events are related, they can be seen within the greater context of social issues and forces. "Why" a pattern emerges is often the result of political, economic, or cultural forces that, while not immediately evident in the trivial or contextual category, may be manifest in another situation. Thus a structural story makes overt the links connecting an event or series of events and broader social issues or policies.

To see how each level is related and how contextual and structural elements are made accessible to the generalist reporter familiar with computer databases, consider the following story on tort reform and its relation to the issue of medical costs in the United States.

Tort Reform

Since the 1970s, state legislators, the U.S. Congress, the American Medical Association, and the Association of Trial Lawyers of America have become increasingly concerned about the rising cost to society of medical treatment in the United States. Thousands of newspaper stories and magazine articles have been written about the problem, many of them dealing with the debate over legislation commonly referred to as tort reform. Sparked by the California legislature's Medical Injury Compensation Reform Act (MICRA), passed in 1975, the idea has been to reduce medical costs, or at least the rapidity of their increase, by placing a limit on jury awards for pain and suffering to victims of medical malpractice. Proponents of tort reform have insisted this limit would reduce the overall costs of medical care by decreasing the stunning increases in malpractice insurance premiums which physicians have been forced to pay. Holding down the amount of court-ordered awards would save insurers money, decrease the cost of premiums to physicians, and in theory those savings would be passed on to society at large.

In this debate, heard each time tort reform is introduced (in states ranging from New York to Hawaii), the two sides have been adamant and clear. Lawyers opposing tort reform consistently argue that increasing malpractice premiums are the result of fair compensation to the victims of bad medical practice; and the answer to increasing health insurance costs, therefore, not legal but medical. The American Medical Association and insurers argue that avaricious lawyers and greedy, if grieving clients are indeed the problem and, further, that the sacred patient-doctor relationship is being destroyed by an increasingly adversarial legal system, which has made litigants of the partnership between caring healer and needy patient.

News reporters cover these issues at legislative hearings and press conferences called by one or another side. They do not take sides or independently examine the central questions raised by the debate. They quote one or another official representative of a medical association, a legal organization, or an insurance company executive who testified at a hearing or called a press conference to state the specific organization's position. These are the "facts" presented to readers or viewers in daily stories chronicling opposing views

Wall Street Journal

A good example of standard reportage on this issue is a *Wall Street Journal* article that reported on a "debate" between the president of the Association of Trial Lawyers of America, Robert Habash, and a "surgeon and a top official of the American Medical Association," Dr. James Todd. The long, two-column story was accompanied by a sidebar on the Canadian system titled, "In Canada, Different Legal and Popular Views Prevail." The whole presentation appears to be a model of contemporary journalism, objectively balancing two opposing views, each articulated by a leading "expert" in his field, in a "debate" over the perceived problem of malpractice liability premiums. The whole is preceded by *Journal* reporter Michael Waldholz's introduction, which summarizes both legal and medical positions through the statements of the participants themselves:

Malpractice liability has lately become one of the most divisive issues among doctors and lawyers.

"Physicians are leaving the profession in unheard of droves because of a system they don't understand, they can't cope with, and which is getting worse," says James Todd, a surgeon and a top official of the American Medical Association. At fault for the burgeoning lawsuits and staggeringly high premiums many doctors pay, he argues, are a legal system that encourages meritless litigation and trial lawyers who profit exorbitantly from malpractice cases.

"Malpractice lawsuits result from malpractice," counters Robert Habash, a partner with the Milwaukee law firm Habash, Habash and Davis and president-elect of the Association of Trial Lawyers of America. Mr. Habash says that present laws help protect patients' rights and ensure their access to the courts. He believes the situation calls for changes in the insurance industry and more careful monitoring by doctors of competence in the profession.

What follows is a debate organized by *The Wall Street Journal* between Dr. Todd and Mr. Habash.

Introduction

This story is, for all its appearance of "objective" debate, a synthetic and mediated product, consistently slanted in its presentation despite the premise of objectivity presumably guaranteed by the body of the text, which is composed entirely of excerpts from the participants' speeches. Even though Waldholz is supposedly silent and "objective," his introduction makes clear what his— or his newspaper's-posture and interests are. In fact, before the body of the "debate" has begun, the biases of both participants and the newspaper are evident. This *Journal* "top" sanctifies as fact a series of assumptions through its summation, thus defining all that will follow.

We do not question, for example, the bylined story's assertion, attributed to *Todd,* that "physicians are leaving the profession in unheard-of droves" because if it were not true, why would the *Journal* print it, and if it were not a problem, would there be any need for a debate at all? Nor do we doubt that these career changes are directly related to the problem of malpractice liability, despite a total lack of substantiation for that position in the text. The lead paragraph— short and direct— insists we accept this linkage.

Todd's assertion that this terrifying image of a future bereft of physicians is due to "a system they [physicians] don't understand, they can't cope with, and which is getting worse" is not substantiated by the story and effectively places the onus for these problems on the debate's "other side," the lawyers and their representative, Habash.

But it is not "the system," understood or not, that is at issue. Rather, this story is about "staggeringly high premiums" and "lawyers who profit exorbitantly"— phrases of the journalist and not of the debators. Waldholz uses adjectives to editorialize in the time honored, *Time* magazine style of condemnation by adjective and modifier. We credit him in part because this is the *Wall Street Journal* on issues of money and business, the commercial daily's métier. We accept on faith that premiums are too high (But too high compared with what? As a function of total gross revenues for doctors? Real income?) and that lawyers profit exorbitantly. Precisely what system is misunderstood by physicians— and the actual state of their confusion— is unstated here, and perhaps it is just as well.

Thus the *Journal* agrees from the start with Todd's position that the issue is malpractice liability premiums, a posture Habash, for his part, rejects. Despite its pretense of objectivity and the reporter's apparent role as moderator, the newspaper has taken a stand squarely on the physicians' side of the argument. In the body of the "debate," Habash insists the problem is elsewhere than in fleeing physicians, in lawyers profiting exhorbitantly, or in a system that befuddles the hardworking physician. He tries to reframe the context of the debate to include prevention of malpractice through tighter regulation of physicians as a class. But Todd disagrees and the body of the *Journal*'s introduction to Habash emphasizes not the lawyer's main argument, that "malpractice lawsuits result from malpractice," but his position on necessary changes in the insurance, medical, and legal industries.

Underscoring the Journal's bias is the simple fact that Todd, a "top official" of the American Medical Association, is given higher billing than the president of the Association of Trial Lawyers of America. One would expect that an as sociation president would be asked to speak first and, where the two speakers are equal in status, the person whose last name begins with the letter closest to "A" would be given precedence. But the first quotes in the introduction are given to Todd and Habash is left for rebuttal. Presumably this order is a result of the fact that the doctor's position, like the *Journal's*, emphasizes the economics of malpractice liability and not the messy and more complex issue of physician responsibility.

The "Debate"

Thus the "debate" begins with a bias toward Todd's posture. He is the first speaker and the one most clearly focused on the "divisive" issue of the cost of malpractice liability. The whole text then alternates, paragraph by paragraph, with statements by one or the other man. We presume, but are not told, that the story is composed of edited excerpts from a longer interview session. Rarely do individuals – especially those so clearly involved in their topic as these men – speak in one- or two-paragraph bursts. Nor, one suspects, would two such men never interrupt each other or allow topics to be changed and discussion over a "divisive issue" to flow as easily as this "debate" suggests. The whole piece is thus an artificial dialogue excerpted, condensed, and formulated to fit both the *Journal's* editorial perspective and its available news hole on a single day. What, then, do the two men say?

Todd argues that juries composed of lay individuals cannot judge malpractice cases, that a doctor's only "peers" are other physicians. Juries of lay people, he implies, are manipulated by crafty lawyers and higher rates are the result. He denies that bad medicine by incompetent doctors is the problem but agrees that "medicine can do a better job disciplining incompetent doctors." The real problem, Todd insists, lies with inequities in the legal system that make everyone resort to litigation. It is that tendancy to litigate that has caused an increase in malpractice suits and the size of resulting awards. The result of these inequities is that physicians are leaving their practice and profession, hurt and befuddled by a system that they do not understand and cannot afford. "If the medical profession is guilty of anything," he insists, "it is overselling its wares. Everyone now expects a perfect result." The people profiting from all this-the real villains in Todd's view—are malpractice lawyers. The principal victim is society-at-large, which suffers through higher costs and decreased care as physicians leave practice (or refuse to practice in a specific state) because of high malpractice insurance costs and the deleterious effect on their lives of contentious malpractice suits.

The answer, Todd says, is tort reform, which would limit the amount juries can award for "pain and suffering" to $250,000, with payment spread over a period of time instead of ordered in a lump sum.

Habash, on the other hand, says that tort reform would not solve the problem which he defines, more generally, as botched operations by incompetent physicians. He even quotes a statement attributed to Todd in 1984 that, "there's just too much incompetence and negligence in the medical profession." Habash insists that the root of the problem is not the U.S. system of litigation but, instead, the fact that bad physicians are allowed to practice medicine. "It's the incompetent doctors who are causing the problem," he says. "In Pennsylvania, 1 percent of the doctors accounted for 25 percent of medical malpractice payments." Thus Habash suggests that if only those "few bad apples" were excised from the community of physicians, the problem would be resolved. Unfortunately, Habash suggests, statistics show that physicians are not doing the job. Medical malpractice suits with high awards thus protect the public, in the lawyer's view, by focusing public attention through the courts on incompetent doctors, and serve the public by championing the victims of bad medicine.

To limit awards in any area would, Habash concludes, accomplish little except "taking rights away from victims." Not surprisingly, Todd takes strong exception to Habash's characterization of claimants in malpractice suits as victims. Habash suggests (and Todd denies) that malpractice litigation is just a convenient target for physicians who don't want to address more central and crucial problems.

Creating the Context

This "debate" is an essentially trivial story. It excerpts, as do most news stories, from a longer discussion between the principal subjects and then records elements of what they said on a single day. It provides, really, no information from which a concerned citizen could choose or judge between the positions offered. The whole is a procession of individual, unexamined, and unsubstantiated data which the reader, like the reporter, cannot evaluate without recourse to independent research. Todd sounds like an honest, sincere guy. So does Habash. Todd is really worried about doctors leaving their practices because they can't afford the malpractice bill. Habash says, in effect, nuts and good riddance. Bad doctors are the issue. Of course, one would expect a lawyer to defend the legal side and a physician to defend the medical profession. There are nuggets of potential information tucked away, of course, that a truly interested reader or reporter could pursue. Did Todd really say, before he became a spokesman, that medicine is riddled with "incompetence" and, if so, did he think then what he denies here-that medical incompetence is a part of this problem? How many cases of malpractice are attributed to a small group of bad physicians? Todd says it's not the issue. Habash says it is.

There is no way to judge between Habash's and Todd's respective positions on the basis of information provided by the *Journal*, and the story joins a huge bank of ephemeral data on a topic that cries to be pulled into a context that would give the reader real information. Who is correct-physicians, represented by Todd, or lawyers, who presumably stand behind Habash? If we put the question another way, can a reporter determine if either bad medicine or litigious patients (teamed with avaricious lawyers) constitute the real, root problem? What are the central issues in the tort reform argument, and to what extent can blame in fact be laid either at the door of doctors (for improper procedures that cause the injuries that result in suits) or of venal lawyers (who encourage legal action at the drop of a hat)? Would a cap on payments for "pain and suffering" really make a difference, and while we're asking, how much is awarded by juries to litigants as a rule? Maybe "pain and suffering" awards are an insignificant part of the typical jury award and thus of the issue of malpractice award costs. The participants in the *Wall Street Journal* debate each had vested interests. What would an objective treatment of this whole subject mean to a reporter?

One way to examine the issues raised by this debate would be to look at the findings of court cases in which juries had made awards to the victims of malpractice. Since this issue is state-wide— tort reform is legislated at that level-and nation-wide because the cost of health care is a federal concern, pertinent cases from most U.S. legal jurisdictions would bear on it. These cases would show how and where blame in fact was laid and, further, allow a journalist to break down jury-awarded monies: so much for pain and suffering, so much to keep a person in hospital, so much for loss of consortium (in the case of a spouse or child) or future earning power for a family's principal wage earner. That research, which would provide one context for the respective statements of both Habash and Todd, could be done in a law library, of course, but legal research is a rather specialized field that few reporters have studied. Since newspapers typically report on large jury awards— and large awards in cases of medical misadventure are the issue— it might be possible to search principal newspapers in each state for stories of large awards. Using traditional, non-electronic methods, that search would require writing scores of letters to city editors or librarians around the country and waiting for them to reply.

To search forty or more newspapers online for stories dealing with court malpractice awards is, however, well within the range of the possible. One service that facilitates such research is Vu/Text, a company that specializes in transferring newspaper files into a computerized database for ease of storage and access. Some of the costs of that exercise are recovered for those clients who agree to allow Vu/Text to offer their files online to other subscribers. At present, over sixty-five newspapers have signed up for that service, and all can be searched globally (at once) for any single search word or phrase.

For the moment, consider that just looking for articles on "tort reform" would return newspaper accounts of legislative debates like the *Wall Street Journal* story— more of the same. If news is, as we contend, primarily the printed record of oral statements, it is unlikely one will find in these accounts an unbiased context for review of the issues enjoined by this specific "debate." Habash suggests the problem is incompetent and undisciplined physicians, but looking for court cases involving physician discipline is not the answer. Stories on surgery and injury or death would be helpful but these phrases are also too general. We talk about deadly "surgical strikes," for instance, so such a search would bring up stories about military exercises. In many newspapers (like the ones where I have worked) there are files of stories, and many involve anesthesia and problems related to its use. Since anesthesia is used in most surgery, perhaps it is a crucial element, and searching for stories involving anesthesia and injury or death to patients should be narrow enough. Searching the whole database with this phrase is worth a try.

Between January 1, 1987, and October 22, 1988, forty U.S. newspapers whose files are stored on Vu/Text carried over thirty stories describing court cases involving death or injury resulting from anesthesia. Several of those stories described court cases in which a single physician was found guilty of up to sixteen deaths or injuries that resulted in court action, so, in fact, the number of relevant cases was far higher than the number of returned stories noted here would suggest. In most cases, the newspaper stories reported on court evidence which showed that death or permanent injury resulted when physicians either failed to monitor their patients adequately during a procedure, used incorrect drugs during a procedure, or otherwise failed to follow established medical procedures.

There were a few spectacularly large awards. One story involved a $28 million award, but the average size of settlements was $4.5 million. Further, the monies awarded were largely for medical expenses to maintain patients who had been permanently disabled by a physician's mistake or to provide continued life support for those who had been left by medical misadventures in a "vegetative state." Patients so injured often received awards in excess of $1 million but, according to these newspaper accounts of statements made in court, those monies were awarded by a judge or jury to pay for the cost of maintaining a disabled person— Todd insists they are not "victims"— in a diminished (quadriplegia, paraplegia, extensive brain dysfunction, etc.) or vegetative state. The amount awarded for pain and suffering sometimes equaled but rarely surpassed and was typically far less than that given by juries to victims for medical maintenance, an area of cost that tort reform would not affect. The whole search took about fifteen minutes, although reading the recovered stories took three hours and analysis of award amounts several hours more. It was, perhaps, a full day's work.

One for the lawyers. Jury awards were based primarily on medical necessity. Compensation to families of those who died or were permanently injured during surgery also included monies for "loss of consortium," which would allow, for example, a widower to hire a housekeeper or nanny to assist him in the care of his children after his wife died in an anesthetic-related mishap. Awards were made for "pain and suffering," and, sometimes, they were large. But the whole of this evidence of reportage of court awards emphasized the cost of malpractice in which the physician(s) were judged to be at fault.

Todd says right off the top in the *Wall Street Journal* story that lay people can't judge medical issues, that only physicians can function as peers for other doctors. So maybe judges and juries were swayed in all these cases by tricky and avaricious lawyers, as the *American Medical Association*'s high official suggests. But in the search for news stories answering the phrase "anesthesia and death or injury," several non-court stories were captured that suggest the opposite. The *Sacramento Bee*, for example, quoted a Harvard Medical School researcher who said that at least two thousand people die annually, and more are injured, because of improperly administered anesthetic. Further, these deaths and injuries were all described as preventable. Dr. John Eichorn told the *Bee* that a review of all anesthetic-related fatalities at Beth Israel Hospital in Boston over the previous decade had concluded that 70 percent of the deaths would not have occurred had physicians followed established standards of anesthetic administration.

Reducing the number of deaths by 70 percent would certainly cut the cost of malpractice insurance by reducing incidents which result in legal action. Further, the story offered strong support for the trial lawyers' association's position that bad medicine, not high awards, was the major villain in medical malpractice awards. But, frankly, I would not want to take a single story from the *Sacramento Bee* (or any other individual newspaper story) to the bank when talking about something so important. Beth Israel Hospital runs a medical database in which articles from all major medical journals are collected and indexed. Checking that service, called PaperChase, for articles by John Eichorn uncovered the critical article which presumably sparked the *Sacramento Bee* interview with him, as well as other, more recent articles that cited Eichorn's research. This body of information (which in turn is based on separate studies done at several geographically distant hospitals) also insisted that if physicians only used appropriate monitoring equipment and followed established procedures, many lives would be saved and permanent injuries prevented. Further, one or more articles analyzed the cost of monitoring equipment that, if used, would radically reduce anesthetic-related problems and found the cost trivial when compared with the savings that would result from decreased litigation. Medical journal articles estimated that health care professionals were responsible for anesthetic-related "catastrophic errors" occurring in surgery from 50 to 90 percent of the time.

The cost of the Vu/Text and Paper Chase searches together was under one hundred dollars and required less than an hour to execute. Reading and analyzing the material returned by those searches took about six hours. Were reporters really industrious, they also could have searched a database like *WestLaw* for the text of cases mentioned in news reports or for the principles of law stated in some stories. Thus, a *Columbus Dispatch* story reported that an Ohio jury was instructed by its judge in an anesthetic related case that the principle of law pertinent to judgments

in this area was *resipsa loquitor*— which means that if something occurred, someone is to blame. On *WestLaw*'s legal database, searching for other cases in which this principle was stated made clear that the issue of compensation when someone is at fault is deeply embedded in the legal system and applicable not only to medical malpractice, but to all injury cases as well. That raises the interesting question of why malpractice awards should be isolated, as Todd thinks they should be, as the only category of personal injury where compensation under the principle would be denied. Further, specific cases searched through West Law provided in-depth treatment of both the precise types of medical injury sustained by individuals and clear statements of the effective causes of those injuries and justification of the awards (whether the money was for maintenance of a person in a vegetative state, for pain and suffering, or for loss of consortium).

All this information, while not necessarily pertinent to any single, specific story, becomes valuable and powerful when a journalist attempts to put a recent, journalistically defined event into a broader context. If, for example, an individual has been injured in surgery and the physician's lawyer says, because the cause of that injury was atypical and unusual that the physician should not be held responsible, the traditional reportorial response has been to quote that statement, seek a "balancing" quote from the claimant's attorney ("Your opponent says the physician's not at fault. What do you say?"), and then go home. Traditionally, reporters could, as a rule, do little more because they knew no more. Now they can understand a bit of the law behind such events and, certainly, draw (as do lawyers) from other cases, legal precedents, and a vast medical literature that make responsibility and liability relatively precise and objective terms.

On the basis of this research, which could be localized by reporters to focus on cases occurring in their circulation or immediate broadcast areas, the conclusions are inescapable. Cases of death and injury in surgery could be reduced significantly-estimates ranged from between 50 and 70 percent-if physicians followed established procedures and used appropriate monitoring equipment when a patient was anesthetized. That reduction would result in savings not only of dollars but of lives far in excess of anything that proponents of tort reform have anticipated for their plan. Reducing incidence of death or permanent injury would eliminate not only large awards for pain and suffering— the sole result of tort reform— but also reduce or eliminate other, costlier awards for maintenance of the injured, compensation for lost ability to work, loss of consortium, burial expenses, etcetera.

Further, failure to follow established procedures may be based on not only physician error but physician incompetence. A significant percentage of supposedly licensed physicians are, in fact, bogus doctors practicing without proper training. Other physicians suffer from alcohol and drug abuse— estimates run as high as one in five— while residents who carry the brunt of hospital work are often forced to work so long without a break that they may literally fall asleep during a surgical procedure. This information is in both popular and technical journals and reports.

Other Approaches

This approach has required the reporter to choose what points require examination, to fashion a hypothesis from the subject's statement, and then to test it against the written record. The database approach forces public information writers to make independent choices as they build a story. Other searches could also have been carried out. A simple question raised by Todd, and amenable to examination, is whether there is a real possibility that the United States faces a shortage of physicians because so many are leaving the profession— for whatever reason. If there is a real possibility of a shortage, then the question may be why those doctors are quitting. Are malpractice premiums the only reason? By searching newspapers for the words "physician and shortage," Todd's concern can be quickly laid to rest. In 1990, for example, Louis Sullivan, secretary of the United States Department of Health and Human Services, told Congress that the current supply of physicians would be at least adequate through the turn of the century. Certainly, physicians were leaving the profession in the 1980s, presumably for a variety of reasons, but not in numbers sufficient to adversely affect the health care of the average citizen. Sullivan also noted, as have others in previous reports, a real and growing shortage of nurses that may impact on long-term health care.

Habash stated that the failure of physician organizations to adequately police their own sometimes results in deadly medicine by bad doctors. Todd, for his part, not only said that physicians can supervise their own professional community but went further and argued that, in his opinion (and the opinion, therefore, of the American Medical Association), no one but a physician can adequately judge another doctor's performance. Is Habash right— are doctors unable to police their own? Or is Todd right when he says physicians and only physicians can regulate their professional brethren? This is a topic which can be framed as a hypothesis and checked against the written record.

One tends to be skeptical of Todd's insistence that physicians and only physicians should review the work of their colleagues.

There is an element of self-protection and self interest in that argument that has been noted by individuals other than Habash. A *New York Times* article, for example, suggested that physicians reviewing the performance of their colleagues is at best a conflict of interest when it asked "whether the medical association, whose central purpose is to represent the interest of doctors, should take the lead in disciplining them." That story did not answer the question, but information found in a basic computer search shows that, at least in the past, physicians have been quite unable adequately to police their own. The *Detroit News* summed up the point nicely when it stated that physicians "reporting an incompetent or impaired doctor to a county, state or national medical organization is like [a motorist] reporting a bad driver to the American Automobile Association. The organizations might deplore the behavior but neither is equipped, legally or politically, to deal with the problem."

Daily newspaper databases carry a wealth of anecdotal, regional stories about the failure of medical organizations in various jurisdictions to discipline or restrict the practices of incompetent or unqualified members. Taken together, they become a damning indictment of Todd's position. The medical literature also concludes that physicians have been extremely reluctant to examine critically the performance or even the credentials of their members. A 1985 report in the *New England Journal of Medicine*, for example, showed that in 1982 some states reported no disciplinary action against even one member per thousand and the number of states that disciplined more than three members per thousand was only fourteen. The report's author, a physician, said dryly that "it is difficult to believe that in any given year any state or territory would not have at least one physician per thousand who posed a threat to the health and safety of its citizens and yet, in 1982, 4 states reported less than that number of disciplinary actions." In 1985 the situation had not significantly improved. In that year, only 2,108 of the United States' estimated 405,000 physicians (.00468 percent) were disciplined, although perhaps 20 percent of U.S. doctors were, according to other studies, abusing drugs or alcohol and at least 6 percent of those who practiced medicine as physicians were, in fact, not licensed and may have had no formal medical training. Thus a significant percentage of the currently practicing physicians to whom

Todd wanted society to turn over exclusive judgment of their colleagues are unlicensed, "bogus" doctors, the very laypersons he insisted could not adequately judge the competence of licensed professionals.

Computer-Research

The information generated online to test statements by Todd and Habash would make a respectable story, sidebar, or part of a series on the issues of contemporary medicine. Whatever approach is taken, the story has become not simply that doctors and lawyers disagree but, rather definitively, that "malpractice is expensive practice." Statements by Habash and Todd, proponents for groups with economic and professional interests in the issues, have been placed in a broader context which allows the writer— hack, flack, or advocate— to examine critically the individual statements. Information resulting from the online search, localized by journalists with examples from their specific circulation or broadcast area, would include the following facts:

- Medical authorities admit that incidence of death and injury resulting from surgery are usually the avoidable result of bad medicine.
- Many physicians do not follow widely accepted procedures or use effective and recommended monitoring techniques. This failure causes as much as 70 percent of the anesthetic-related deaths occurring nationally in surgery.
- One result of these failures has been increased insurance costs as malpractice suits multiplied, causing, among other problems, the "medical insurance crisis."
- Medical associations have been lax in disciplining their members, weeding out "bogus" or inferior practitioners, and, generally, in assuring fulfillment of the profession's institutional and instrumental goals: to heal the sick through administration of specific protocols and procedures.
- Physicians agree that if proper medical procedures were followed in surgery and if anesthetists used appropriate monitoring equipment, incidents of injury and death-and

therefore the number of court awards involving malpractice—would decrease dramatically.

Further, these statements are "facts" not in the sense that newspapers typically use the word but, rather, in one approximating the objective sense it carries in logic and science. Typically, a "fact" in news means someone in a position of authority stated that "x" was true. It is a fact only to the degree that the "fact" reflects a true statement at the level of the journalistic event— that is, what was actually said by the official, president, coroner, chief of police, CEO, professor, or designated spokesperson. The validity of that statement in relation to the antecedent subject is outside the journalist's typical arena of inquiry. It is a datum bounded by both the level of information of its source and the time frame of that statement. Newspaper "facts" are like the Watergate defendants' defense: everything is modified by the phrases "at that one point in time" or "in that time frame." If the police announce that a man's death was suicide, the fact is not necessarily that of an individual's successful action to end his own life. In the absence of other information from dissenting but still official sources, one may assume the truthfulness of the police chief's statement, but without corroborating evidence, nothing more.

The "facts" in this computer-assisted story are a little different. They put the issues raised by Todd and Habash within the context of a score of medical studies, public reports, and court decisions written and rendered over time. There are to the stories, decisions, and reports returned by this search a depth and breadth which require of the print reporter, broadcast journalist, or magazine writer a critical focus and input as the statements of a Habash or a Todd are weighed against outside information. The reporter or editorial writer can say with some certainty that, to the best of our knowledge, something is true not because an official says it is so but that it is true on the basis of a wide range of public information. Thus a computer-assisted story on the subject of tort reform, which subjected the statements of Habash and Todd to an electronic review, might include the following:

Malpractice is "Malpractice"

A newspaper staff investigation suggests strongly that those lawyers who argue that "bad medicine" is at the root of the medical cost crisis are correct.

Forcing physicians to follow established procedure would save hundreds of lives and the millions of dollars required to maintain individuals placed in a "vegetative state" by improperly administered anesthesia during surgery.

Medical experts admit that the failure of physicians to follow basic procedures or use readily available equipment that medical studies and medical schools recommend is responsible for more than 50 percent of the deaths or permanent injuries that result from surgery in the nation's hospitals.

"There's just too much incompetence and negligence in the medical profession," Dr. James Todd, a high official in the American Medical Association, stated in 1984. Here are examples of what incompetence and negligence mean to individuals:

The story would then include a localized discussion of issues like:

- to cases involving failure to monitor
- cases involving use of inappropriate drugs
- cases involving equipment failure leading to death
- the failure of medical associations to supervise their members or to assure that members have proper credentials and training.

Changes

It is important to see the limits as well as the strengths of this approach. The general agenda remains in the hands of lawyers, physicians, and legislators who have raised the issue of medical costs to society and framed it in terms of compensation to victims or their families. Problems are still defined not in terms of an individual's quality of life or the root causes of illness and preventable injury (many of which are social and environmental) but in terms of an economic bottom line. The main issue— cost of compensation after medical misadventure— was defined by the speakers and followed by the reporter. The story has become not how to eliminate illness resulting in deaths and injuries but, rather, how to cut medical insurance costs by evaluating a class of medical events. Nobody has questioned that economics is the essential issue in the malpractice debate or that lawyers and physicians are the appropriate people to make these decisions. The position of nurses, for example, has not been solicited on the issue of medical costs or procedure. Nor has the idea been raised of scrapping fee-for-service medicine for a more socialized medical system like Canada's or New Zealand's, a change which would, some believe, increase the quality of health care while decreasing total cost to the nation. The *Wall Street Journal*'s sidebar on the Canadian medical system was limited solely to statements on that country's system of malpractice litigation. Nobody has entertained suggestions that supervision of physicians-and their licensing— be taken from medical organizations and given to an independent body composed, perhaps, of nurses, emergency technicians, lay people, and physicians. The physician's present status in society and the means by which medical services are rendered remain unquestioned.

Further, the agenda in which medical and legal officials focus on malpractice as the critical factor in rising health care costs has been retained without examination. There is a wealth of stories in both the professional and popular literature describing the degree to which other elements contribute to national medical costs. For example, both professional journal and news writers have shown that in some cases Directed Release Groups (DRGs), introduced in the 1980s in the United States as a cost-cutting measure, have resulted in an increase in deaths or post-operative complications by forcing the too rapid release of patients from hospitals. Further, the issue of not only iatrogenic (physician-created) disorders but also of nosocomial illness (those caused by the hospital environment) is not addressed, though it is the root of a whole class of illness, adding to the nation's total medical bill. These range from the spreading of infections on hospital wards by hospital staff members who fail to wash their hands between patient visits to the disastrous effects of incorrect medication of patients by hospital and pharmacy staffs. Leading systemic causes of injury and illness— automobile accidents and sustained abuse of tobacco and alcohol— contribute significantly to lost work hours among the populace, injuries leading to hospital admission and thus the general national health bill. To address the issues of health care costs would require an examination of these and other problems, which are, in fact, discussed in medical and social literature. But because the story's "hook" is a legislative debate focusing solely on the cost of malpractice insurance rates for physicians, this computer-researched story is limited in the main to that context as well.

But within the parameters of the specific legislative agenda — tort reform — this online approach has led to significant changes in text and procedure. Reportage has become active rather than reactive. Positions are not simply relayed, oral statement to printed paragraph, but examined from the perspective of an enormous body of information drawn from the medical, legal, and popular literature to bear precisely on the essential point: people are injured or killed in hospital and seek, in person or through their survivors, compensation for those injuries or deaths.

Rather than simply quoting a doctor, lawyer, or representative, reporters can now closely and critically question the participants. Their knowledge of the issues, supported by targeted electronic research, is sufficient to ask appropriate questions and to know when the responses are incorrect. It would have been interesting to ask Todd about Eichorn's study, for example. It would have been fun (as well as interesting) to point out to the AMA official that tort reform's cap on pain and suffering would barely dent the total amount awarded, during the year reviewed here, in malpractice suits. Certainly, medical journal articles, information from the Federation of State Medical Boards, and newspaper summaries all suggest strongly that physicians perform laxly as peers policing their own profession. Personally, I may find Todd's suggestion that lay people should not sit in jury on medical cases offensive. Politically, I could argue that it flies in the face of several hundred years of legal and democratic tradition that defines "peer" as not simply a fellow professional or classmate, but rather as a member of the same society. Professionally, I now can take him apart on this point, using evidence available in the public domain to show that physicians have not, in the past, been able to police their own adequately and that the failure of doctors to follow what they themselves agree are appropriate procedures in anesthetic administration has significantly affected the incidence of injury and thus of malpractice in general.

Hack journalists trained to quote subjects uncritically, to write ephemeral stories based on the unquestioned statements of authorities or officials, have been empowered by information approximating that possessed by their subjects. The form is not destroyed – they still quote interview subjects who largely define the agenda, but both the questions a reporter might ask and the context in which the responses are framed can now, for the first time, occur from within the broader context of that information already in the public domain. The difference, quite simply, is between a lapdog and a watchdog press.

Newsroom Effect: The Beat

Perhaps as importantly, this method, based on electronic information has broken down barriers that in the past have kept reporters locked in a "beat system." The general assignment reporter has covered and brought together material that would normally have fallen into the separate domains of the court reporter (what is the liability? what do the courts find?), legislative reporter (where tort reform is to be debated), medical reporter (Eichorn's and other researchers' work is noted), financial reporter (rising health care costs as a function of insurance, effect on business payments for medical insurance), and a general, human interest writer (one who can pull from the cases described in the literature or personalize a story through local, individual tales).

In short, not only are individual data from a variety of sources no longer necessarily isolated, but reporters once blocked by the newsroom's internal fiefdoms ("Ask reporter Ralph – he's business." "Ask reporter Koch – he's our medical man.") have been freed to pursue a story across those internal barriers. Because data comes from outside as well as inside the realm of the cultivated source, the reporter's traditionally absolute reliance on personal relations with officials is also lessened. This change will affect, perhaps radically, the relations of news people to their individual sources or experts because no longer can the head of the local hospital, who has cultivated reporter "X," be assured that "his" or "her" reporter will be the one present when tough questions are raised. As reporters move beyond the traditional system of "exclusive" beat information and absolute reliance on the official sources each has cultivated in his or her "beat," the traditional news subject's ability to control and slant stories by feeding information to a specific reporter will be diminished to the degree that news people can gain independent background information. Creating an information system that decreases reliance on any single source or the necessity for cultivating ties to a professional category weakens the beat system, diminishes reportorial fiefdoms, and gives news people a method for the objective evaluation of public statements.

Writers have found a context broader than the narrow political viewpoint of adversaries or the definitions of the newsroom itself. They are empowered to examine, discuss, or focus a story through intelligent questioning based on a large background of objective information. Writers, in short, have the opportunity, if not independently to set the general agenda, then at least to modify it, and in the process to become the gatekeepers of their own stories—wherever they may lead. The electronically generated, informational background allows the newsperson, advocate, public relations writer, or interested citizen to access a context greater than that ordained by a partisan but necessary source or subject.

Story Levels

Another way of understanding what has changed is to see the degree to which this database approach has altered the story's signifier and what that image signifies. *Signifier* is defined by semiologists as the original subject, the boundary event that becomes, through the mediation of the news story, a sign. In the case of a photograph, for example, the signifier is a pattern of dots on paper that makes an image we take, at the most elementary level, as a photograph representing "x" at a moment in time. That photo, however, is not a value-free representation any more than Todd's statements were value-free, but one to be interpreted and perceived through social and political filters. Semiology provides a perspective allowing for the decoding of cultural events and was developed from attempts by linguists to describe the structure of language. In a very general sense, it is the type of intuitive abstraction that good political cartoonists employ when creating and applying symbols across the text of news reports to individual illustrations. As a system of understanding, semiology was pioneered by Roland Barthes and offers a useful perspective on precisely what cultural artifacts, in this case news stories, do or do not say. In the *Wall Street Journal* story, the signifier is a class: lawsuits that are filed by lawyers against doctors. The headline, "Malpractice Liability: Can the Law Serve Both Doctors and Patients?" makes this clear. The ability of the law to serve patients is, however, not the focus or the subject of the story because, as the lead paragraph states, malpractice liability is itself defined and treated as a divisive issue between doctors and lawyers. In the body of the text, Habash introduces the issue of patient suffering but Todd refuses it. Objecting to the word *victims,* Todd addresses only the social and practical cost of malpractice suits. Both men steer clear, perhaps by previous agreement, of any case examples. So while the story's signifier is the burgeoning case load of medical malpractice cases, what is signified is increasing cost to physicians and society.

The story's sign, at the most elementary level, is a dollar sign: cost in insurance premiums (to doctors) and in physician care (to society). At a more abstract, political level, however, that dollar sign is interpreted in very different ways by the two men. Todd and the *Wall Street Journal* interpret the subject of malpractice liability as a signifier composed of "burgeoning lawsuits" and "staggering premiums" (malpractice liability), which, in their turn, signify merciless litigation" and exorbitant profits for members of the legal profession. Doctors can't do their job. They're leaving their practices in droves. Malpractice liability (and, by extension, avaricious lawyers playing on the trauma of the patients mentioned in the headline) is robbing doctors of their work and the population of medical care. In Todd's analysis, the whole signifies, at a more general level, embattled, humanitarian physicians beset by onerous costs and avaricious lawyers-the whole business that interferes with their job of caring and treating.

Habash's recitation defines the second and third levels more generally. While accepting the basic sign, he, like Todd, virtually ignores the patients. In his version, "bad doctors," not "burgeoning lawsuits," are the signifier of this tale. He quotes federal statistics which suggest 5 percent of the nation's physicians are incompetent. He quotes "an outstanding physician [Todd]" on "incompetence and negligence in the medical profession." The problem is not medicine in general or physicians as a class but a few bad apples in the medical barrel. What is signified by incompetent physicians is injured patients. At a political level, this signifies the necessity for lawyers to represent the injured and lawyers thus become not the problem but the answer, signifying redress and not, as Todd argued, the problem.

What is signified in Habash's view is the lawyer as guardian, attorneys as defenders and protectors. Todd's statements signified the physician as healer, the good doctor under attack by a "system" which is beggaring his profession. Thus both men reinforce the myths of their respective professions throughout the whole argument. Todd has the healer befuddled by laws, lawyers, and malpractice suits, followers of a healing art who cannot understand (although clearly Todd does— very well) the issues behind increasing malpractice premiums. For his part, Habash cleverly enforces and underlines the advocate's image as guardian both of the injured (the client) and (because the law helps weed out bad doctors) of medicine itself.

The whole is pretty much a standoff. What the story does do supremely well is allow the issue of medical care to be defined in terms of cost and to create a text that affirms simultaneously the social posture of both lawyers and physicians, two primary categories of *Journal* subscribers. The context of the story has, as its elementary signifiers, a physician, a lawyer, and a *Journal* reporter together. It signifies reasonable and responsible discourse. After all, the lawyer, the doctor, and the reporter are sitting together, "debating," finding common ground and defining honest differences. In this process the *Journal* (through its reporter's participation) is coequal, a facilitator and partner among professionals in the search for solutions to society's problems, which are, the whole says, at base business related. Signified is an entire process of problem identification and solution in which the publication takes on the role of both society's informant and its surrogate. The story signifies, in its present form, the newspaper as consensus builder in the realm of power because, after all, it brought together a high official of the American Medical Association and the president of the Association of Trial Lawyers of America. Habash says that Todd is "an outstanding physician," although on what he bases his assertion is unclear. Todd clearly listens to and respects Habash's opinion, even though he sees lawyers as a class as the problem.

The *Daily Journal of the American Dream* comes off the clear winner because the whole exercise signifies its power, "objectivity," and attraction to wealthy clients who are or serve physicians and lawyers. Lost in these abstractions from the start, however, was the issue of injured patients who may file suit against physicians and then use lawyers as their representatives. When introduced into the debate at all, patients were ciphers, mentioned as a class by Habash and then only in the briefest, most general terms. Also ignored were questions regarding the context that causes specific health problems, as well as attention to other factors directly affecting the social cost of health care (e.g., fee-for-service medicine, underutilization of nurses). These subjects are central to the cost of medical treatment (and the efficacy of American medicine in general) and, at another level, the overall cost of health care in the United States. The whole has been dehumanized, reduced to an abstraction of professional stances which are not challenged and costs which are not critically considered.

A reader in 1986 could scan this story or study it and come away uninformed. Doctors will agree, presumably, with their surrogate while lawyers will support their leader. Uninvolved readers can say with satisfaction that "there is right and wrong on both sides" but cannot come away with anything other than the occasional, disembodied factoid. For example, the government says that at least twenty thousand of America's four hundred thousand doctors are incompetent (whatever that means); 1 percent of the doctors in Pennsylvania account for 25 percent of the malpractice claims (Are they all in high-risk specialties? Is Pennsylvania unique?); and physicians are leaving the profession in droves ("Not in my neighborhood," a reader might say dismissively. "I support five of them myself.").

The whole does not inform from the start because it presents no data in context, no information other than self serving statements by representatives of two groups: physicians and lawyers. It deals not with illness, the sick, or those injured by medicine but rather with an aspect of the cost of bad medicine to society. It is smoke and mirrors, like Todd's argument that only physicians are qualified to judge the performance of their own class. The *Journal* has presented information that affirms its role as chronicler of society's commercial issues, but at the cost of the type of information news publications are pledged to provide (full and unbiased) if they are to fulfill their institutional and instrumental goals. The real loser in this approach has been the United States as a dynamic social system whose legal and scientific communities act to assure the life, liberty, and potential for its citizens' contentment. Attempts by the medical, legal, judicial, and legislative communities to define and then redress the root problems of society through research, case law, medical protocol, etcetera – the wealth of data uncovered in the computer search – are ignored in this traditional news approach. This lack of context implies by that exclusion that cost is the only issue and that what is important is the self interest of wealthy, professional groups.

Story Levels: Contextual

The story resulting from the computer search changes the system of signifier, signified, and sign throughout the whole. It places the question of malpractice litigation and the resulting costs within the context of an aspect of contemporary surgery in which a large percentage of suits originates. The basic signifier is "individuals injured by improperly administered anesthesia during surgery." What is signified is not money or dollars but corpses or critically disabled people whose deficits are the direct result of physician malpractice. At another level of meaning, those victims (that is what they have become, despite Todd's objections) stand for the failure of physicians as a class to monitor their own and enforce upon individual members even the most basic standards of competence. Physicians are not, in this version, part of the solution but instead constitute a central aspect of the problem. Lawyers become, at this level, tangential to the problem. If the issue is not costs but the cause of the injuries that give rise to the suits, then the question of avaricious lawyers is not even relevant.

Table 4.1. Goals and Myths: Malpractice

	Institutional A	*Instrumental* B	*Functional* C
Reporters 1	To serve through providing information	that is unbiased and complete	Earn adequate hourly wage
Physicians 2	To cure the sick and injured	Through recognized	Make a profit through fees

	Institutional A	*Instrumental* B	*Functional* C
		protocols and procedures	charged per patient
Lawyers 3	To defined the injured or wronged	Through successful litigation	Make a profit by fee or percentage of awards per case

At one more level, physicians are seen not as Todd insists they must be, as caregivers besieged by financial concerns and a legal system they cannot understand but, rather, as a class of technicians who lack appropriate monitoring and control. In a contextual story, lawyers are neither agents of avarice or of justice. They become a conduit for the redress of the injured and, as such, are valued neither positively nor negatively because the issue of the nature and causes of those injuries has become the central issue. From such contextual or structural reportage comes a radically changed image of the newspaper. Here the signs affirm not the other professions but rather that of the journalist, whose contextual investigation "suggests strongly" that a specific problem exists that can be precisely defined on the basis of objective documentation, and one which therefore can be clearly explained. By examining medical texts, legal cases, and the printed reports of colleagues from other geographical regions, the newsperson has gathered a series of cases in which individuals were injured. By drawing on the published work of medical and legal experts, the public information writer can suggest authoritatively how those injuries might, in the future, be diminished or eliminated. Cost has become not the issue but a result and, in the process, the newspaper has fulfilled, at least to some degree, its instrumental goal of objectivity. It has examined an issue, identified its components, and then reported from within a context that fit the "facts" together to create a coherent description of the issue at hand. It has, simultaneously, approached its institutional goal by providing information of social importance in such a way that both layperson and official may be informed by the story the newspaper puts forward. Things might even change.

Todd, for his part, emphasized to the *Journal* the physicians' *institutional* goal and warned that because the physicians *functional* goal was under attack (malpractice suits cost money and time; malpractice premiums are expensive), many doctors were abandoning their professions and thus their socially desirable, instrumental goal. In short, they were refusing to attend to the *instrumental* goal because malpractice insurance costs were making it uneconomical for those physicians to continue to cure the sick. Habash suggests the real problem is at the physicians' *instrumental* level, that the recognized protocols are not being employed and, therefore, the physicians' *institutional* goal (to cure the sick) is not being fulfilled. In fact, he says, the reverse often occurs and people are made sicker. That argument is amenable to computer information searching and is the one both examined and tentatively confirmed by our story.

Todd and the *Journal*'s introduction emphasize the lawyer's functional goal and downplay or deny the institutional goal and institutional myths of the legal profession. They ignore the root cause of a "burgeoning" number of lawsuits or the reasoning behind the high awards that have resulted in increased premiums. Thus they define lawyers earning contingency fees as the problem. Habash, for his part, skillfully counters by emphasizing his profession's instrumental goal— defense of the injured through socially approved litigation— and allows the reader to perceive the institutional value of these acts. He is also careful-a good technique in legal arguments— to take the high road. By complimenting Todd— "an outstanding physician"— he does not attack the institutional image of physicians as healers and helpers (something many people believe in) but rather the instrumental failure of a subset (bad doctors) who injure the legal profession's clients.

The advantage of the story based on computer-generated information is its ability, through proper searching of popular, professional, and technical literature, to make overt the difference between what people say in defense of their own institutional myths, and what they may, in fact, want at the functional level. Further, it allows the layperson to compare institutional goals with the evidence of observable performance at the instrumental level. Actions at this level are typically well documented and therefore particularly amenable to contextual, computer-generated analysis. The *Journal*, with no real information of its own, credited and placed prominently in its introduction Todd's statement that physicians are abandoning their practices because of "a [malpractice insurance] system they don't understand, [and] they can't cope with." But Todd, a physician as well as spokesman, clearly understands it very well. The issue as he states it is one of functional economics (they don't want to pay more) and the degree to which instrumental goals (people are injured, not cured) are being unfulfilled. It is also one, as Todd suggests, of power and control. Will courts with lay juries continue to judge physicians demonstrably incapable of overseeing themselves? Or will physicians be freed from general, social accountability, as Todd argues they should be, presumably to judge themselves in solitude? From this perspective, the issue is one of balancing the autonomy of a profession with the social accountability of its individual members— whose record in self-regulation as a class is, on the evidence, anything but reassuring.

This computer-assisted, contextual approach has laid bare the grammar of the "debate" and thus allowed the reader to evaluate its constituent parts. Through the perspective of outside research it has made overt the interests of the respective speakers and the means by which one or another used the *Journal* as a forum to advance a specific profession's agenda or interests. Sigelman's sociology and

Barthes'semiology provide different languages which allow us to analyze the whole. But both gain, in this case, through the ability to test the conclusions and examine the debate's dialectic through reference to outside data. Indeed, this extended exegesis would not have been possible without the use of these technologies. Through this process the newspaper and its reporter have gone from being a silent conduit for the polemics of others to an active participant in a social debate. The newspaper, through its reporter, now listens to the positions enunciated by interview subjects and not only relays those positions but places them in a more objective context. It accepts oral statements as a starting point and tests them in the context of what has been written by "experts" on the general subject and against what has happened of a similar nature in other circulation or broadcast jurisdictions. Thus the newswriter and the publication acknowledge and approach, perhaps for the first time, the journalist's instrumental goal of unbiased, objective coverage and, through this, the institutional myth has a chance of becoming a reality. The effect of this approach on publishers' and writers' functional goals is at present untested.

Structural Context

The contextual level is one in which statements by interview subjects can be examined against the records of previous cases and their analysis in a general or professional literature. If Habash says a small number of unqualified physicians cause a large number of complaints, that statement can be checked. If Todd says that physicians can adequately police their colleagues and judge the competence of their fellows, that statement, too, need not be accepted on faith. A structural story might take the whole further and attempt to determine the degree to which elements causing a specific problem are, in fact, merely symptoms of a deeper social perspective or context.

If the issue is the cost of health care to society at large, examining the cost of malpractice as a single problem will not serve. As the contextual approach made clear, health costs are a subset of larger issues in medicine and in society. Using a series of electronic databases, it would not be difficult to define the problem by first examining the major types of illness (nosocomial, environmental, viral and bacterial, accidental, etc.), defining general categories of health care costs (pharmaceutical, physician-related, nursing, etc.), reviewing the costs of specific medical procedures, and referencing the whole against the demographics of illness (at what ages are people most likely to become ill and to what extent are their medical bills paid for by society at large).

Further, there are nations with federal health insurance programs where indices of health are higher while health care costs are lower. The efficiency of those programs, and thus their potential suitability for the United States (or any other country), can be determined through the examination of any number of health service indices. Armed with this information, the public can judge for itself the wisdom of adopting a federal health insurance program. The structural issues thus become efficient use, appropriate compensation, and adequate supervision of health care professionals as a class, of political allocations and decisions. Classes of disease are defined as the result of environmental, industrial, and social policy choices. In this whole, Todd's agenda and Habash's perspective are but single elements of the greater, immediate whole, and the issues of cost which they present will be seen very differently from a structural perspective.

Thus, in the structural story, the writer or broadcaster takes full control of the agenda. The designated speaker's signifier is diminished as the reporter defines and redefines the context of an issue as one of root causes and systemic problems. In this process, which tests immediate concerns against antecedent knowledge, the system of signifiers and signs traditionally accepted as public fact becomes obviously biased data. A structural story by definition changes the initial focus from that of an individual issue to the more general, cultural perspective by absorbing the original speaker's signifier into a broader class of events or research. One example is the current American war on drugs, declared in the early 1980s by President Ronald Reagan and carried on with enthusiasm by his successor, President George Bush. A brief overview of its coverage and the issues that it raises is an instructive lesson in the limits of orally transmitted news.

War on Drugs

Throughout the 1980s, the chemical addiction of U.S. citizens to a long list of controlled substances— heroin, marijuana, and cocaine being the best publicized— was trumpeted as a critical danger to the national body. The interdiction of drug supplies through the use of military, police, and judicial resources, a growth industry during President Reagan's tenure, escalated during the term of his successor, President Bush, who used the "drug war" as an excuse for, among other things, the invasion of Panama and the removal of its leader, General Manuel Noriega. Between 1980 and 1988, the United States spent several hundred billion dollars to first interdict narcotics during the transportation of supplies to their market and then to prosecute those responsible for the wholesale preparation and distribution of controlled substances. In 1989, President Bush asked the U.S. congress for $9.5 billion more and his 1990 budget included direct allocations of $10 billion in drug war monies. These funds were allocated during a period of systematic federal cutbacks in funding for social programs, education, and general services.

The war against illegal drugs has been covered at each step by daily journalists who typically report the arrest and trial of dealers in their circulation area, lament the continued presence of drugs in their home region, and editorially laud government and community efforts to remove a chemical tumor from the body of the American politic. As Jeff Greenfield of ABC News noted, national television coverage of the war on drugs has been voluminous, if un-edifying. In a two-week period in 1989, for example, the three major networks carried 163 drug-related stories and several "special reports" on their national news shows. CBS named its coverage, One Nation under Siege," and ABC titled its stories, A Plague upon the Land." Regionally, trivial stories across the nation have recorded, in newspapers and on broadcast news shows, the amounts and estimated street value of illegal substances seized by local or federal police departments in thousands of separate raids. They have also disseminated, without consideration or thought, thousands of official statements made by law enforcement officers and politicians insistent on the necessity for increasing police and military action in the war on drugs.

As Massachusetts reporter Al Giordano said of his fellow journalists involved in covering the war on drugs:

> *With a few exceptions, they have neglected their self-proclaimed task of providing objective or critical coverage of the issue. Although there is a wealth of academic research that finds most casual users of non-nicotine drugs do not become addicted, press coverage continues to stigmatize addicts and scapegoat users of illegal drugs for social problems that existed long before crack arrived. Journalists have failed to differentiate between types of illegal drugs and have accepted legal definitions of drug abuse as medical and factual – which they are not.*

There are two basic patterns to the ephemeral story on drugs. One chronicles, on the authority of local police, federal investigators, or army officials "who" was arrested (today), the value estimated by officials of the drugs seized, and "what" a police chief, president, army officer, or administration "drug czar" said about those drugs (yesterday). The second quotes those same officials when they reiterate the danger-to the individual and to society – of any drug use, the importance of decreasing chemical dependency among the citizenry, and the official position that a "drug-free America" can only be reached through interdiction and the apparatus of the judicial system.

This reflexive reportage clearly serves a legitimizing function, affirming the official postures not only that drugs create an evil, chemical dependency among users but that police action and a tough judicial posture are the only possible cures. In January 1990, NBC broadcast a miniseries – Drug Wars: The Camarena Story – which presented both a fictionalized account of the death of a Drug Enforcement Administration (DEA) agent, Enrique Camarena, and the attempts of his fellow officers to bring his killers to trial. Following the nightly series segment, NBC national news anchor Tom Brokaw hosted and participated in "panel discussions" on the drug problem, which were broadcast from a DEA laboratory. Clearly, NBC News, through its participation in these "discussions," was lending its considerable prestige and voice not only to the U.S. government's war on drugs but also to its foreign adventures in drug interdiction. In one segment Brokaw insisted, for example, that Mexico, like Panama, was a drug villain ("In every part of the country there is a local Noriega, a commandante, a general, a governor getting rich."). In this series NBC's principal newsman, and by extension NBC News itself, functioned as an uncritical advocate for both the DEA, whose agents were portrayed (in both the fictional show and the "news" segment) as universally virtuous, patriotic, and hardworking, and for the administration, which has made the war on drugs into a patriotic crusade. In the NBC series, as in most daily or weekly news reportage of the drug, there was little objectivity and virtually no analysis of the assumptions of the war on drugs, no consideration of the structural or contextual issues that it raises.

Like local news stories trumpeting brave police arresting dangerous drug dealers, NBC News participation in this docudrama's creation of a federal martyr, agent Enrique Camarena, affirmed government action by accurately reflecting official positions without any consideration of the two principal assumptions of the war on drugs: that chemical dependency is a problem in and of itself and that police and judicial action can stop the traffic in illegal substances.

An even simpler question would be whether the program of interdiction has been successful. In 1990, when President Bush asked Congress to allocate an additional $10.5 billion for the war on drugs, one way to deal intelligently with the story would have been to ask if, in a decade of escalating action, there had been any hint of success.

The answer is, in fact, no. Those searching for stories on the efficiency of the war on drugs would find, for example, an American Bar Association report, issued in 1988, which stated bluntly:

> *Police, prosecutors and judges told the committee that they have been unsuccessful in making a significant impact on the importation, sale and use of illegal drugs, despite devoting much of their resources to the arrest, prosecution and trial of drug offenders. These extraordinary efforts have instead distorted and overwhelmed the criminal justice system, crowding dockets and jails, and diluting law enforcement and judicial efforts to deal with other major criminal cases.*

From 1980 to 1988 the cost to customers of most controlled substances (marijuana, cocaine, heroin) dropped as supplies increased, despite the increasingly expensive and constant efforts of local, regional, and federal law enforcement agencies. Interdiction is, apparently, an appalling failure. Further, it is clear from a search of newspaper stories including the words *drugs* and *arrest* or *death* that the war on drugs is not a tightly focused fight. There are, for example, battles to stay the supply of cocaine (from Colombia), marijuana (from Mexico or Hawaii), heroin (from Asia) or, most recently, "crystal methamphetamine" (from Korea). At varying times in the decade, the war on drugs has been defined with reference to each of these substances, as well as alcohol, model airplane glue, crack (synthetic cocaine), tobacco (a "legal drug"), etcetera. At different times each drug has been targeted as a real and present danger, its increasing use supposedly signifying, according to news reports of the day, an ever greater imperative to allocate public resources to the war.

Individuals will, apparently, switch with alacrity from one drug to another depending on cost and availability. That explanation is the only one for the progression of "targeted" drugs, and one found frequently in newspaper stories. A more appropriate question is: Why do individuals use drugs at all? As Greenfield of ABC News said in a Nightline report on the "timid" state of contemporary journalism:

> *A more skeptical press might have asked questions. If drugs have triggered a sudden huge surge in crime, why are national murder*

and robbery rates down in the last two years? Why were there fewer burglaries in New York and Los Angeles last year than there were back in 1980? They might have asked whether the violence of drug-dealing gangs stems from drug use itself or from the battle to protect the huge profits of dealing in illegal drugs. They might have asked whether drugs are a cause of crime, or a symptom of deeper social pathologies.

Some spokespeople on the fringes of official dissent have raised these issues. Rev. Jesse Jackson, for example, told a congressional panel that "Bush's plan [to stop drugs] does not adequately address 'material and spiritual poverty, which are the preconditions for the drug crisis.'" That statement suggests that drug use is, in fact, a symptom resulting from "material and spiritual poverty." But his is a relatively solitary voice, an apparently unsubstantiated opinion isolated in an ephemeral story from the other side. In the same month, however, the *Wall Street Journal* had a long front page article on how an Omaha businessman, Ben Gray, hired the head of a local, drug-oriented youth gang because, Gray told the *Journal*, in his opinion the drug problem was "institutional racism and double standards." If drug sellers could be brought into the social and economic mainstream of society, he reasoned, they would give up the quite dangerous business of selling and distributing controlled substances. So this story at least had some meat, a single case study of one man and one drug dealer whom the businessman tried to convert.

The article quoted Gray's gang-leader-turned-employee, Robert Penn, and Federal Bureau of Investigation (FBI) supervisor John Pankonin, who both said drugs are a problem rooted in poverty and that, to decrease drug use, issues of poverty need to be addressed. In the words of the FBI agent: "What alternative have I got for them? What job have I got for a high school dropout that will allow him to get up at noon and make $300 dollars in the afternoon? I don't like to admit it, but they're pretty good capitalists."

This suggests that, on the basis of both the FBI field officer's and Penn's experiences, activist Jackson may be right: poverty and alienation are indeed factors in the continued sale, if not the use, of controlled substances. This possibility is especially interesting because throughout the 1980s, newspapers and magazines also chronicled the government's elimination of a whole series of programs aimed at decreasing poverty through increasing literacy, prenatal care, and so on. A result of Reagan's "supply-side" economics and Bush's wars on both drugs and taxes was the destruction of a "social safety net" whose unraveling coincides with increasing drug use, increasing supplies of controlled substances, and increasing federal and regional expenditures in the war on drugs. In fact, there seems to have been an inverse correlation: the more that funding for social programs was cut, the more money was spent on drug interdiction. Further, throughout the 1980s (as several writers make clear) the street prices of most controlled substances – crack, cocaine, heroin – fell. A graph charting these trends would show an increase in money spent for drug interdiction by the government and a decrease in the cost of individual drug dosages as a function of supply outpacing demand. Not since the sale of liquor was prohibited has so much money been spent for so little effect.

If it is all a shuck, if the drug busts, drug wars, and drug legislation are futile exercises unless socioeconomic problems are addressed, why cover the subject at all? A search of magazine articles on drugs and interdiction turned up a tentative answer by *Harper's* editor Lewis P. Lapham, who described the current war on drugs as a safe, political ploy that makes good copy. "Because the human craving for intoxicants cannot be suppressed – not by priests or jailers or acts of Congress – the politicians can bravely confront an allegorical enemy rather than an enemy that takes the corporeal form of the tobacco industry, say, or the Chines, or the oil and banking lobbies." He also blames the media for their slavish coverage of drug busts and drug hysteria but acknowledges that:

> *The drug war, like all wars, sells papers, and the media, like the politicians, ask for nothing better than a safe and profitable menace. The campaign against drugs involves most of the theatrical devices employed by* Miami Vice – *scenes of crimes in progress (almost always dressed up, for salacious effect, with the cameo appearances of one or two prostitutes, melodramatic villains in the Andes, a vocabulary of high-tech military jargon as reassuring as the acronyms in a Tom Clancy novel, the specter of a crazed lumpen proletariat rising in revolt in the nation's cities).*

Great writing and beautifully crafted opinion, but not really substantial. Similar views are also expressed by Charles T. Salmon, who reviews the work of sociologists interested in media coverage of the drug phenomena. But consider, for a moment, the assumptions in Mr. Lapham's piece. Who says the human craving for "intoxicants cannot be suppressed?" Is there, in fact, such a craving at all? What are the biology, psychology, and pharmacology of addiction? Are they the same for all drugs or different for each one?

If the policy of interdiction is a failure, perhaps demand is where the real story lies. Therefore the appropriate contextual question might be: Why do people take drugs at all? The war on drugs is based on an assumption that a broad class of controlled substances (heroin, marijuana, cocaine, etc.) is chemically addictive, creating an absolute physical need on the part of addicts, who will do anything to satisfy their habits. A search of the pharmacology and psychology literatures (using search phrases written as "addiction and (heroine or cocaine)," or "addiction and habituation") suggests that this assumption is, at best, a very partial truth.

Addiction researchers seem unanimous on two general points. One is that chemical dependency is not the single, critical factor in repeated use of either heroin or cocaine. The second point is that prohibition and interdiction cannot and will not be effective in the curtailment of drug use. Were unrelenting chemical dependency the necessary result of the ingestion (or injection) of proscribed substances, it would be impossible for individuals using cocaine, heroin, marijuana, etcetera, to cease their use voluntarily. But clinical studies have shown consistently that chemically dependent mammals regularly give up drugs on their own when the conditions of their life improve. For example, animal studies have shown that laboratory rats kept in comfortable surroundings do not become addicted while those isolated in small cages rapidly become dependent on morphine. Studies of human addiction have had similar results. A follow-up study of U.S. military veterans, addicted during the Vietnam War, showed that the vast majority voluntarily stopped using controlled substances after their return to the United States. Individuals belonging to selfhelp groups, which attempt to modify their members' social context, cease inhalation of cocaine, for example, without adverse affects, just as Alcoholics Anonymous assists alcoholics, once freed of their immediate dependency, from again using alcohol as a stress release. In addition, the vast majority of young drug users voluntarily cease use of currently illegal drugs as they mature. Hospital patients are increasingly allowed to self-administer morphine following surgery and not only do they not become addicted to the analgesic but, in fact, they used less narcotic than physicians typically ordered for their comfort. The stated conclusion of these and other studies published in the technical literature has been that individuals became addicts as a response to stress and tensions in their personal lives. U.S. military personnel in the 1960s and early 1970s, for example, used drugs as an escape when their quality of life in Vietnam was intolerable, but when their tours were completed, most voluntarily became drug-free as their lives returned to relative normalcy.

This suggests that interdiction cannot work because those whose quality of life is such as to require relief will use almost any substance that offers escape from an unpleasant and stressful reality. A partial list of drugs whose use newspapers have campaigned against includes alcohol, heroin, airplane glue, morphine, marijuana, cocaine, crack cocaine, amphetamines as a class, and crystal methamphetamine as a specific substance. Street users regularly switch from one drug to another, often on the basis of availability, just as newspaper coverage switches from articles on one drug or drug class to articles on another (marijuana to heroin to cocaine to synthetic drugs) on the basis of what police are confiscating in the current season of drug busts.

The Story

The clear conclusion, based on these and other studies, is that to decrease drug use, it would be necessary to create a series of social programs, for clients of various income levels, that support and help improve lives so diminished that narcotic use became desirable. To the degree that controlled substances are sold or used as a means to escape poverty, social programs whose aim is the long-term elimination of society's economic disparities would need to be implemented. But social programs themselves have been a major casualty of the drug wars. As money was funneled into the war on drugs, the war on poverty became ever more tenuous. And, of course, the war on drugs is based, as was 1920s-style prohibition, on legal penalties and interdiction. Just as prohibition failed to stop the use of alcohol, so must current and structurally similar policies be ineffective in stemming the use of heroin or cocaine, because interdiction does not address the primary causes of any substance's abuse. Jackson was, in retrospect, quite correct. Drug abuse has social, economic, and psychological roots not addressed and, perhaps, exacerbated by Bush's policies.

Table 4.2. Drug Cops and Crime Reporters

	Institutional A	*Instrumental* B	*Functional* C
Crime Reporter 1	To serve through Publishing or broadcasting	records of police antidrug activities	and earn salary through exciting, prestigious, socially important work
Drug Squad Cop 2	To protect and serve the people	by arresting drug users and suppliers	is a valuable social service worthy of a decent wage and society's respect

It is not that the futility of administration policies or the false premises which are at the heart of the administration's war on drugs has gone unnoticed. Even conservative magazines ranging from the *National Review* to the *Economist* have carried articles arguing for some form of drug legalization as a cost-effective alternative to, in Giordano's words, the "prohibition-related crime" that current drug war policies have spawned. In an open letter to the administration on September 7, 1989, economist Milton Friedman argued in the *Wall Street Journal* that repressive administration policies in the war on drugs— more police, more jails, harsher penalties for drug users, military adventurism-"only make a bad situation worse." But these pieces are opinion, like Lapham's argument, submitted through the press and quickly forgotten in the daily march of new statements at news conferences covered by reporters. There is no memory to the oral argument, no careful comparison to be based on it. As in the debate between Todd and Habash, it is barely considered grist for the editorial mill. Populations was prepared for publication in that year. But it took two years for my employers to run a different and greatly modified version because, as *Province* assistant city editor William Holden, said testily "I just don't believe it, no matter how many eggheads you quote." Holden's aversion to academics, intellectuals, researchers, and other "eggheads," as well as the comments of other *Province* editors, was instructive.

When the story finally ran, the *Province*'s city editor, Donald MacLaughlin, insisted it also include an interview with a local official of the Royal Canadian Mounted Police (RCMP) involved in drug enforcement, who said simply, "I don't buy it." The RCMP officer, like Holden, sneered at academic research and argued that his experience on the streets was sufficient to assure the newspaper's readers that chemical addiction was the real problem and police action the necessary solution. Running this interview served two purposes. It guarded against the *Province*'s apparent endorsement of some flaky academic finding— Holden's "egghead argument" — and, more important to MacLaughlin, assured the *Province* would not lose valuable police contacts that, he said, the newspaper needed. To run the story without giving the police a rebuttal would have been not only "biased" but politically unsound. The newspaper needed police sources, and allowing the RCMP to critique the conclusions of years of careful research assured the whole could be finessed as an "egghead" story in which the politically valuable police were given a chance to insist upon their raison d'être, drug confiscation and interdiction. Another assistant editor, Bud Jorgensen, was more than willing to accept the position of researchers, but he insisted the story could not run without information on the economics of the drug business: how much was spent on enforcement and how much drug users spent on the streets. If the academics were correct, Jorgensen reasoned, then the taxpayers money was being misspent. The salient question for him was, by how much?

Within this one admittedly anecdotal example, the variety of perspectives affecting news judgment can be seen. MacLaughlin was concerned about the newspaper's losing valuable police connections, without which it could not continue to report on drug busts and other RCMP activities. Since these were crucial to its style of ephemeral reportage, those factions had to be placated. Holden did not give credence to research on principle, trusting instead to the weight of materials published in his and other newspapers in which drugs had been socially defined as a menace. What more, he reasoned, did one really need to know? Jorgenson, a more experienced and perhaps a better-read editor, understood that whatever the conclusions of the researchers, readers and advertisers wanted an economic focus: how much was spent on these chemical prohibitions and what did this research mean to some "bottom line"? Thus the final copy had to balance a number of non-textual constraints in its attempt to present objective "fact" based on a series of studies and researcher positions within the broad context of the daily news process.

In retrospect, all these editorial concerns were justified. Police were angered because the story attacked not only their view of the world in general but, specifically, their instrumental goals. The myth of the drug enforcement program is that, institutionally, police protect the public by (instrumentally) stopping the flow of harmful substances to an unwitting public. Functionally, RCMP and city police drug officers earned their salaries through a system that deemed it necessary to pay them wages to fight drug suppliers and to capture both suppliers and users.

News people attempt to fulfill their institutional objective (service to the public) by instrumentally publicizing the "successes" of antidrug officials involved in interdiction. A story challenging the assumptions of the drug interdiction program attacked not only the police officers' livelihood, and thus the individual officers' functional support, but also the instrumental myth that governed both the officers' and journalists' professional lives. As Holden was at pains to point out, the story made a mockery of the hundreds of articles and stories the *Province* had run. If the newspaper in fact served the public (institutionally) and made its money (functionally) by publicizing drug arrests, then what would it mean if the newspaper said with any consistency that researchers had known for years these arrests not only were not going to stop drug traffic but would, in fact, have no effect whatsoever (despite the enormous financial cost of interdiction) on drug use? And if drugs are themselves a symptom and not the cause, why was the newspaper devoting substantial news space to stories quoting police, politicians, and civic leaders who might, for one self-interested reason or another, decide to "speak out" on the evil of drugs? The amazing thing, in retrospect, is that my story ran at all.

It is from this perspective that reportage through the 1980s of not only the drug war but, by extension, government policies and actions in general can be understood. To the degree that reporters, editors, and television anchors are limited to information based on the official view, they repeat those official statements without consideration. Their research is limited to "checking facts" in the newspaper morgue or broadcast station's library. And, in both, the principal information base is prior "facts" from previous stories quoting the same sources. There is, simply, no context from which the journalistic event (the press conference, media opportunity, official statement, or press release) can be judged. News research becomes, in the main, a tautology in which the statement of an official today is compared with the "facts" he or she uttered yesterday. There is, with these traditional resources, no possible connection between the boundary event (the addicted or habituated individual) and the journalistic event (the trumpeted war on drugs). It is as if contemporary news were a physics experiment in which light (information) is reflected from mirror to mirror until its final intensity (the story) is measured. One mirror is the journalistic event, a second is the reporter's perception, and the third, perhaps, is the editor's. Information on the original boundary event, the objective context of a prior occurrence or process, is not within the traditional system. So the whole reflects but does not probe, presents but cannot inform, because there is no way to examine the information presented or compare the illumination's source with its final transformation.

This changes when computer-assisted data is included. One result in this case, like that of Todd and Habash, is that the system of meanings alters dramatically. In the *Province*'s typical drug bust story, believed by Holden and protected by MacLaughlin, for example, the elementary signifier is arrestees in chains, led to jail or the booking desk. What is signified by the standard news photo or arrest story is active police closing down drug dealers. At a second level, that news photo image creates a signifier emphasizing not the workaday, mundane officer following orders but the institutional myth of the police, whose motto is To Serve and Protect, as social servant fighting for the individual citizen in the communal war against drugs. Finally, the police are officers of the courts, civil servants whose allegiance is to the jurisdiction that employs them. The success of the RCMP officer (patrol cop, FBI agent, or army private) affirms, at the level of myth, the government's protection of its citizenry and its waging of a war (however senseless, however counterproductive) on behalf of each of us. Ultimately, each drug bust legitimizes by what is signified: government active on the behalf of its members.

The electronic story changes these levels of meaning by changing the interpretation of that original signifier. If drug abuse is a social problem brought on by poverty, lack of opportunity, and failed lives, then the constantly repeated news image of drug dealers arrested or in jail signifies not protection but failure on the part of society's protectors. If interdiction cannot work, then the antidrug machine is spending money not on the problem (poverty, lack of opportunity, racism) but on a symptom. Then the police do not signify protection but become, themselves, signs of a broader social failure to address the issue, dupes whose financial compensation (the functional goal) is a reward for largely valueless work. From this perspective, the police drug raid story cannot signify the honorable motto To Serve and Protect, but becomes, rather, the mercenary's "bust'em and get paid." The whole makes of police what radicals have charged, an army of occupation in the ghetto where the majority of police actions occur, including drug interdictions. Finally, Mr. Bush's government, which proclaims its responsibility for the war on drugs, is signified in turn not as caring but as indifferent, not concerned but opportunistic. They fight the visible symptoms and not the problem itself, a futile exercise whose only result is waste and continued suffering.

These transformations occur on the basis not, however, of radical rhetoric but of studies in recognized journals, even articles from the *Wall Street Journal* and other newspapers that have been pulled into a structural or contextual whole. These changes occur as the story gains depth through structure and context, the conjunction not only of a class of specific events (fifteen drug busts; new drug "epidemics") but of the relation between narrowly defined occurrences and their "what" and "why" written over time.

In this brief analysis, the general issue of police and news objectives and goals has been focused on a single type of reportage and a single type of police activity. In the previous example, the general operational myths of lawyers and physicians were used. But it is important to remember that these are examples whose real utility is to demonstrate the effect of new technologies on news in general and not simply a medical or police story, interesting though they may be. To the degree that the information generated by online resources allows for the examination of the institutional and instrumental myths, it also forces the writer to seek a greater specificity in the definition of a problem or argument. The whole indeed may be hampered by the cultural filters and individual perceptions that news professionals bring to their post, or by the economic necessities that limit individual media outlets. But those assumptions and, to a lesser extent, the economic restraints themselves, are the end result of a historical tradition growing out of the era of the first printing revolution. News is a system of information transfer whose historical function has been to assist in the dissemination of the officially spoken word to geographically dispersed peoples. It grew from the printing revolution and its form remains rooted in the postures of that era. It is argued here that new technologies will result in new economies and cultural forms whose end effect will be to change the cultural assumptions and traditions on which news, a part of the public information system, is based.

Conclusion

It is clear that online technologies can significantly affect the content of the news and the ability of contemporary journalists to approach the instrumental goal of "objectivity" that all, in theory, espouse. The typical news story, based on what one or another source said at a specific time and place, is by definition limited to an individual's comments and thus to that subject's specific perspective and information resources. Attempts to "balance" such statements are usually limited at present to fielding other comments, delivered orally, by actors of official import in a specific context (e.g., drug enforcement) or at a specific event (e.g., a district court trial). Current journalistic practice reinforces and is limited to the traditional, supporting media role of relay or conduit for the orally presented statements of officials and experts. Even when the information to be translated from distinct event to public report is printed, it often is treated as if it were a verbal presentation. Thus information from press releases, typically prepared in the standard news narrative's "he said" or "she said" form, is included uncritically in any individual story by newswires. Objectivity, the instrumental goal, is thus impossible to achieve in any but the most limited of senses.

Electronic databases, which make available to the reporter a wide variety of journals, newsletters, and newspaper texts, present the opportunity for a radically different, far more instrumentally satisfactory reportage. Through the "structural" or "contextual" story that this technology makes possible, online resources place the description of any isolated event within the context of a class of similar occurrences so that the journalist is informed by the work and research of other writers — colleagues and academics – involved in and knowledgeable about the event or event class in question. The assertions of news subjects are seen as not necessarily "true," as verified "facts" in and of themselves, but as hypotheses to be examined within a literature's context. This represents a potentially profound shift in the way data can be treated by public information writers and a significant change in the way data is incorporated into the public sphere. At the very least, this potential informs reporters or editors in a significant way, empowering them, through this electronically-gathered, background information, with a perspective that allows them to question critically an official posture, no matter how politically powerful its official source may be.

Table 4.3. Means and Goals

	Institutional *A*	*Instrumental* *B*	*Functional* *C*
Reporters 1	To serve by Providing information	which is complete and unbiased coverage	of what officials say
Police 2	To Serve and Protect	By arresting crooks and getting them convicted	through investigation of traces of prior events

The result is a diminishment of the source or subject's power to define any story's content in such a way as to advance arbitrarily that person's personal standing or the posture of the subject's professional group. If one accepts as general divisions of interest the categories of institutional, instrumental, and functional goals, this procedure may emphasize the speaker's personal, financial interest in a project or proposed legislation while making overt the degree to which their instrumental procedures or policies are perhaps the real issue at hand. For news writers, the end result is not only an ability to approximate journalism's own instrumental (and thus institutional) goals but an increasing freedom from the profession's history of absolute reliance on the professional or political subject as crucial and sole information source.

Criticism of coverage in this case presumed that the methods by which the press fulfilled its instrumental and institutional goals were the same as those of the police. But reporters do not have the legal authority or professional expertise to investigate homicides. Just as police were hampered by a lack of evidence against the victim's husband until Stuart's brother came forward, reporters were limited to police reports andeven without any other evidence— had a fantastic story. Similarly, the news professional does not have the institutional goal of To Serve and Protect, as do the police. Rather, the reporter and editor offer to the public, in the traditional news paradigm, information provided by official, police sources.

Thus criticism of *Boston Globe* reportage depended on a confusion of police methods and instrumental goals with those of the news people who covered the case (B1 and C1). Reporters are not investigators. They report (B1) what police officials find (C1). In cases like the Stuart case, this is an uncomfortable truth for news professionals to accept. Most would, like the *Globe*'s Goodman, prefer to argue a failure in reportage and presentation than admit a structural limit to their profession's abilities. But, as the analysis of the *Wall Street Journal*'s story made clear, the confusion of methods and goals is a consistent aspect of contemporary journalism. In this book's context, what makes the Stuart case unusual is that reporters covering it would have gained nothing from online search techniques. It was a totally unique event and thus not conducive to any contextual or structural research. There was, in short, no class of prior events that a reporter could have used to make sense of the whole. While one may know, statistically, that spouses are usually the primary suspects in a murder investigation, the likelihood that a man would shoot himself in the stomach after killing his pregnant wife but before calling for help on a mobile telephone— all as part of a bizarre murder plan— makes the whole situation atypical.

It is far more common to assign reporters to cover events or issues for which there is a body of information amenable to online research, and, in those cases, the journalist's role and function can change. Thus, in the tort reform story, the *Wall Street Journal*'s Waldholz was limited to information presented by Todd and Habash. That much of it was incomplete or incorrect did not matter because the reporter's methodology— the means by which he met his profession's current institutional and instrumental standards— was limited to information received orally (" Todd said"; " Habash said") without a consideration of antecedent events. The story's event was the "debate," not the issues it pretended to cover. The reporter did not and was not expected to write or consider, for example, malpractice as a class or the resulting cost of multiple injury suits. Thus his instrumental goals of objectivity and completeness could not be met. These limits were largely removed when, through the use of data obtained online, the biases of the debate's participants and the limits of their perspectives became clear. Then the reportage became, or had the potential to be, structural or contextual, not ephemeral and perhaps even misleading.

As the example of the drug story research made clear, news is affected by historical, social, and economic patterns that influence what is printed or broadcast in individual cities. Stories must still be passed by editorial gatekeepers and be accepted as relevant to the degree that they are not only placed on the media's agenda but placed there prominently. Concern over traditional sources, distrust of "eggheads," worry over the possible offense of other sources, and a disposition to interpret stories through their overt, economic relevance all affect what is written and, of course, what will be researched. But that story did run, despite the reservations of the newspaper's editorial staff. To the extent one can speak of journalism as divorced from these restraints and argue solely to the instrumental and institutional myths, it seems clear that these technologies have the potential to forge a new and perhaps more complete news.

5

Impact of Online Technologies on Publishing

Introduction

At all stages of the news process – story conception, research, finding and interviewing sources, establishing source credibility, information analysis and presentation, even distribution of finished articles – journalists are using computers in increasing numbers. This is despite the many technical barriers that have made online access difficult in news organizations. Large newspapers, especially, place typesetting terminals on journalists' desks. These terminals are critical production tools: direct connections between the internal production-oriented network and outside networks are technically difficult and potentially dangerous. These connections have only recently begun to appear, allowing journalists to move seamlessly between the Internet and other on-line networks, and internal production systems.

It is clear, however, that the major barriers are technical. There are, for instance, no obvious differences between male and female reporters' use of on-line services when they are on the same beat. Perhaps the stereotype is because such services have tended to be more heavily used among sports and business reporters than among journalists on other beats. And sports and business sections tend to have higher percentages of men on reporting and editing staffs.

There are also no obvious gender (or race) differences among those using analytical software such as spreadsheets and relational database programs for computer-assisted reporting. Women and minority-group journalists author many such stories. At Columbia, where we have been teaching mandatory spreadsheet and database use to all students since 1987, we see absolutely no difference in student course performance by gender or race.

But all that is computerized is not analytical, or even reporting. Journalism jobs that are specifically in new media organizations are often glorified production positions, especially when those new media organizations are associated with newspaper Web sites. The field is still evolving.

This chapter concentrates on print journalism, especially in newspapers. It includes data on magazines (and some asides about broadcast) for comparison.

With Don Middleberg, head of Middleberg & Associates, a New York-based public relations firm, I conducted two large surveys of print reporters – one in August 1994 and one in September 1995 – to quantify these gains. These surveys, of 6,000 and 3,800 respectively, are the largest of their kind. They generated more than 1,500 usable responses – high for mailed surveys. Various tests, described later in this chapter, allow us to assume that the responses mirror the overall sample. All U.S. daily newspapers were queried in each year. The 1994 survey also included all U.S. weeklies with circulation larger than 2,500. There were 1,500 magazines surveyed in 1994, and 2,000 in 1995. The magazines were randomly selected from the nation's 14,000 generally circulated titles (avoiding house organs). Sampling error is detailed later in the chapter. But, in general, reported percentages for the overall sample each year are plus or minus 4% at the 95% confidence level.

To summarize the "good" news, assuming that greater access to a broader variety of information sources inherently makes for better stories: There has been an enormous increase in print journalists' use of on-line sources of late. Almost a fourth of the respondents (23%) to the fall 1995 survey say they or their staffs use on-line services daily. More than two thirds say they use such services at least once a month. Those totals were significantly higher than for the survey taken in the summer of 1994. The growth has been mainly in daily newspapers; monthly (or more frequent) use by newspaper staffs rose from 44% to a startling 71% in the 14 months between the two surveys. In this chapter, where inclusion of weeklies in the 1994 survey distorts year-to-year comparisons, we compare only dailies to dailies each year.

Despite press reports predicting the demise of value-added on-line services in the face of Internet growth (and especially growth of the Internet's World Wide Web), the press itself favors value-added commercial services for its searches. In 1994, the leader in our survey was CompuServe. In the survey conducted in the fall of 1995, to the surprise of no one who has been following America Online' s

(AOL) marketing blitz, AOL surged ahead. By fall 1995, twice as many journalists responding to our survey ranked AOL first (40%) for commercial services and Internet access, compared to the Internet alone (20%). CompuServe ranked in third place by fall 1995, at 19% (it had been first, at 35%, in 1994). Of course, many use AOL to access the Internet despite its high cost relative to local providers, because it is easy to set up and obviously available. This tends to inflate AOL's scores.

The situation is likely to remain fluid for some time. Since the fall 1995 survey was completed, AOL and CompuServe have stepped up their offers of free accounts to news organizations. Both have also improved access to the Internet from inside the commercial services. AOL even is expected to offer limited access to AOL features from the World Wide Web (WWW).

Once editors and reporters go on line, they are interested in gathering reference materials, finding raw data (in particular, government figures and legislative doings, and corporate biographies), using e-mail and seeking out new sources for interviews. In that last function, editors and reporters will often use old-fashioned on-line Internet utilities such as Listservs and Usenet newsgroups, as well as the WWW.

One might think that younger, more computer-literate journalists would be leading the charge into the computer age. There is some anecdotal evidence, and evidence from our non-representative sampling at professional meetings, that this is so with respect to use of on-line services. There is no evidence, however, that this is so with respect to use of analytical techniques such as spreadsheets. A quick look at bylines suggests, in fact, that older journalists use numeric analysis more than younger ones do. This may be due to the increased responsibility which older, more experienced journalists have for major analytical stories at news organizations – or due to poor math and logic skills among recent graduates.

The 1994 survey was the largest ever for computerization of print media – more than 6,000 writers and editors were queried. The 1995 survey concentrated and expanded upon coverage of magazines and of daily newspapers. Thanks to the exceptional response rate (about 500 of 2,000 magazines and more than 300 of 1,815 newspapers in 1995 – almost all of them dailies), we were able not only to track overall use of on-line services, but also to gain a better understanding of how journalists use these services. The magazine section of the 1995 survey was the largest ever conducted of magazines in cyberspace. Responses to the newspaper section of the 1995 survey cover 40% of U.S. daily newspaper circulation.

The 1995 survey calculations are based on 751 responses, out of more than 800 received (some responses lacked answers to questions on circulation and frequency, and thus could not accurately be matched to the 1994 cohort). The 1994 survey results were based on 725 usable responses, also out of about 800 received.

Although we have informally sampled broadcast media, and found substantial growth in on-line services provided by and used by broadcast media, we see no consistent pattern in such use. That is, outside the networks, whose on-line use is growing rapidly, we see no particular pattern between a broadcast or cable outlet's adoption of on-line services for research or for disseminating add-on services, and the outlet's staff size, market size (as measured by Arbitron's Area of Dominant Influence and share), or years in market. Instead, entirely new services are springing up within broadcast and cable markets. And in traditional organizations, the existence of a "champion" seems more important than other variables. By "champion," we mean an individual who understands the process and economic benefits of going on line and who is willing to press for including an on-line component in the organization's media product lineup.

On-Line Reporting

As already noted, 23% of those surveyed in fall 1995 said they or their associates use on-line services roughly once a day or more. Another 24% said they use such services at least once a week on average. Overall, 68% said they or their staffs use on-line services at least once a month.

This reported level of use was up considerably from the 1994 sampling, which showed that only 50% of print media journalists used on-line services at least monthly. Both values are plus or minus 4% with a confidence of over 95%. So at worst, the growth was from 54 to 64%, or roughly a 20% annual growth rate. More likely, the annual growth rate was closer to 35%.

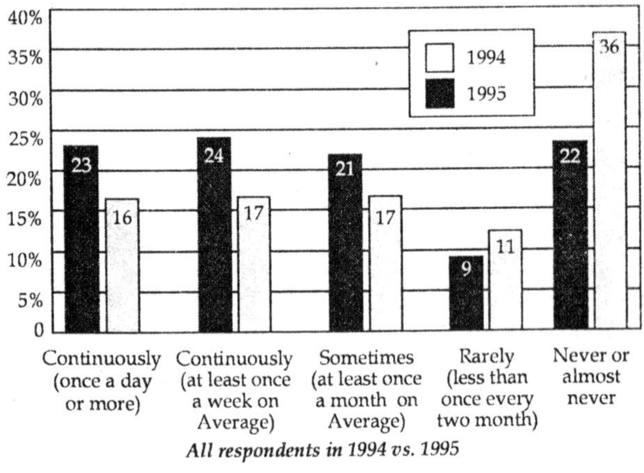

Fig. 5.1. How often do journalists search for information on line

The growth was wholly attributable to newspapers, not magazines. For magazines, monthly use of on-line services was steady within the statistical limits of the survey, (69% in 1994, 65% in 1995). For daily newspapers, however, it rose dramatically, as already noted, from 44% to 71%. (See methodology, below, for discussion of sample differences.)

What's more, respondents from newspapers (and their staffs) were much more likely to use on-line services at least weekly by fall

1995 (56%) than summer of 1994 (22% for the entire newspaper sample, 31% for dailies).

Although the Internet gets most of the publicity, and although pundits predict the eventual decline and or demise of commercial services such as CompuServe and AOL, journalists overwhelmingly use these value-added commercial services. Internet use is obviously expanding, however. By the time this book appears, CompuServe and AOL should both be offering more seamless connections to the Internet, especially to the WWW. In fact, the relative position of all commercial services except AOL dropped from 1994 to 1995. Direct Internet use by journalists increased somewhat. This use has probably been accelerating since the 1995 survey; AT&T and MCI are among many communications giants that started low-cost access services to the Internet in the past year.

Most journalists who access the Internet do it through a commercial value-added provider such as AOL, CompuServe, or Prodigy — and not through a local or national Internet "provider" that offers an Internet on-ramp but little or no value- added services. Local "on-ramp" providers are much more likely to be used than are the few large national or regional providers. During the fall 1995 survey period, there were about 600 local providers in the United States. Newspapers were beginning to become local Internet providers themselves.

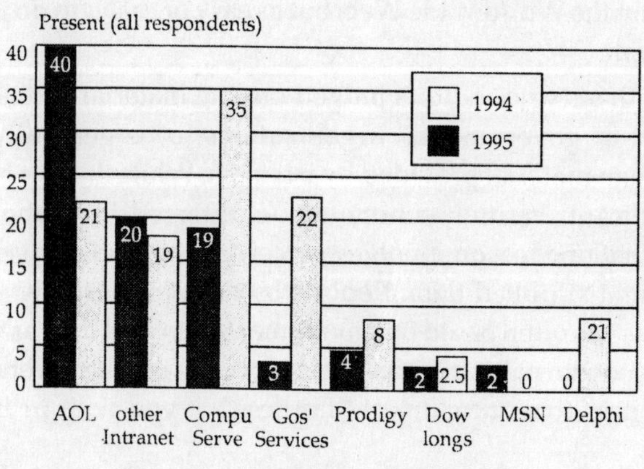

Fig. 5.2. Which on-line services do reporters use

One third of the Internet users in our sample accessed the Net through their employer's host. News organizations are probably similar to other organizations in this regard. That is, other studies have shown that employees of organizations that have their own hosts tend to use the Internet more often because the extra cost of using it, once a host is in place, is minimal.

More than two thirds of the 1995 respondents said they used the internet (69%, or 519 out of 751 respondents) for one reason or another. This is a larger number than those who said they or *their staffs* used the Internet frequently. (Remember, 68% said they or their staffs used on-line services, including the Internet, at least once a month in the 1995 survey, and 50% said they did in the 1994 survey.) The responses suggest that knowledge of the Internet is higher than "frequent" use by a fairly wide margin. What's more, almost all who said they use it, do so for both personal and business reasons. The bulk of Internet use by journalists is for article research, e-mail, and finding sources or experts, but this is not the same as saying that 69% of all print journalists use the Internet specifically for journalism.

One fourth of those who use the Internet said they do so to retrieve press releases, essentially replicating electronically a traditional journalistic task. More than a third of those who use the Internet use it to access Usenet newsgroups – something that is possible on the World Wide Web, but as easy or easier to do in a text only system.

In both surveys, editors judged on-line material provided by nonprofit or governmental organizations to be generally more reliable than material provided by business. While the gap is small, it's significant. Written comments volunteered by respondents suggest that one reason involves perceived comprehensiveness of government-supplied data. Reports by nonprofit groups – even activists – are often based on government-supplied data as well. In general, non-journalist Internet users expect comprehensiveness and inclusiveness (one measure of "fairness," if you will) in Internet postings.

Some comments by respondents to this study, and some more general studies of journalists' sourcing habits, suggest that journalists are more leery of "business," because profit-making organizations have a more vested interest than do nonprofits and government agencies in getting their points of view across. Journalists should, of course, take nothing for granted in any data, no matter what the source. Nevertheless, the survey results specifically suggest that businesses placing material on-line for editorial use should be extra careful about accuracy and errors of omission; credibility is key – and fragile.

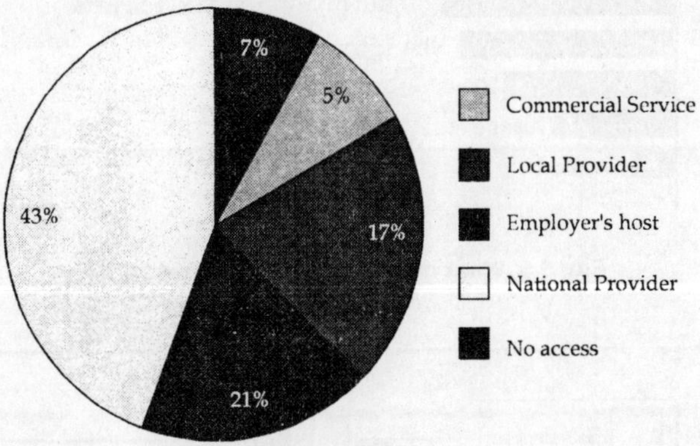

Fig. 5.3. How do you access the Internet

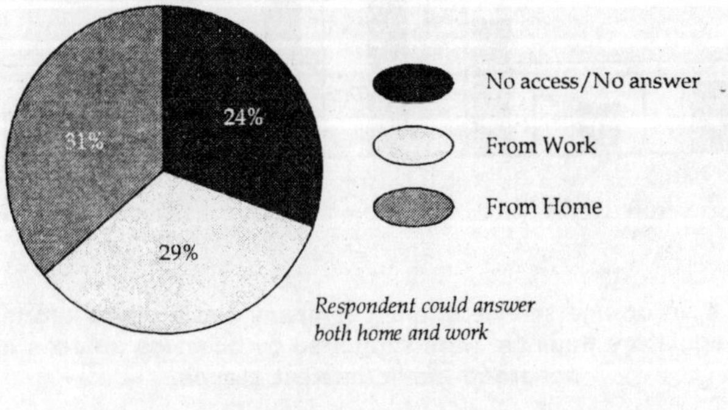

Fig. 5.4. Where do you access the Internet

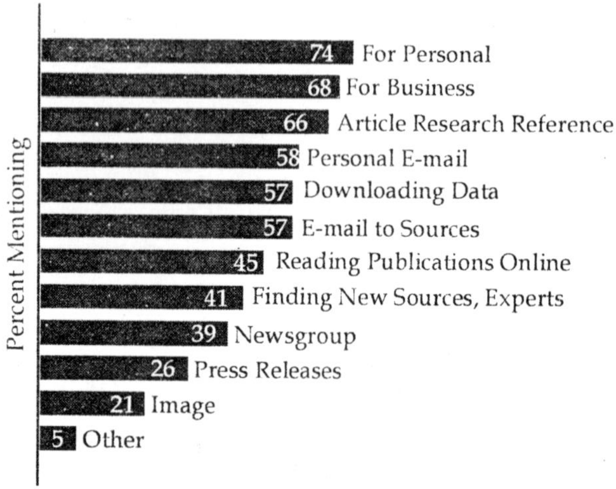

Fig. 5.5. What do you use the Internet for

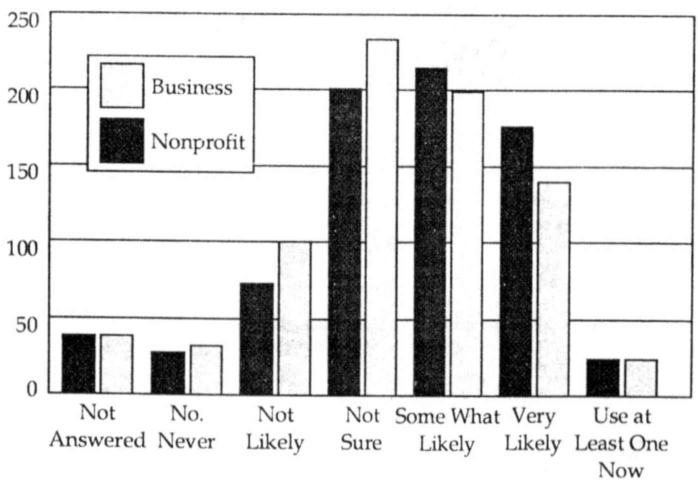

Fig. 5.6. If an on-line service offering company and product information, or regulatory findings, were supported by business sources or nonprofit/ public interest groups

About 46% of the respondents said in 1995 they were at least "somewhat likely" to use business services on-line. That's down slightly from 49% in the 1994 survey, but the difference is not statistically significant. When asked if they would use services provided by nonprofit or public interest groups, 57% said in 1995 they were at least somewhat likely to do so. That's down slightly from 1994's 59%.

On the flip side, only 3% said in 1995 they would flatly refuse to use such a service. The few scattered comments from the 20 or so "refusers" in the 1995 survey suggest that they may like to report only from live interviews, and not from documentary sources of any kind. The chart below provides actual numbers of respondent answers for the 1995 survey. Of the 751 in the analyzed sample, 35 did not answer this question.

The key uses cited by our respondents in 1995 for such on-line services provided by business or nonprofit organizations would be for reference (mentioned by more than 40% of the respondents), press releases (mentioned by more than 34%), and raw data such as Securities Exchange Commission (SEC) filings and Environment Protection Agency (EPA) material (mentioned by more than 27%). In other words, raw data and source documents have the most pulling power. Images are gaining in importance.

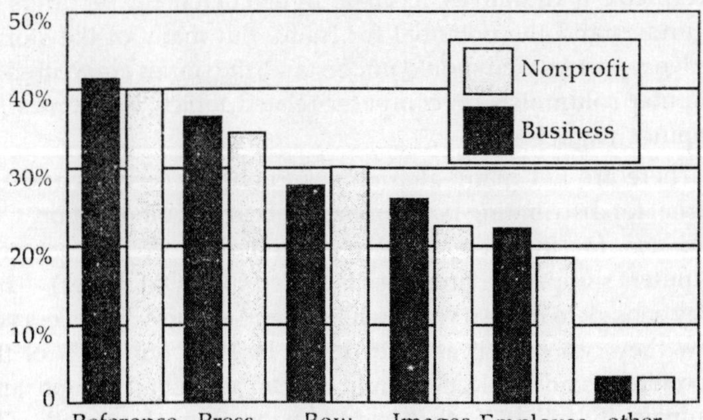

Fig. 5.7. Journalists' use of on-line services supported by business or nonprofits

The survey itself did not address the issue of how, exactly, journalists treat information from Internet sources that are less formal, such as e-mail, Usenet newsgroups, and Listservs. The problem with such "sources," is that reporters have no sure way of knowing the true identity of the source. That 60-year-old professor a reporter finds on a Listserv or in a newsgroup posting may really be a 13-year-old seventh grader. An e-mail address that looks genuine may have been forwarded through Fidonet or a third-country Internet server specifically set up for the purpose. Such forwarding is easy to do on the Internet or through a telephone-accessed electronic bulletin board. In the forwarding process, the e-mail address of the original sender is stripped away and replaced with a fake.

In responses gathered at professional meetings, reporters have been near unanimous in their insistence that firm identification be achieved before such sources are quoted. This, they say, would be achieved by, at the very least, an exchange of phone numbers followed by the reporter's call. Follow-up communication, once the source is interviewed by phone or in person at least once, could be by e-mail, respondents say. The chain of questions and responses is much harder to fake.

Nevertheless, many stories do find their way into print quoting unverified e-mail sources. It can be argued that many reporters do not understand the potential for fraud. But many of the stories involve reporters who should understand; the stories are written by computer columnists on computer-related topics, sometimes for computer magazines.

There are not many alternatives to on-line services and the Internet for distributing large amounts of current information. CD-ROM use, for instance, greatly expanded in 1995 (most new computers shipped for home use included CD-ROM drives) – but not by enough to make it worthwhile to send editors CDs unless you know they can read it at their desks. In 1994, only 17% of the respondents said CD-ROMs could be read at editors' or reporters' terminals. By fall 1995, that hadn't changed much overall. (The survey indicated 15%, but the results were

lower in 1995 mainly because freelancers were not included in the 1995 survey; freelancers working at home were far more likely than the norm to have CD-ROM drives.)

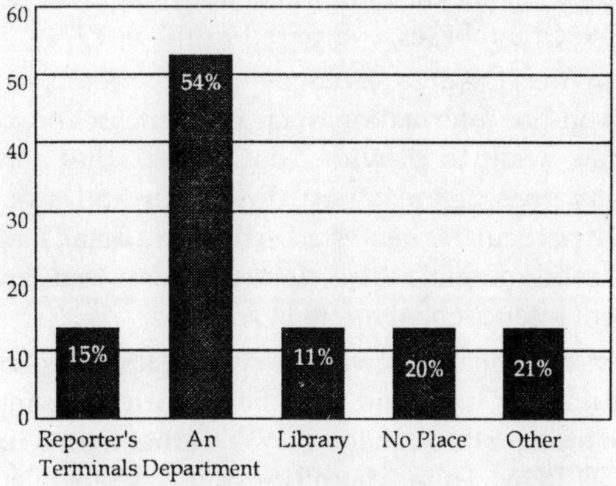

Fig. 5.8. Where can CD-ROM disks be read

However, availability of CD-ROM drives in newspapers' art departments increased dramatically, by 22 percentage points from 1994 to 1995. In the 1995 survey, 54% said CD-ROMs could be read in the art department. In the 1994 survey it was 32%. This is in line with increasing demand for art to be supplied electronically rather than in the form of a slide or reflective art.

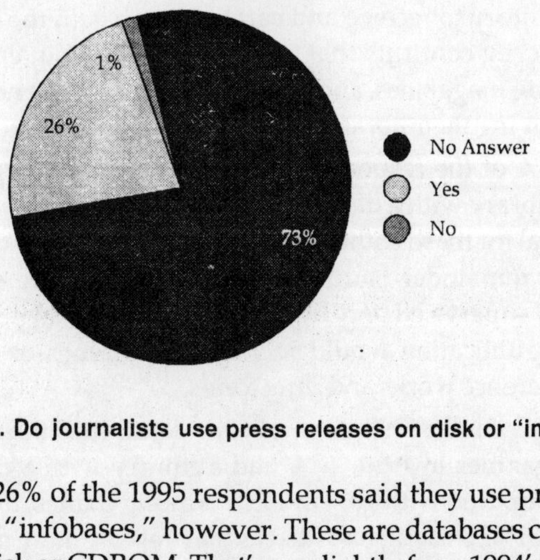

Fig. 5.9. Do journalists use press releases on disk or "infobases"

Only 26% of the 1995 respondents said they use press releases on disk, or "infobases," however. These are databases contained on a floppy disk or CDROM. That's up slightly from 1994's 22", but not by a statistically significant amount. Among magazine respondents in 1995, 21 "used infobases, compared to 18" in 1994.

Slow growth in this area has not matched expectations. Although providers of on-line information, such as businesses or government agencies, may want to provide "databases" that contain such materials as catalogs, organizational directories, and laws, the media have not been particularly interested in the extra detail that electronic delivery has made possible. Also, users complain that each infobase has a different interface that has to be learned.

Providers of infobase software, such as AskSam, Folio, Zylndex, and MicroRim, say the trend may be toward allowing users to "search" an infobase through the WWW, rather than sending users a disk or a CD-ROM. Folio, MicroRim, and AskSam all have "Web server" products designed to do just that.

Libraries and Librarians

Media use of reference materials is generally weak in other ways as well. Most important, library services in media organizations are shamefully inadequate. Online services can help reporters access such reference materials. But you can't send a disk to a media librarian and expect the information, or availability of it, to become common knowledge in the organization, because there may not be a central repository to receive and catalog the disk in the first place. The 1995 survey confirms that news libraries are an endangered species among magazines, and becoming more so. But newspapers began improving their library staffs in 1995 compared to 1994.

Only 27% of the respondents in 1995 said their organization has a news library with a designated librarian, compared to 23% in 1994. The total for those without a news library at all was unchanged at 47%. The remainder had news "libraries" that are essentially unstaffed, or supervised only by a secretary. A typical news library for a small publication would include back issues or clips, and standard reference works and directories.

The sample for the 1995 survey, however, omitted most weeklies. Among magazines in 1994, 17% had a library with a designated librarian, compared with 10% in 1995. Among dailies, the rise was from 27% to 61%. This suggests that as they receive more material on line than they have in the past, and as they seek to post material of their own, daily newspapers have started to re-invent and to re-invigorate their library systems. A quick nonrandom check of 12 medium-size dailies with news libraries and designated librarians suggests, however, that not all of the "designated librarians" are actually fully trained "traditional" library science/library service personnel; many may be trained only in database or Internet access. Only one of the 12 dailies (circulation 25,000 to 60,000) had actually employed a library-school graduate to oversee its library.

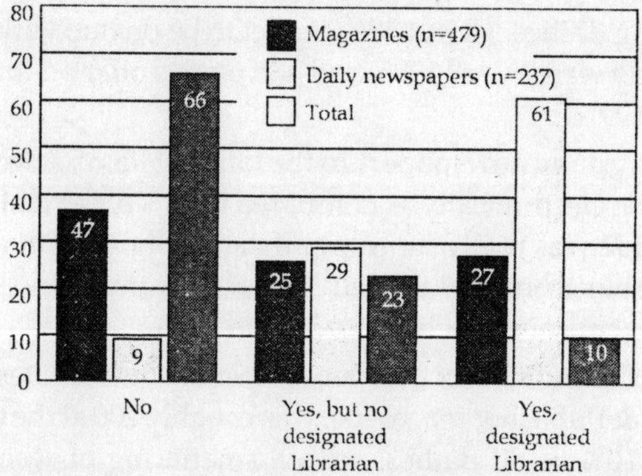

Fig. 5.10. Do media organizations have a news library

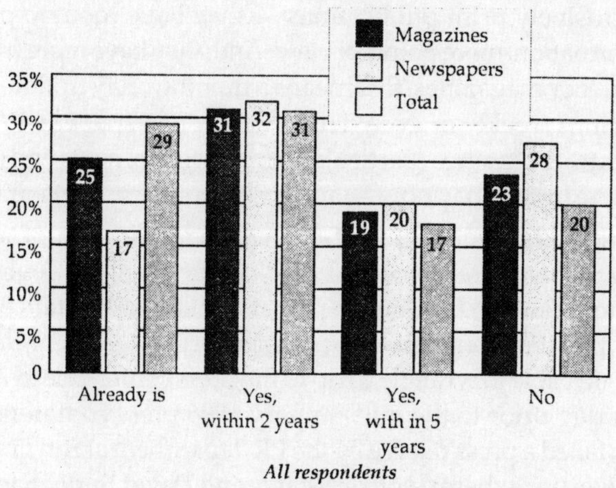

Fig. 5.11. Do you expect your publication, or sections of it, to be distributed electronically

Print Media On-Line

It should come as no surprise that newspaper and magazine organizations' plans for electronic distribution exploded in 1995. Some 46% of the 1994 sample had no plans to go on line a year ago. That percentage was cut precisely in half, to 23%, in the interval between the two surveys. Some 29% of magazines in the sample were distributing electronically by fall 1995, and another 31% expect to be doing it by fall of 1997.

Among dailies, all but 30% expect to be on line within 5 years; 15% already were by fall 1995, and half plan to offer on-line products by fall of 1997.

Among daily newspapers in the fall of 1995, 15% were already distributing electronically – compared to 13% of the dailies in 1994. The flip side was really more significant -- those with no plans to distribute electronically totaled 51% of the sample in 1994 among dailies; that number declined to 30% in 1995.

Steve Outing's list of U.S. newspapers with Web sites, compiled for Editor & Publisher magazine, was roughly 200 at the end of 1995 – about 10% of all dailies, with a smattering of weeklies. This confirms our respondents' answers.

The needs of on-line publications will, in the near future, differ from exclusively print publications – they have room to publish more information, more points of view. And, they have more frequent deadlines. For magazines, this means a monthly may update its on-line offerings weekly or even daily. A daily newspaper's Web site may update its offerings (particularly for business, news and sports) two or three times a day now – and continuously in the near future.

Continuous updating may change the definition of a news embargo. The *San Jose Mercury News* Web site (Mercury Center) was the first to report on Jupitersize planets orbiting two stars 35 light years away, even though the paper's science reporter, Glennda Chui, had not been able to wrangle a trip to the press conference in Austin, Texas. A day prior to the mid-January 1996 press conference, she had been faxed a press release by the PR department at San Francisco State University, where Geoffrey Marcy and David Butler had made their findings about the planets. Taking advantage of her friendship with Marcy, she interviewed him early on the morning of the press conference, then published her story on the Web just as his press conference began (and the embargo ended) a few hours later. The piece did not appear in the paper itself (the *Mercury News*) until the next day. Chui's "scoop" was discussed in *Science Writer*, the quarterly newsletter of the National Association of Science Writers.

Most newspapers with Web sites of their own do not yet allow the Web site to scoop the paper. Mercury Center was an early exception. In one sense, this episode is similar to a live radio or TV report from the site of the press conference. But there is a difference. The live broadcast is unfiltered by reporters. Chui filtered the Mercury Center report, but it still appeared at the same time as the event itself unfolded. Clearly, embargo rules may have to be redefined – and so do the operating rules of newspaper and magazine Web sites. The segment of a publication's readership that wants a certain type of news – astronomy in this case – will seek it out on the Web, ignoring the local, late, publication source. Thus, the local newspaper must "scoop itself' on its Web site or risk being scooped by someone else.

Today, few newspapers are doing much original reporting on their Web sites at all. In fact, in the name of avoiding union work-rule entanglements in a fluid, ever changing, technology-based endeavor, newspapers have tended to set up their Web operations as distinct and separate entities, apart from the main newsgathering, news writing activities. They have tended to hire HTML coders – and pay them more than reporters – even though coding is a skill that takes only a few weeks to learn.

Where there has been original reporting, it has been reporting that tends to exploit the nearly unlimited news hole of on-line publishing. We see school-by school surveys, street-by-street stories, neighborhood-oriented advertising. It was easy to envision a "lawyer's version" of the O.J. Simpson story as it unfolded, or a feminist version, a Black version ... a Minnesota version. Unfortunately, most of the extra material tacked onto such a story theme may very well be archival, with little "added value" – rather boring for a typical reporter to assemble.

The next step, just beginning to happen, is the exploitation of on-line tools such as video and audio to make stories more vivid, and even fill-in-the-blank forms to personalize stories. What will the property tax increase mean exactly, to you as a reader and a property owner? What about changes in Social Security for someone at precisely your age, income, and state of residence?

It can be argued that such matters can be covered on paper, with sidebars and tables. But why would a reader accept an "approximate" answer from the local paper when he or she can have an answer that is exact, and when competitors are willing and able to provide that exact answer? Video and audio are, frankly, being overused on the Web – often provided for its novelty value. But as television and radio have proven again and again, the printed quotation is not always an adequate reflection of a source's tone or circumstance.

And what about new storytelling techniques? If I really wanted to explain New York City's budget history and budget priorities, for instance, perhaps I could do so by licensing a game such as Sim City, adding an appropriate set of New York City-like starting values, and allowing readers to download it from my Web site. Sim City is an interactive game that allows users to set policies for a model city of their own. The game reacts to the policies in a realistic way. In fact, much of the math behind it was developed by Jay Forrester at MIT in the 1960s. Few have read his book, *Urban Dynamics*. But millions have played Sim City.

Where do reporters and editors (or publishers, if these are to be new staff categories in the newsroom) get the new storytelling and math skills? And how will they manage the resulting organizations?

Many magazines are already there, as these surveys have shown. They tend to be smaller publications, however, with free (controlled) circulation. Their "print" business models require that 25% or more of revenue go into physical distribution and into circulation-building, mainly by direct-mail promotion. Those two expense categories are cut substantially by Web publishing. The "Web" business model should, in fact, be well suited to publications that are advertiser-supported, or that, like most newspapers, use subscription revenue to roughly cover or come close to covering manufacturing and distribution costs.

Smaller magazines have seen this already. They have tended to merge Web publishing with on-paper publishing staffs. They have also been more willing to explore new editorial techniques, using their uniqueness and editorial quality to preserve or gain a following.

Magazine reporters and editors like to respond to our surveys by pointing out that their Web offerings are new publications in a new medium. The on-line product (whether it is *Columbia Journalism Review or Wired*) is not the same as the print product.

What will the reporter's contribution be, to this new age of math and games? On a magazine, the journalists often have specialized fiscal knowledge sufficient to handle the task. Newspapers may for a time have to resort to "new media syndicates" selling explanatory interactive features – and may be limited to stock, one size-fits-all features instead of features customized precisely for their readers. One analogy in the newspaper business today would be the small paper that must use unedited or barely edited wire copy for national and international stories.

Weeklies and small dailies vary greatly in their sophistication when it comes to computer use; there is no clear pattern by location, circulation, or staff size. It appears instead that weeklies, like broadcast organizations discussed earlier, embrace new media technologies when they employ a "champion." The existence of that champion is somewhat random.

All this stands job-hunting advice for new media journalists on its head. The exciting, fun jobs for 1996 are with smaller news organizations, while major news organizations, particularly large dailies, are hiring but offer, on average, jobs that are more mundane for the present.

Not since the late 1960s, when advances in printing technology and list brokerage made small-circulation specialized magazines cost-effective, has there been such a revolution in the media business. The revolution in magazine publishing took a decade to unfold. The new media revolution is happening faster, but it will not occur overnight.

Methodology

The 1995 sample newspapers included all daily newspapers in the United States (including "Sunday-only" papers published with dailies of a different name), and several weeklies with a circulation greater than 2,500. The job titles among the 1,815 survey forms mailed to newspapers were evenly divided; 907 business editors and 908 managing editors. We saw no significant differences in responses from the two job titles. The usable responses represented publications with a total daily circulation of 23.8 million and Sunday circulation of 24.8 million – more than 40% of the nation's total newspaper circulation.

We also mailed questionnaires to 2,000 magazine managing editors in 1995. The magazine sample was not random; it was weighted toward business (but noncomputer) publications; we tried to avoid small-circulation publications from narrow-interest groups. The sample did, however, include general membership publications of major professional organizations – particularly if those publications were produced by commercial publishers. Only three of the 479 usable magazine responses were from publications with a circulation less than 10,000. Total circulation of our respondents' magazines was 128.9 million – more than 10% of all magazine copies sold in a typical month in the United States. We consider magazines covering the computer industry as a special case; including them would have inflated the survey results on computer use by journalists.

Unlike the 1994 survey, we did not mail specifically to weeklies in 1995 (there were 1,500 "non-Sunday, non-dailies" in the sample of 6,000 in 1994). Thus, when we compare newspapers in the 1995 sample to 1994, we specifically exclude weeklies in the 1994 sample to make the results comparable, where inclusions would have skewed the sample.

We also did not mail to freelancers as we had in 1994 (in 1994 we mailed to 1,500 freelancers who belonged to Investigative Reporters and Editors; this was roughly half the group's list). The response rate from freelancers had been low, and it is impossible to find a truly random sample to target with a survey.

Although we have been conducting informal surveys of broadcast or cable media for the past 2 years, we have not included broadcast or cable media in either survey except for some broadcast-oriented freelancers in 1994.

Focusing on dailies and magazines, providing more response time, and surveying mainly after Labor Day (the 1994 survey had been mailed early August) increased our response rate considerably, from 14% in 1994 to 22% overall in 1995. August is normally a good time to survey the media; in 1994 we wanted to survey before congressional election races heated up. But surveying in August 1995 would have caused us to run afoul of the August 24 U.S. introduction date for Windows 95 and the Microsoft Network on August 24. Survey forms mailed and returned in 1995 are summarized in the table:

	Number mailed	*Usable respon-ses*	*Incomplete responses*	*Returned as undeli-verable*	*Response rate**
Magazines	2,000	479	17	128	26%
Newspapers	1,815	272	42	36	18
Total	3,815	751	59	164	22

* *Total responses (complete and incomplete) divided by number mailed minus undeliverable.*

For the sample as a whole, the results reported from respondents would be expected to be within plus or minus four percentage (+/- 4%) points of the responses expected from the entire universe of these categories of newspaper and magazine editors, 95% of the time – assuming that the sample is truly random. Here are the issues to consider with regard to the sample:

Non response bias: The overall response rate for the 1995 survey, at 22%, is far above average for mailed surveys of this type. The response rate for magazines, at 26%, is outstanding. Furthermore, circulation histograms – the number of responses at each circulation range – display no obvious abnormalities.

Nevertheless, the newspaper responses represent a higher percentage of all newspaper circulation (40%) than they do of the sample to which surveys were sent (18%). Magazine responses, on the other hand, represent a lower percentage of all magazine circulation (more than 10%) than they do of the sample surveyed (26%).

Thus, we paid close attention to response variation by circulation size. Except for questions on in-house libraries and production techniques, we saw no significant response variation by circulation size for newspapers, within limits of sample size, and only small variations for magazines. The "incomplete responses" noted in the table above lacked circulation data, so we could not match them to the overall circulation profile or to the 1994 responses. But we could use them to check for nonresponse bias.

We also offered respondents a copy of the complete survey results; they returned cards to us, certifying that they had completed the survey and sent it in separately. The 604 cards returned showed no obvious bias to one city or zip code.

Sample selection: While the newspaper sample both years was designed to cover all dailies and their associated Sunday editions (even when published with different staffs or under different names), the magazine sample was not "random," as discussed earlier. Compared to the magazine industry as a whole, the sample's circulation (the number of copies distributed, whether on the newsstand or by mail) is below average. But compared to subscriber-only publications, it is above average. The circulation frequency, however, mirrors the subscription-driven part of the industry.

There are about 12,000 magazines published in the United States that meet our criteria; we surveyed only 2,000. Even so, this represents the largest survey ever conducted of magazines in cyberspace.

We emphasize that the universe of responses from magazines in 1995 was slightly different than for 1994. We made no effort to keep to the 1994 magazine sample (several hundred titles had disappeared). And 1995 responses represent a slightly higher average circulation. Thus, the magazine sample is not completely random. Because the sample did not include computer-related magazines, however, the lack of randomness probably understates online use by magazines.

Frequency, times published per year	*Number of magazines in sample*
12	221
6	97
4	33
10	28
8	16
9	14

Frequency, times published per year	*Number of magazines in sample*
11	11
52	10
13	7
2	5
7	5
3	3
18	3
24	3
26	3
5	2
14	2
1	1
15	1
23	1
51	1
Total	**467**

Cover design by Jennifer Sterling

Sub sampling: It should be obvious (but in published surveys often is not) that information from subsets of the overall sample is less reliable than for the sample as a whole. We provide complete cross-tabulations for our sub samples, In general, percentages from each individual cell in a cross-tab should be considered suspect when the cell size is less than 50 – unless the percentage reported is very high or very low (above 80% or below 20%). Users who are interested in subsets of the data may wish to combine cells to get a valid cell size.

Questionnaire bias: We have minimized bias by exhaustively testing the survey; the fall 1995 version is similar in wording and layout to the 1994 version. In addition, there has been extensive and continuing pre-sampling of nonrandom audiences (mainly at professional meetings of journalists).

The high response rate and low incidence of blank (unanswered) questions also suggest that the survey form was germane (asked the right questions) and understandable.

Timing: As the 1995 survey was being answered, Microsoft Network was just starting up, AOL was continuing its saturation marketing (a disk in every magazine, computer box, and – it seemed – anything that moved or stood still), and CompuServe was cutting its fees to match AOL. Prodigy and Delphi were trying to define a marketing strategy. The number of Web pages catalogued by the Lycos search engine grew from 8 million to 12 million (in 6 weeks!). In short, life was about normal in the on-line business. Since the survey was done, Microsoft's CEO Bill Gates has declared that the Internet looks like a good marketing bet, and that value-added services such as Microsoft Network must become more Internet integrated. The number of Web pages catalogued by Lycos grew to 60 million by August 1996.

6

PRACTICAL APPROACHES TO ONLINE PUBLISHING

Introduction

Most online publishers seem to have a "field of dreams" philosophy: Build a World Wide Web newspaper, and readers will come. But building an online newspaper is more complicated than building a baseball diamond in an Iowa cornfield.

Since its humble beginnings in Geneva, Switzerland, in 1991, the World Wide Web (WVW) has garnered millions of WVW pages, all vying for readership. Developed by the European Laboratory for Particle Physics (CERN) to enable users to share information using a simple "point and click" system, the WWW allows online users to retrieve text, graphics, video, and audio data through an easily navigable browser software package. With the explosive popularity of the WWW among businesses, organizations, and individuals, an online publisher must dream beyond simply getting to that first information base in order to attract a loyal following.

A successful online newspaper must have excellent, local information; it must be designed well; it must be interactive; and it must successfully build a community around the information and interaction. This chapter is a case study of one such online publication.

The Campus Press, a weekly student-produced newspaper at the University of Colorado (CU) at Boulder, circulates 8,000 print copies on the CU campus. It began publishing a weekly WWW version in the fall semester of 1994. Early in the spring semester of 1995, nearly 900 on-line readers of *The Campus Press* viewed an average of 5,000 documents each week. The criteria for building the online *Campus Press* and other successful on-line publications are described below.

Information, Interaction and Community

Building an on-line newspaper involves more than shoveling all the stories and press releases available into a WWW publication and hoping people will become regular readers. Publishing an on-line newspaper requires the nurturing and development of information, interaction, and community. These are the same elements necessary for a successful print newspaper. The difference on-line is that these relationships can be quicker and more binding on a larger geographic scale.

Newspapers build readership through content. What binds a newspaper to its readers is information about the readers' community as well as the readers' trust in that information. This information can take the form of local stories, or national and international stories related to the interests of the community; but it can also take the form of reader-contributed material, such as letters to the editor, announcements about cultural events, or, in some newspapers, news about clubs and organizations. This reader-contributed content – which is a type of interaction among readers, the newspaper and others in the community – can also take the form of display advertising and classified advertising, where the reader has almost absolute control over the content. At present, the advertising information makes up about 60% of most newspapers; but with rising newsprint costs, some newspapers are having to cut the amount of news in a paper to as little as 30% of the content.

An on-line newspaper has a virtually unlimited "news hole." Instead of editing stories to fit the available space or condensing the geometry of the actual page layouts, editors can revise stories for completeness. On-line stories can be linked electronically to archived, background stories and to analyses. Similarly, ongoing stories can be condensed, depending on how many good, background stories are linked to the breaking news. On-line story summaries become important as a way for busy people to browse quickly through a publication; if the reader wants more information, it's only a click away. Thus, on-line news publications have distinct advantages over hard copy versions. With the online *San Jose Mercury News* or the online *Boston Globe*, for example, users can enter keywords to expedite searches for classified or news information. With the *Los Angeles Times' TimesLink*, users can search years' worth of archived articles quickly and conveniently using keywords. In addition, on-line letters to the editor can be published instantly. Readers can send their comments to a common area, called a newsgroup, where the comments can be read by any subscriber. This material, in turn, can be edited and later used with permission in the print version of the newspaper.

These features enhance the reliability and credibility of on-line publications. As some observers continue to criticize the Internet for its abundance of unsourced or unreliable information, users will increasingly congregate around information they can trust – such as that found in traditional media sources, including the local newspaper. With the established reputations of local newspapers at stake, users will be likely to rely on their on-line newspaper to provide not only credible local information, but also to find and edit the credible information that is available on the Internet.

While print newspapers are often constrained by the rising costs of newsprint to the spatial detriment of community-oriented content, on-line newspapers have the space they need to devote to building strong ties to the community. For example, community areas could be created within these newspapers where clubs, organizations, or other interest groups could post announcements, full meeting agendas, or other information. Civic and government organizations also could post information on, for example, city council meeting agendas, volunteer opportunities, or recycling centers, that users may not otherwise know how to obtain. Likewise, students in grade schools could become involved with building online pages as a way to bring young readers into the newspaper.

On-line newspapers also could provide live forums for discussion, where people could click into a conversation and participate by typing their comments and watching as they appear instantly onscreen through chat software. The print newspaper could announce topics for discussion related to current events; some of the on-line comments could be edited and used in the print publication. On-line newspapers also could feature special guests in the chat forums. For example, the mayor of a community could be a guest in the chat area, similar to talk radio hosting an important political figure, and on-line readers could ask the questions. Or, members of a band might appear as guests in a chat forum as a way to publicize an upcoming appearance.

It is through this kind of instant interaction – contributed reader content, newsgroups and chat – that an on-line newspaper could build a strong community of readership. The on-line journalism phenomenon has helped to publicly illuminate the fact that most of the content in both print and on-line newspapers is reader-contributed. Letters to the editor, advertisements, calendar events, and press releases by far constitute the bulk of both types of newspapers; thus, the concept of journalism itself may change as more readers recognize that they dictate, in large measure, newspaper content. So, while the usefulness of on-line resources remains questionable for journalists seeking a tool to aid in their critical public role, online newspapers themselves do help to foster community building. For the cost of a phone call, out-of-towners could maintain contact with their communities through their hometown newspapers; online public forums within these newspapers could be created to serve as a "virtual" town square; and users could access text, audio, and video data through one medium. Clearly, the fun and ease of using the Web, in concert with its lack of spatial constraints, could allow online newspapers to facilitate community bonding.

The same is true for advertising. Readers could submit ads on line. Many advertisers, in fact, send their material via modem to print newspapers. The WWW could make this process easier by supplying on-line forms. As with news content, there aren't the same space or photo limitations on-line that there are in print, since the FCC has not limited the amount of bandwidth publishers may consume. Perhaps more importantly, on-line ads could be interactive. With a simple click, a reader could ask for more information, send a fax to the advertiser, or order something from an advertiser. Classifieds that offer this interactivity have the potential to surpass the response rate of print classified ads; an on-line reader has only to click on a classified to respond. While complete interactivity is not yet a reality, many of these features are now available through, for example, the *Raleigh News* and *Observer's NandO Net*. It's important to note that the ability to send an advertiser a fax from the WWW means the advertiser doesn't need Internet access to get responses from an on-line ad. Many major advertisers, such as General Motors and Microsoft, already have built WWW pages. They are seeking popular WWW sites and are willing to pay for a link from those sites to their advertising. For local on-line newspapers, providing this link would be similar to publishing national advertising. But local advertising has always supplied the bulk of revenue for newspapers. A local newspaper could offer a local advertiser server space and assistance building ads on line. A local on-line newspaper also could offer print/on-line combination opportunities. For example, a print ad might refer the reader to an on-line catalog. Ultimately, an on-line newspaper might better serve a print newspaper community by offering more news, more opportunities for readers to contribute and participate, and more ties between readers and advertisers.

Why Publish on The World Wide Web?

Although computer-mediated communication has allowed general users to connect to each other and to vast storehouses of information for more than a decade, many people have been deterred by the complexity and a morphousness of navigating the Internet through Unix commands. The WWW has all but eliminated this reluctance. For example, shortly before a University of Colorado football game in the fall of 1994, a group of 150 School of Journalism and Mass Communications alumni gathered in a computer lab for a demonstration of the online *Campus Press*. Few had ever been on the Internet. Some had never tried computers. After a brief presentation, everyone was smiling and surfing through the newspaper. Soon they were taking virtual Internet journeys to different parts of the globe. Why should newspapers be concerned about this kind of transformation? Here are a few of the reasons:

- Building WWW pages is easy. The University of Colorado had offered students, through their free university e-mail accounts, a chance to build their own Web pages in the spring of 1995. By summer, there were 1,016 registered pages. Commercial Internet providers, such as America Online, are now offering their customers the opportunity to build their own personal pages for free.

- The number of commercial newspapers that publish on the WWW has grown at a phenomenal rate; approximately two new newspapers per day come on-line, according to Steve Outing, of *Planetary News* and *Editor & Publisher*. Outing tracks on-line newspapers and publishes a WWW site called Media Info Interactive. In the time since the introduction of Mosaic in 1993, a free Internet browser application that allows the display of headlines, photos, text, sound, and movies in a format that simulates a publication, the number of commercial newspapers publishing on the WWW skyrocketed from zero to 424. Of those 424 newspapers, 326 are U.S. newspapers. Most major newspapers in large markets are now on line; for example, *The New York Times*, the *Philadelphia Inquirer*, the *Los Angeles Times*, the *Boston Globe*, the *Houston Chronicle*, the *Miami Herald*, the *Denver Post*, and both the *Chicago Sun Times* and the *Chicago Tribune*.

Access to the WWW over the Internet is cheap and getting cheaper. Universities provide free, unlimited accounts to students and faculty. Commercial Internet providers charge from $5 a month plus a $2-an-hour access charge, to $35 a month for unlimited access. As of the summer of 1995, businesses could put their information on the WWW for as little as $50 a month. When telephone and cable companies start offering Internet access, rates are expected to decline as competition sharpens. Presently, AT&T is working to develop new Internet access technologies, such as symmetrical digital subscriber loop (SDSL) and cable modems. Bell Atlantic is already testing SDSL technology in homes for approximately $10 per month. However, Internet Service Providers (ISPs) are developing browsers and other Internet software platforms that are compatible with any operating system, so competition between them is indirect. Although ISPs depend on telephone companies and potentially even cable companies for connections, while telcos and cable companies depend on ISPs to supply Internet services, provide new customers, and for technical support, pricing competition expected to intensify.

Why should Newspapers Explore Publishing On Line?

- Fear. What if an entrepreneur enters the market and captures a big chunk of classified advertising on-line? It could happen. Producing an on-line version of a local newspaper could help the newspaper retain, if not increase, its advertising market share. Moreover, producing both a print and on-line newspaper could create synergistic benefits for both. Each could be used to generate visibility for the other; each could trade content, especially content generated by on-line readers. For example, the *Fayetteville* (North Carolina) *Observer-Times* introduced its Web version of the paper in its print version. Using a print ad featuring computer mice driving on a road with accompanying copy reading, "New Highway Connects Fayetteville to the World," the *Observer-Times* touted its new electronic version. The paper also conducted a "community meeting" to introduce the service and to teach citizens how to use the Internet (Outing, 1995b). Also, on-line copyright issues become less problematic when print and on-line versions of the same newspaper share copyrighted content. Because new copyright issues are still being debated within legal circles, pre-existing copyrights that are legally recognized in print probably will subsequently be recognized in the on-line environment.
- It's cheap. Many commercial Internet providers are hungry for good content and eager to work with newspapers on pricing. There are no printing press costs, no circulation costs.
- There is nearly unlimited space. Plus, stories can be linked to analyses, or to related archived material.
- News can be more immediate on-line than in print.
- Print, video, and sound can be used to enhance the on-line newspaper.
- There are more opportunities for entertainment, such as interactive games.
- Celebrities can log in for interviews conducted by readers.

- Elementary school children are learning all about computers and the Internet. To them, it's as easy as using a VCR. When they reach prime newspaper readership age, they are likely to continue their preferences for interacting with sophisticated new media rather than with traditional newspapers.

Of course, it makes no sense for a local newspaper to also publish an online WWW edition in an area where there is little Internet access. Thus, it is important for a newspaper to learn about the number of Internet users in its circulation area; Internet use could be probed in every newspaper readership survey conducted.

Industry estimates indicate that about 30% of U.S. households have computers; about one third of these computers have modems, and about one third of these computers are used to access commercial on-line services or the Internet. (Soon, having access to a commercial service will mean having Internet access; all of the commercial services are shifting to offering WWW access.) However, with access to on-line services in the work environment and increasingly in public areas such as kiosks, libraries, and even cyber cafes, the gap that distinguishes users from those with no access is rapidly closing.

The number of Internet providers in an area also can be an indication of access. Some providers will talk openly about how many users they have. In Boulder, for the *Campus Press*, it was easy to decide to put out an on-line edition. The University of Colorado provides about 32,000 free Internet accounts for students and faculty; there are 38 computer labs tied to the Internet throughout the university and in dorms; and the Boulder area has several government labs that are tied into the Internet (the National Center for Atmospheric Research, the National Renewable Energy Laboratory, and the National Institute of Standards and Technology).

On-Line Campus Press Readership

A counter keeps track of the number of "hits" on items that are read in the on-line *Campus Press*. It's like having instant marketing data. Using a statistical analysis program called Getstats, an on-line readership survey of the *Campus Press* was conducted between February 24 and March 30, 1995. The survey indicated that the popularity of sections in the on-line *Campus Press* are, in order, fun (which includes entertainment stories from the print version, plus many entertainment items from the Internet), the coffee house (which is a chat area where readers can "talk" to each other), news (which contains news stories from the print version, as well as related Internet stories), sports (which includes stories from the print version, plus related Internet links), community (which is an area for campus clubs that is not duplicated in the print version), internet (which includes Internet search resources), calendar (which includes the calendar from the print version), services (advertising), opinion (editorials and letters to the editor, plus feedback from online readers), weather (which includes up-to-the-minute National Weather Service data, as well as ski reports), and mail (which is a way for readers to access their email accounts).

Generally, readership is lowest between 3 a.m. and 5 a.m., peaks at 11 a.m., declines slightly over the lunch hour, picks up again between 1 p.m. and 2 p.m., then drops sharply between 4 p.m. and 5 p.m. Generally, the largest readership is on campus computers, then high-tech businesses and a commercial on-line service. There also is a small but consistent national and international readership.

What do these numbers mean? Many people access the *Campus Press* at work, with the highest readership between 8 a.m. and 5 p.m. Many of the readers are off campus. Most of the readers are seeking entertainment and communication with each other. News and sports are important components. The readership is largely local. A look at comments sent by readers reveals a little more information. One reader, who stated he was from Oslo, Norway, said he is a CU grad who enjoys following CU sports on-line. Another reader, an alumna living in Georgia, said she enjoys following the news about CU. Another reader, from Chicago, said he enjoys reading his son's column on line because he doesn't get the print version. A reader living in the southeast said that she'd like to meet other CU alumni living in her area. Students and others from around the country have asked for housing or other information about Boulder.

This kind of information is similar to the information newspapers obtain through expensive readership surveys. But the computer can generate the numbers instantly, accurately and for free with the use of statistics programs available from the WWW. If an advertiser wants to know whether an ad has been read, and some basic information about who read it, the computer can churn out the numbers in seconds. On-line newspapers, just as print newspapers do, can use this marketing data to help build a larger readership.

The Future

The WWW, since the formal introduction of Mosaic in 1993, has already caused a revolution in on-line publication. But the revolution is getting a bit stale as the number of new WWW information sites grows. As the amount of information expands, the credibility of the Internet tends to decline. There is too much information of little, no or questionable value. This represents the coming decline in interest in the Internet; it also represents the opportunity for newspapers, which can supply credible information. Newspapers need to apply the same careful reporting and editing techniques that they always have when producing an on-line publication.

They also need to demonstrate the same kind of savvy in knowing their readership, be able to change and grow according to the on-line readership demands, yet keep the priority focused on content. Similarly, newspapers need to design on-line publications that go beyond the on-line designs produced by computer technologists. Many print newspapers, when they first converted to powerful personal computers and pagination, made the mistake of producing gaudy, cartoon-colored pages because it was technologically possible. The same thing is occurring now on the WWW. On-line publications need to be designed not by technologists, but by people who have a good understanding of news presentation and design and who are not designing pages simply because the technology makes it possible. Advertising opportunities need to be more well-developed in new publications. On the one hand, large-scale advertisers are creating their own Web sites. On the other, local advertisers are doing very little. And if they are, they are more than likely doing it through their local Internet provider, rather than through the local newspaper.

Finally, newspapers need to build alliances with television stations. Currently, there is a trend for television stations to create WWW sites. As on-line video becomes the next World Wide Web trend, newspapers and television need to work together. This venture is a reality at the University of Colorado; journalism students in both print and broadcast produce full news stories accompanied by related video reports as part of the on-line *Campus Press*. Print and broadcast students, in concert, produce audio and video clips within the *Campus Press* on-line environment; soon at the University of Colorado, on-line publication will evolve into multimedia production. The priority will be on news information, interaction and community. With that formula, perhaps more readers will come — and will return often.

7

Computing in Publishing

Introduction

This chapter addresses three questions: (a) Why, in just a few short years during the 1980s, did personal computers go from almost nowhere to nearly everywhere at hundreds of American colleges and universities? (b) What consequences did their rapid diffusion bring about? (c) Were those consequences revolutionary? My theoretical stance toward these questions stresses the social construction of technological realities. A starting point (but only a starting point) is one of the most powerful explanatory principles of sociology: "If people define situations as real, they are real in their consequences". Known as the "Thomas Theorem," it was employed by Robert Merton in a blistering critique of self-fulfilling prophecies that feed ethnic and racial conflict. But the sociological insight that underlies the theorem—namely, that reality is inter-subjectively defined, not objectively given—has broad if not universal application. Within the past decade, that essential insight has been applied in counterintuitive fashion to objects of social reality that presumably were more or less immune to it, namely, technologies. The central insight of the Social Construction of Technology (SCOT) perspective is "that technological artifacts are culturally constructed and interpreted". The "interpretive flexibility" of technologies means not only that different groups react differently to the same artifact. It means also that the very definition of a technology—its design, content, and functionality – is itself the product of complex negotiations among networks of engaged .

Technocratic-managerial decision making models of the diffusion of innovations have limited relevance to understanding why computing captivated – and captured – academia during the 1980s. Such models stress administratively determined, hierarchical patterns of technological innovation, driven by managerial interests in rationalizing production and controlling employees. They provide little analytical leverage for understanding the social processes through which personal computing became so widespread so quickly in higher education throughout the 1980s. Such models fail to capture the full complexity of academic computerization because they tend to reduce legitimation problems to implementation problems, rest on an inadequate concept of how technologies are institutionalized in "loosely coupled" organizations , focus more on outcomes than on processes, and may present a misleading picture of actual decision making.

Far from selling itself on technical merits alone, personal computing encountered a great deal of skepticism and even resistance on U.S. campuses. Certainly, major academic computing initiatives of the kind undertaken by leading colleges and universities in the early to mid-1980s required technology, money, and administrative leadership to pull off. But these initiatives also required something else of comparable and pre-conditional importance: institutional legitimation. Although there are literally hundreds of studies of the implementation, impact, and evaluation of computers in higher education, the legitimation of academic computing has received no attention in the social scientific literature.

This chapter first examines the experience of one university in the vanguard of the academic computing movement of the 1980s: Brown University. Along with Carnegie-Mellon and MIT, Brown was widely regarded as one of the three pioneering experiments in campus wide computerization. They shared this distinction for two major reasons: the ambitiousness of their visions and the magnitude of their projects. All three universities signed semi confidential multimillion-dollar contracts and grants for equipment and cash with IBM and other computer vendors in the early 1980s that were intended to provide core funding for their long-term computing initiatives. Arguably, Brown's "computer revolutionaries" articulated the most ambitious vision of academic computing in the future. It was a vision that became emblematic, nationally, of the enormous potential of the new technologies, yet the vision was controversial on the Brown campus itself. Given the initial conditions, successful implementation of its bold computing strategy was hardly a foregone conclusion. Yet if the academic computing revolution were to become a reality among liberal arts-and-sciences institutions, it probably had its best chances for success at Brown.

Realities of Sketches

What was Brown's vision of academic computing in 1983? In its cover story for the September 1983 issue, the *Brown Alumni Monthly* made this enthusiastic pronouncement: "Today Brown is poised to begin an experiment that may have as equally strong an impact on the life of the mind as the Gutenberg Press. The University has embarked on a proposal to spend $50 to $70 million in the next 6 years to equip each faculty member, student, administrator, and staff member on campus with a powerful new type of personal computer".

So, beginning in 1983, the university began gearing up for a massive, long-term effort to build what its proponents called a "network of scholar's workstations" on campus. These workstations would be highly sophisticated and powerful, but easy to use; they would be a type of new computer that would functionally "leapfrog" existing personal computers; and they would revolutionize scholarly work. The scholar's workstation vision was of a campus that, by the end of the 1980s, could become a showcase for the "wired university" of the future, with 10,000 workstations linking all "knowledge-workers" (scholars) in the university community to one another. Analytically, the workstations vision simultaneously embodied a selective critique of current realities, a conception of desirable future possibilities, and a strategy for translating current visions into future realities. Normatively, the vision embraced a universalistic conception of the scholarly community, while affirming that community's capacity to nurture the individuality and creativity of each scholar. It was a technologically driven vision, but with technology as a means, not an end. From the beginning, it was a vision that resonated with the institutional culture and identity of Brown, yet also one that projected beyond its campus to encompass eventually all of higher education. Brown would lead the way by making its campus a hospitable socio-technical laboratory for new educational experiments with scholar's workstations. Others would soon follow, it was assumed, because the vision was irresistible and its realization was within reach. The workstations project vision was first spelled out in a March 1983 proposal to the California-based System Development Foundation (SDF) titled *Experiments with Scholar's Workstation Networks in a Wired University*. The SDF proposal was a manifesto. Its foreword described the magnitude and significance of the project: "We are planning for a social and a systems experiment: an attempt to find out what a university of the year 2001 would be like if the most modern computing were exploited to the fullest in order to augment people's thinking and learning, and if we rethought many of the ways we work, teach, and do research in the university". Later in the proposal, the authors pointed to the project's revolutionary implications: "At Brown we believe the actual quantum jump in education and scholarship will be the use of the computer as a pervasive, multi modal medium. If developed properly, the environment created with networks of scholar's workstations can catalyze the most fundamental change in education and scholarship since the Gutenberg press". The proposal listed three major "improvements" being sought through "interdisciplinary experimentation" with scholar's workstations:

1. Integrated methods for creating, accessing, filtering, synthesizing, and manipulating information;
2. More efficient processes and tools for learning, teaching, research, and the routine daily tasks that often impede or take valuable time away from the above; and
3. Enhanced group interactions with more sharing of work and more joint exploration of ideas.

When these objectives are realized, students will play a much more active role in the classroom than they do now. The classroom will be extended to the dormitory and even off campus. The new dynamic media for both education and scholarship—as well as the new ways for individuals to communicate and interact with one another—will fundamentally change the university as we know it.

The vision of academic computing in higher education articulated in the SDF proposal would in fact inspire and rationalize an experiment that sought nothing less than a sea-change improvement in the quality and conduct of academic work, employing innovative computing tools as its chief instrument. The proposed experiment, the SDF manifesto cautioned, would be a risky one, but nevertheless one well worth pursuing at Brown:

> *We realize that this is by far the most ambitious undertaking that we as a University have attempted, not only in terms of the impact on the entire University but also in terms of the human, financial, and material resources required. While our discussions have certainly illuminated the magnitude of such an undertaking, they have also reaffirmed the sense among the highest leadership of the University not only that Brown can do the job, but that it can do it well.*

The proposal estimated that capital costs for the project would be $32 million, with estimated yearly fixed costs of $7 million for staff, equipment, and maintenance. In addition to requesting startup funds for computer equipment and infrastructure, the authors proposed the creation of a new campus-based organization to initiate, manage, and legitimate the Scholar's Workstation Project. In June 1983, the Institute for Research in Information and Scholarship (IRIS) was established for this purpose. SDF did not fund the proposal, but starting in 1983 both Brown and IRIS received multimillion-dollar support from IBM as well as funding from several other corporations and foundations, including Apple and the Annenberg/CPB Project. IBM's initial 3-year $15-million agreement was in fact the largest corporate grant ever made to Brown.

As Bill Shipp, one author of the SDF proposal, emphasized 3 years later in a memorandum to the faculty workstation committee, "We had to come up with *some approach that at least had the potential to benefit all of the academic disciplines*. What could we market? The concept of building a better computing environment that improved support for scholarship seemed to match both the marketing needs and the faculty's needs. We had to become leaders in academic computing".

When the vision was first presented to the Brown community in mid1983, there were no prototypes of the anticipated scholar's workstation, although Sun and Apollo workstations, plus earlier Brown experiments with hypertext systems on campus, served as interim working models of some of the capabilities envisioned for future workstations. In addition, Apple Computer gave Brown 50 Lisa computers in 1983-1984 to distribute to selected IRIS staff and Brown faculty for a pilot project in the distribution, use, and support of graphics-based workstations. But it was another 3 years before a prototype (IBM's RT) was available for wide-scale campus deployment. In the meantime, as IRIS director Bill Shipp pointed out in a memorandum, "PCs and Macintoshes [would] serve as 'place holders' until *real* workstations were available and affordable". In the absence of "real workstations," the vision articulated in the SDF proposal helped shape campus expectations about what academic computing could eventually become. Indeed, in this capacity the manifesto embodied the reciprocal notions of technology as text and text as technology.

Three years after the proposal, and just 1 month before the installation of IBM RT workstations in two university departments, IRIS director Shipp offered an intriguing metaphor for the Scholar's Workstation Project (SWP) in a memorandum to Brian L. Hawkins, vice president for computing and information services at Brown:

> *From one point of view our "experiment" is just about as much of an experiment as the electrification of rural America. Electrification did not guarantee productive uses would be made of electrical appliances, but it did offer people living in rural areas many opportunities for altering their work. Computers don't guarantee much either, but they do offer opportunities. And many believe computers offer far richer opportunities than did other technological developments such as automobiles and rural electrical distribution systems.*

Yet the vision itself, both in its encompassing generality and in some of its specific promises, was contested for some time by many faculty and students as well as by computing services and technical staff nurtured on mainframe based timesharing computing concepts and systems. Faculty skeptics were concerned about the possible conflicts of interest between the university's mission and IBM's research, development, and marketing needs – a concern fueled by the secrecy surrounding the initial agreement with IBM and the confidentiality provisions of proprietary information and equipment. Student opponents conjured images of an Orwellian distopia, "Brown Tech," as well as more mundane (and relevant) implications like the burden of computing costs as a looming factor in possible financial aid reductions and tuition increases.

Perhaps the sharpest, most influential student assessment of the scholar's workstation project appeared in a 1983 full-page *Brown Daily Herald* editorial, "What's Wrong With Brown's Computer Plans". The author, Jonathan Rotenberg , a Brown senior and president of the 11,000-member Boston Computer Society, criticized the SDF workstation vision for its technological unrealism, institutional inappropriateness, and elitist hyperbole: "Reading all the literature that has emanated from the project's organizers, one gets the impression that the computers will do everything. They will help people in every mode of thinking and working in a college environment. In short, you name it, the computers will do it". Although several of Rotenberg's specific criticisms eventually turned out to be wrong (including his negative assessments of the cost and feasibility of networking and his dismissal of what he called the "extremely cumbersome and tedious" new "'mouse' pointing devices"), his was an influential voice among the chorus of voices raising basic questions and doubts about the scholar's workstation project.

Nearly 7 years later, in its April 1990 issue, the *Brown Alumni Monthly* ("Computer Technology", 1990) reported: "In 1990, instead of using high powered workstations, most people at Brown now write and communicate on simple personal computers such as the Macintosh and IBM PC . The powerful, desktop workstations that were the focus of the 1983 feature haven't disappeared; about 500 of them are in use, most notably in the sciences where their computational capacities are needed for faculty and graduate-student research". Even the 500 workstations, however useful and powerful compared to those available in 1983, were a faint reflection of the scholar's workstation network of 10,000 interconnected machines envisioned in 1983. To be sure, enormous technological and administrative changes in computing took place at Brown between 1983 and 1990—initiatives that led to an academic computing environment that other colleges and universities may have envied ("Computer Technology", 1990; Shields et al., 1991,

1992). Brown's project was not alone, by any means, in falling short of its expectations, but because its vision was so grandiose, the gap seems so large.

Technological Legitimation

From the start, the university wide acceptance of the Brown workstation's vision was hardly a foregone conclusion. Yet even today, with historical myopia, academic computer revolutionaries may have forgotten the controversy generated in the early to mid-1980s, before computing became securely institutionalized. For some, it seems, the pervasive presence of personal computers in higher education and especially their rapid rate of diffusion during the 1980s requires no special explanation. After all, it might be argued, colleges and universities, like the rest of society, merely responded to a compelling technological imperative: the immense capacity of computers to improve productivity, efficiency, and the quality of work. By this logic, it was not only rational but also inevitable that academia would embrace computing with gusto: Investing in computers was a predictable response to technological advance. ("Academics of the world compute! You have nothing to lose but your typewriters!") And because it is a widely shared cultural presumption in the United States that technological advance is a central, indeed dominant, social force leading to other social changes, higher education's embrace of computing could be treated as simply one instance of a general process: technological innovation driving socio-cultural change. Such an assumption, however, would be mistaken.

The saturated rhetoric of revolution coupled with the demonstrable technical changes that personal computers produced in academic work during the past decade obscure the fact that the first step in the institutionalization of the "new computing", namely, normative *legitimation,* was by no means inevitable. Academic computing policies and their implementation do not operate in an institutional vacuum; they are not self legitimating. Computing policies acquire legitimation not only through successful implementation and demonstrated effectiveness but also through their compatibility with institutional culture. By institutional culture, I mean those broadly shared beliefs about the academic mission and collective identity of a college or university – what its members value about it and which images it self-consciously projects to the outside world. Institutional culture shapes peoples' visions and expectations of academic computing in terms of an institution's mission and identity. Academic computing visions draw on key symbolic dimensions of institutional culture as a way of influencing beliefs about the general value of computing and the more specific translations of these beliefs into computing policies and their implementation.

Social analyses of new technologies increasingly have emphasized the indeterminancy of innovation-and-diffusion processes and consequently the necessity for innovators to "construct a meaning-framework for their artifacts to *create* a need that did not previously exist", and to connect an inclusive network of inventors/ designers, advocates, and potential users within a shared "technological frame". The legitimation of academic computing involved a symbolic reconstruction of the computer's appropriate place and function in higher education beyond the sciences, engineering, and administration. Specifically, as Pfaffenberger argued, this involved a "reconstitution strategy, promoted by the personal computer industry's founders and embraced by many of the technology's users, [that] sought to invert the equation of computers with central authority by creating a new computer that would foster decentralization. Timing was critical, of course: IBM, the epitome of huge centralized computing, came out with its PCXT in 1983, followed within a few months by the debut of Apple's long-awaited Macintosh in early 1984.

The futuristic technological virtuosity of the Brown workstations vision therefore had to be constructed and justified not only on instrumental grounds but also on normative-ideological grounds. Academic computer revolutionaries – principally located in the computer science department and the provost's office – realized the essential connection between legitimation (the scholar's workstation vision) and implementation (the creation of IRIS). They also realized the necessity of quickly recruiting a network of supporters and experimenters in other crucial sites on campus – "building a critical mass" was the operative phrase. This was supposed to be accomplished through a two-pronged strategy: an experimental hypertext-hypermedia instructional computing project, called the Intermedia .

Project is to deploy workstations (and later PCs and Macintoshes) to as many individual faculty and departments as possible, via the Faculty Workstation Project.

What, then, were the decisive normative claims that helped give legitimacy to the vision? First, the very notion of a scholar's workstation served as a compelling technological metaphor of institutional transformation. It rested above all on two crucial pillars of legitimation: universalism and pluralism. The scholarly community was conceptualized to include all knowledge-workers (essentially anyone working at a desk), each of whom would benefit from computerization. No kind of academic work, group, or discipline would be excluded. In contrast to the centralized, hierarchical, and elitist computing cultures of the past, no longer would computing – now, specifically, *personal* computing – be regarded mainly as a research machine for scientists and engineers.

The pluralism and universalism of the vision even promised to transcend the deep antinomies of U.S. society, culture, and academia: individual autonomy and communitarian solidarity. By linking thousands of desktop personal computers together over local, national, and international networks, the dream of an electronic global village seemed almost within reach. The instrumental capabilities of the powerful new technology could build new "virtual communities" both within and beyond the campus, yet accommodate the intellectual diversity and creativity that he at the core of academic work. In short, according to the vision, a network of scholar's workstations would nurture the values of both individualism and community. It posed no challenge to core academic values or interests; indeed, it would enlarge and enliven the application of those values.

Organizational mechanisms of various kinds were established to enlarge the network of participants and to mobilize support for implementing the vision. In addition to the creation of IRIS, several university planning and advisory committees, consisting in some cases of students along with staff and faculty, were commissioned; computing-attitudes-and-experience surveys were conducted to inform the policymaking process and to reassure the campus community that there was nothing to fear; personal computers and workstations were distributed to individual faculty and departments; and "computing-across-the-curriculum" became a rallying cry, symbolized by the high-profile Intermedia Project.

Furthermore, the Brown computing vision was consistent with the university's ethos of innovation in both computing and the curriculum. It also offered the potential for enhancing the university's national and international prestige. The financial feasibility of massive computerization was vindicated by pointing to the largesse of corporate vendors (like IBM and Apple) and private foundations (like the Annenberg/CPB Project), thus muting the voices of skeptics who argued that rapid computerization would divert financial resources from crucial human needs, especially faculty and staff raises, student financial aid, and the library. The coupling of economic feasibility and academic integrity—of material and ideal interests—provided the kind of legitimation that eventually enabled proponents of rapid computerization to seize the day. Yet, all of this preceded the availability of a concrete piece of computing equipment or software, let alone an integrated network, that came close to embodying the articulated vision.

An obvious question thus arises: Was the rhetoric about an academic computing revolution mostly hype and hucksterism, as some prominent skeptics suggested at the time? There was certainly a great deal of that, but also a great deal more. The grandiose visions were more than empty hyperbole or self-deception. They were believed by their proponents, who regarded their visions as not only desirable and necessary but also feasible. After all, they were touting the potential of a powerful, fast-changing technology—a technology, moreover, that had already helped to bring about dramatic changes in the rhythm, if not the quality, of academic work. Thus, why not think that even more radical technological advances and consequent socio-cultural changes would come about in the near future, as the technology moved forward inexorably? Above all, why not be an institutional agent in promoting that change? As Pfaffenberger pointed out, it was a time when innovative leaders in the personal computer industry—and, by extension, academia—were trying to redefine the symbolic meanings associated with dominant centralized computers by "reconstituting" their ideological implications through the ostensibly more benign attributes of personal computers as decentralized, democratic, and participatory technologies. "Though some industry founders advanced [a mythology of personal computing] for cynical reasons, others took it quite seriously, and saw themselves on the leading edge of a major wave of social change".

In short, academic computer revolutionaries were not electronic hucksters or crazed futurists. Nor, despite some of their occasional rhetoric, were they cultural revolutionaries. Instead, they might best be characterized as "instrumental idealists," based on two longstanding mainstream U.S. cultural predispositions that help to account for the subtext of the revolutionary rhetoric they employed: technological idealism-cum-utopianism and instrumental activism. First, their imaginations were captured by a kind of technological hubris, common to the culture generally but not historically to academia that, before the personal computer, had tended to regard things technological with an elitist cultural contempt. Academic computer revolutionaries really believed that new computing technology would transform the academic world. Yet at the same time, their technological idealism was joined and thus tempered by their instrumental activism: a means-oriented, goal-directed, technocratic realism about the need for pragmatic, strategic, aggressive leadership to bring about the envisioned transformation. It was the combination of these two rationalities – a kind of Weberian instrumental means-oriented activism coupled with a uniquely American idealistic ends-oriented technological utopianism – that led to the early successes of these instrumental idealists of academic computing. Together, moreover, the two rationalities were the foundation of a legitimation and implementation process that institutionalized a new mode of networked computing in higher education during the 1980s.

From Legitimation To Implementation

By the end of 1985, 2 years after the public announcement of SWP, the workstations vision was securely legitimated on the Brown campus. It was virtually taken for granted that networked, desktop computing was not only essential but also desirable. To be sure, the pressure for specific legitimations had not vanished. Chiefly, these focused on the need to justify the unequal allocation of computing resources to the various campus segments and the related (chronic) need to justify growth in computing expenditures in light of competing budgetary priorities.

From 1986 on, the main challenges became allocation and implementation problems—how-to issues: how to fund, deploy, and manage growing demand for more and better computing resources within existing budgetary constraints; how to persuade or convert reluctant adopters ("laggards," in Rogers', 1983, terminology); how to organize and provide access to better (decentralized, distributed, powerful) computing services. The need for generalized legitimation in terms of core academic values of teaching, learning, scholarship, and research had been superceded by more mundane concerns. The initial and uncertain legitimation-through-reconstitution of the campus computing revolution thus evolved into a complex but more routinized and regularized process of technocratic implementation and deployment—addressing how-to problems with can-do solutions. Implicitly, if not explicitly, it was now presumed that computing per se had become self-legitimating, an undeniably good thing that merely needed to be deployed to users in the right packages. The early rhetoric of legitimation, emphasizing "cutting-edge" computing, had shifted to a rhetoric of implementation stressing "appropriate" computing, and also requiring a different level and focus of justification. In the abstract, an appropriate computing policy is one that implements an affordable campus computing environment after prudently weighing the diverse costs and benefits of plausible computing packages in light of existing technological options and the university's computing needs, available resources, and other budgetary demands. Thus, a computing policy is appropriate to the degree that its implementation leads to "effective" and "successful" outcomes. This expansive redefinition of the technological frame made it difficult to oppose appropriate computing even though there was no fixed consensus about what that might be for a diverse campus user community.

The allocation of computing resources and the impact of computing on the university's budgetary priorities continued to provoke debate. Despite major equipment grants from IBM and campus computer store discounts for individual purchasers of

Macintoshes and PCs, both of which contributed to the proliferation of personal computers on campus, the university spent over $6 million on computer operations in 1986. Since 1984, the need for greatly increased staff and facilities to support burgeoning campus computer use had been emphasized by high-level administrators. But the rising costs of computing were also occurring alongside rising costs of needed maintenance and expansion of the university's physical plant as well as recognized needs for increased faculty salaries and student financial aid. These fiscal constraints, coupled with the absence of expected workstation technology, meant that the vision of achieving more-or-less universal access to sophisticated computing tools for everyone on campus would remain elusive.

Nevertheless, the legitimacy and utility of distributed computing was no longer seriously contested, as it had been for some time following the announcement of the scholar's workstation project to the Brown community in 1983. Recognition that the only advanced IBM workstation available at the time (the UNIX-based RT) was not an appropriate computer system for all academic work did not produce disenchantment with computing per se. On the contrary, the campus community embraced computing more enthusiastically than ever before. "Heightened expectations are persisting," a computing administrator remarked in late 1987. Echoing this sentiment, a geology professor observed that "the RT has raised the expectations of most people in this department." The RT experience, in short, introduced a large segment of campus computer users to a new and appealing concept of computing. The appropriate computing environment came to reflect a blending of technological needs, budgetary constraints, organizational diversity, and institutional culture. And the central mechanism for implementing this strategy was not the scholar's workstation but rather the Faculty Workstations Project (FWP) coupled with a major reorganization of computing and information services.

The implementation strategy was decided ultimately by technical constraints and choices. From the start, the idea was that there would be a "family" of compatible (networked) workstations with different price and performance levels to serve the varying work routines and computing needs of different groups of scholars: faculty, staff, and students in all disciplines. In fact, it would be another 3 years before even a single type of workstation (the RT) was available for campus deployment. Yet, in the absence of real workstations, the vision and the symbol of the scholar's workstation helped legitimate the goals of the FWP, while also shaping campus expectations about what academic computing could eventually become. By the end of 1989, however, there was still no compatible family of workstations but rather a diverse mix of only partly compatible workstations and microcomputers.

The Brown University case exemplifies and illuminates the recursive interaction between technological legitimation and implementation. Academic computer revolutionaries on that campus—the instrumental idealists—self-consciously and successfully constructed a broadly inclusive technological frame around the notion of a universally accessible, decentralized network of powerful, user-friendly desktop computers and workstations. With substantial material inputs from large computer vendors, the vision animating the whole project seemed, for awhile, not merely utopian but also feasible. The shift from cutting-edge to appropriate computing—from legitimation of the vision via the Scholar's Workstation.

Project to implementation of the possible via the Faculty Workstations Project—did not delegitimate the key symbolism of the original vision as much as it redefined what could be accomplished under realistic constraints. In retrospect, during a 5- to 6-year period between 1983 and 1989 the academic computing "revolution" at Brown was not so much a technical reality as it was a socio-technical construction that eventually included a diverse network of supporting actors and fellow travelers, forged ultimately by the ramifying strength of weak ties. But that period of spellbinding technological virtuosity was and still is a long way from having an "impact on the life of the mind" equivalent to the Gutenberg Press, let alone "the most dramatic change [for higher education] since the founding of the University of Paris and Bologna. Some eight or nine centuries ago," as Johns Hopkins' president, Steven Muller, mused in 1984.

Academic Computing Into The 1990s

Brown University's experience, though unique in several respects, was nonetheless emblematic of the academic computing movement's aspirations for higher education. What, then, shall one conclude sociologically after a decade of experience with academic computing? Assessments and forecasts from academic computing proponents and interest groups now tend to be more guarded and less millenarian than those of the 1980s. Nevertheless, most academic computing analyses are still tendentious, usually authored by writers who continue to invoke a rhetoric of revolution and who, in collaboration with vendors of computing products and services, seek to sustain high levels of financial investment in and ideological commitment to computerization. "They employ a rhetorical strategy of curt confidence to communicate their viewpoint and to help inspire readers to trust in a 'computer revolution' made by acquiring and using computer equipment under commonplace social conditions". The remainder of this chapter proposes some broad stroke answers to the question of the consequences of academic computing from the vantage point of the early 1990s by examining U.S. higher education at large, drawing especially on recent national data and reports about campus computing. I examine consequences for students, faculty, and administrators, with special attention to issues of cross-institutional inequalities and electronic networks. My assessment is intended as suggestive and preliminary in lieu of systematic and comprehensive social scientific evaluations.

No Social Revolution

Appropriating Marx's distinction between the means of production and the social relations of production, one general conclusion stands out: *Although there was a computational revolution in the means of academic production, it was not accompanied by a revolution in the social relations of academic production.* "Dumb" typewriters and terminals were almost universally replaced by "smart" microcomputers and workstations, laser printers replaced ditto machines, and for the first time ever mail was something you could send and receive on a screen, where "nodes" and "user ids" replaced city and street addresses. These and other un- precendented technical innovations – in text production, graphics, data processing, database searching, networks, and instructional computing – were proof that the technical means of production in academic life had been irreversibly transformed within a matter of years, not decades.

But the technical innovations that so transformed the means of production have not had a comparable impact on the social relations of academic life and work. The latter have resisted fundamental change, and certainly transformation, quite effectively. Indeed, computer revolutionaries' over-technicized view of socio-cultural change led them to conflate technical means and social relations. They even seemed to assume that rates of technical computing innovation, measured in months and years rather than in decades and generations, could be transposed to the realm of social relations. But there was no technological imperative, *no deus ex machina*, no revolution.

The structures of influence and authority within colleges and universities have remained relatively untouched, except for new administrative and technical roles and units created to manage academic computing and information services. Academic and financial administrators still control the bulk of organizational decision-making authority at most colleges and universities. For the most part, too, professors still control the content of their curricula and the evaluation of their students. Students have not, in any demonstrable way, gained more input into these matters, in contrast to the 1960s and even 1970s, when curricula and student evaluation procedures were dramatically reformed to give students more control of their academic lives. "In most respects, the social relations between teachers and students in classrooms or courses with access to computer systems are not fundamentally different [from] those without such equipment". Moreover, the great debates on U.S. campuses in the early 1990s—about racism, multiculturalism, political correctness, outcomes assessment, and budgetary crises—were fueled by political, economic, demographic, and cultural currents that in general bore no direct or explicit relationship to computing technology issues (academic budgeting being an obvious and critical exception).

Nor is there much evidence to suggest that computing-across-the curriculum has in any thoroughgoing way infused scholarship or pedagogy with a stronger impulse to reflect critically on the cultural mission of higher education. On the contrary, "corporatist" values coupled with an "entrepreneurial ideology of expertise" have if anything become more pronounced in American higher education—not only because of computing, of course, although extensive ties with vendors have played an important part in the overall process. Higher education administration in the 1980s and now especially in the 1990s seems more conservative, technocratic, and entrepreneurial than ever before. Extraordinary investments in computing-and-information infrastructure, capital, staff, and services, along with unrelenting pressures for their expansion and upgrading, have reinforced technocratic and entrepreneurial values. Campus-vendor relations are more routinely businesslike: "Campuses are investing in technology but are asking more questions before they do. Companies are giving away fewer machines and are less eager to finance projects on campuses unless the colleges are willing to invest in the efforts, as well. The days of a 'higher-ed handshake with the palm up' are over, says a software executive".

The role of computer vendors in higher education must be viewed within the broader context of growing ties between academia, industry, and the state that accelerated during the 1980s and show no sign of slowing down. For example, National Science Foundation (NSF) initiatives in several areas, including the establishment of university-based engineering, science, and technology centers, have been significant. In computing, the NSF established four national centers for supercomputing applications and is being advised to broaden significantly its academic support for high-performance computing. The National Research and Education Network (NREN) program supports high-speed "test-bed" networks on several campuses. And a number of federal agencies will play major roles in developing the National Information Infrastructure. Peters and Etzkowitz, referring to the spread of industry-oriented centers on U.S. campuses, remarked that "the implications of [government attempts to be responsive to industry and the economic environment] are that many more research universities are actively trying to integrate into the industrial technical system and to assume a role in economic development".

Instructional Computing

After the early wave of entrepreneurial largesse and millenarian anticipations subsided, the academic computing movement seemed unable to attract large numbers of dedicated new cadre. The vast majority of faculty, to be sure, regard computers as indispensible for research, writing, and communication; a significant minority also use computers in teaching. But it is hard to find academics who are not themselves academic computing leaders discussing the relevance of computing to the larger cultural mission of higher education. This was most tellingly confirmed by the then Vice President of EDUCOM, Steven W. Gilbert, in an *Open Letter to Ernest L. Boyer, Russell Edgerton, and other leaders in higher education,"* reprinted in the April/May 1990 issue of *EDUCOM's The EUIT Newsletter*:

> *What prompted this letter was my recognition that even within the context of a respected higher education association [American Association of Higher Education] that is "friendly" to information technology, when it was time to discuss the future of post-secondary education and approaches to transform teaching within colleges and universities, computers and other information technologies had disappeared from the horizon.... This technology was not being rejected, it was simply omitted.*

Gilbert also pointed out that "access and utilization issues for information technology are still not mainstream concerns for researchers and policy makers".

That was not the first time he lamented the higher education community's neglect of academic computing. In an earlier newsletter, Gilbert observed that faculty members' adoption of computing was slower than academic computing advocates expected or wanted: "The number of faculty ready and eager to integrate computing into their instructional efforts is not increasing at the same rate as the development of new capabilities in computer technology and systems". And in the next newsletter Gilbert criticized the higher-education publication *Change* for ignoring information technology in its special issue discussing higher education policy changes for the next U.S. president to consider. Gilbert was right. Faculty were not then and are not now drawn in great numbers to instructional computing or courseware development. This is the perennial teaching-versus-research bind in a new electronic guise. A 1991 national survey of about 1,100 U.S. colleges and universities, conducted by the Center for Scholarly Technology at the University of Southern California, confirmed previous reports about the difficulty of getting faculty to use or develop their own computer-based instructional tools. "Relatively few institutions [15%] offer any rewards or incentives to faculty to encourage the development of instructional resources". Follow-up surveys in 1992 and 1993 found little or no change in the percentage of institutions offering professional incentives for faculty courseware development. Moreover, in 1991, less than one third of U.S. campuses had "a formal plan for integrating desktop computers into the curriculum" or "formal projects for developing desktop instructional software/ courseware".

The clear if implicit message is that colleges and universities should be offering more incentives and rewards, but the normative claim seems to downplay a compelling sociological reality: Academic disciplines, through their professional associations, ultimately define the products that count as legitimate academic work. Disciplines are conservative social structures that resist challenges to redefine and broaden the criteria according to which their members may expect to be rewarded. The "publish-or-perish" imperative that still governs promotion and tenure decisions is not now, in most disciplines, defined expansively enough to include instructional products as publications. By themselves, universities have neither the incentive nor the power to alter unilaterally the enduring reward structures (and time demands) that ultimately explain why only a minority of faculty members are attracted to courseware design and development. Although influential individuals and interest groups certainly are urging that the imbalance of research over teaching be corrected, the traditional paradigm is still dominant. Unless disciplinary cultures accept the desirability of courseware as a legitimate professional product for their members, there is not likely to be much movement in this direction no matter how sophisticated software development tools themselves become. Suggestions that instructional computing should be used for labor-substitution – "as a way of improving courses without having to shrink class sizes and hire more faculty members" – will not be embraced by the professoriate.

Another reason for limited faculty involvement with instructional computing and courseware development may be that the pedagogical benefits of computer-based learning have been exaggerated. There is not much evidence thus far that computing has altered, let alone transformed, the cognitive-intellectual processes and capabilities that students nurture and develop in college. Despite quantum improvements in the power, versatility, and elegance of instructional computing technology and software authoring tools, what Kulik, Kulik, and Cohen concluded over a decade ago in their meta-analysis of the effectiveness of computer-based college teaching probably is still true today: "For the most part the computer has made a small but significant contribution to the effectiveness of college teaching. Overall, however, the accomplishments of computer-based instruction at the college level must still be considered modest". Another researcher questioned whether specific attributes of the computer per se (as opposed to instructional methods, content, and/or novelty) explain learning gains; he also suggested that learning effects reported in the literature may be exaggerated because journals are reluctant to publish studies that do not demonstrate significant differences in outcomes between experimental and conventional courses. Apparently in recognition of these problems, in 1993 EDUCOM announced a new initiative and focus for its Educational Uses of Information Technology (EUIT) division: "a new effort aimed at demonstrating that computers can make instruction more effective and more efficient". It is by no means inevitable, however, and not even highly probable that the newest instructional computing technologies will produce measurable learning gains that are dramatically better than those of past experiments using older computing technologies. A healthy skepticism toward "hypermedia learning" is advisable, enthusisatic endorsements not withstanding.

Inequalities in Computing Access

Many early academic computer revolutionaries believed that the spread of microcomputers would have a dramatic egalitarian effect on access to computing resources, a sentiment captured by Apple's adline billing its Macintosh "the computer for the rest of us." Instead, an unanticipated effect of computerization on college campuses probably has been to exacerbate cross institutional technological inequalities, and hence also inequalities in the competition for other resources: students, research grants, faculty, and prestige. There is a partial, albeit important, exception: better access to computing resources by women, minorities, nonscience, and engineering majors. Yet even their enhanced access is not universal within institutions nor equally distributed across them. Access to the Bitnet or the Internet networks, for example, is much greater for faculty and administrators than for students at most colleges and universities. Students in every type of college or university are also far less likely than faculty and administrators to "have or own" a computer. Moreover, Green and Eastman found, both faculty and students in business and engineering are perceived as better prepared to use computer technology more effectively than their counterparts in the humanities and the fine/ performing arts.

New cross-institutional inequalities also have arisen, according to the Center for Scholarly Technology's national surveys. Green and Eastman concluded that "research institutions and more affluent campuses invest a greater proportion of their desktop computing resources in their faculty" than other institutions. Their surveys also showed that access to networking at universities, both private and public, is significantly greater than at private and public colleges, but that students, faculty, and administrators at private universities are most likely to "have or own" a computer. They also found that in both 1990 and 1991, financially strapped public colleges and universities were more likely to reduce their campus computing budgets than private institutions. In 1991, for example, nearly two thirds of public research universities and over one half of public 4-year colleges reduced their campus computing budgets, in contrast to computing budget increases at 45% of private research universities and 49% of private 4-year colleges (35% and 21%, respectively, reported reductions).

In light of these inequalities it is with only some exaggeration that Douglas Greenberg , Vice President of the American Council of Learned Societies, wrote that "current technologies now provide only limited access to a select group of high-prestige scholars in high-prestige disciplines in high prestige institutions". Broadening controversies about funding and access to national electronic networks — the Internet, the National Research and Education Network (NREN), the proposed National Information Infrastructure (known by its metaphorical moniker as the "national data superhighway") – highlight new sources of cross-institutional and sectoral inequalities. The NREN – a multibillion-dollar joint private- and public sector project to develop a super-high-speed electronic network linking educational institutions, libraries, businesses, and laboratories – requires participating organizations to upgrade their network hardware systems. For some campuses, the costs are prohibitive, thereby leaving them behind in this latest venture in electronic leapfrogging. The Telecommunications Policy Roundtable, a group of nonprofit organizations formed in 1993 to represent the interests of the "technologically disenfranchied," is "afraid that a national network [the "data superhighway"] developed by market forces would not reach the poor and minority communities or include the services that educators, librarians, people with disabilities, and others want". Such expressions of escalating concern for equity issues were highlighted in a 1990 report by the Congressional Office of Technology Assessment (OTA). "OTA found that changes in the U.S. communication infrastructure are likely to broaden the gap between those who can access communication services and use information strategically and those who cannot".

On balance, then, despite unprecedented technical innovations in the means of academic production, the diffusion of microcomputers on American campuses has scarcely reformed, let alone revolutionized, higher education. Instead, probably the net effect thus far has been to reinforce prevailing stratification systems, institutional values, and hierarchies of authority. "Computer-based ways of work and new services sometimes overturn specific practices, but they do not readily overturn key social relations.". Nevertheless, there is no doubt that academic computer revolutionaries successfully constructed the idea of a computing revolution in higher education, engaged in persuasive technological framing to legitimate and implement it, and even now continue to characterize what happened (and what can occur in the future) as revolutionary. The Thomas Theorem coupled with the socially constructed character of technological realities aptly account for the self-fulfilling prophecy "academic computing revolution." Yet an alternative interpretation, presented in the preceding pages, certainly lends support to Kling and Iacono's assessment: "Instructional computing has not yet revolutionized the social organization of schooling in any meaningful sense. And we do not see substantial changes from computerization likely in the near future because computer-based systems have been adopted in ways that fit pre-existing relationships between students and teachers, curricular arrangements, etc.".

Concluding Reflections

My examination and assessment of the putative academic computing revolution has not been an exercise in mere historical exegesis and critique. Despite the evidence of experience from the 1980s, the computer still serves as a key symbol of transformation and transcendence through technology. To cite just three typical expressions of the recent hubris: "Exploited to the full extent of its potential, information technology can literally give every scholar a global reach, almost instantaneously placing him or her beside any desired collaborator anywhere, or in direct contact with any storehouse of knowledge". In October 1990, the theme of EDUCOM's annual meeting in Atlanta was "Preparing for the Renaissance." And in 1993, writing about the emerging potential for "hypermedia learning," a professor concluded: "A great new force will, in the years immediately ahead, change the nature of learning and what it means to be a faculty member". The visions of the early 1980s may have passed, but others—equally far-reaching and arguably utopian-have arisen to take their place into the 1990s.

Above all, now the new visions seem to be animated by the idea of something like a "virtual academy," integrated by super-high-speed networks in seamless local environments of "ubiquitous computing" stretching around the world—a true electronic global village, presumably ushering in a new era in human history. According to *The Chronicle of Higher Education*, a report issued by the Higher Education Information Resources Alliance argues that "networks allow users to communicate inexpensively, unconstrained by time-zone differences, distance, or location". The report goes on to suggest that "geographical and cultural barriers between departments are being broken down by the ease and cultural neutrality afforded by networked communication". Invoking an unqualified logic of technological determinism, one background paper for the alliance's report claims that there is "no way to predict where and how far technology's evolution will take us, but this is a given: It will be extensive, expensive and inevitable". Contrary to the effusive technophilism of the report, networks are no more "culturally neutral" than interstate highways, and both are extremely expensive to build, maintain, and extend. There is no doubt that the importance of networking issues is growing throughout academia, and that more colleges and universities are offering networking services each year. But one should not forget that administrators and faculty (especially in the sciences, business, and engineering) have better access to these networks than students; and that in 1993 over one third of all U.S. higher education institutions still had no campus network whereas 30% lacked access to Bitnet or Internet. Even when (if ever) universal access is achieved, transformation of the social relations of academic production, including equal access to network services by students, will not necessarily follow. There is no technological imperative.

As Jeffrey Alexander observed, "Expectations for salvation were inseparable from the technological innovations of industrial capitalism. In this technological discourse, however, the machine has been not only God but also the devil . The computer is the newest and certainly one of the most potent technological innovations of the modern age, but its symbolization has been much the same". What is perhaps most striking about the symbolization of academic computing has been the virtual absence of distopian or satanic discourse. Yet now, in addition to the hubris, there are signs of a cautious instrumental realism about academic computing from some of its most thoughtful leaders.

The new realism, driven largely by budgetary stringencies and post revolutionary ideological thermidor, was reflected in several presentations given at the 1993 EDUCOM meeting in Cincinnati. The keynote speaker, Blenda J. Wilson, president of California State University at Northridge, emphasized the urgency for a "very disciplined approach" toward computing and other technologies on college campuses: "I hope we will be guided by the maxim, We *don't* have to do everything that is possible to do". Might this be a new phase in higher education's reception of computing, one characterized by a deflationary adjustment" and its accompanying resymbolizations. Alexander detected such a shift in today's popular discourses about the computer, what he termed its "routinization". Yet as the current debate about electronic networks shows, routinization is by no means an all encompassing theme of contemporary discourses about computing. The present phase does not signify the end of instrumental idealism even if it does seem to command a need for instrumental realism. In all likelihood, instrumental idealism and instrumental realism will coexist in dialectical tension as alternating currents of discourse in the social construction of academic computing.

8

Searching Strategies: Electronic and Traditional

Introduction

The ability to examine the precise tensions through which news is synthesized has, in turn, been based on a distinction among story levels defined as ephemeral or trivial, contextual, and structural. The argument has been advanced that each is defined, in large, by the source of information used by the reporter or writer. This book's theme— that electronic libraries are a unique information source that empowers writers and changes their relations to the subject— requires that the nature of these databases and the means by which they are accessed be discussed in some detail.

This and the next chapter attempt to describe the effect computerized databases will have on the information potentially available at each of the three story levels: trivial, structural, and contextual. This description requires not simply a listing of those computer files currently available online but, in addition, a description of the general levels of information they represent and, simultaneously, the search strategies that are used to find specific data in the "electronic library." Just as the printing revolution not only made libraries possible but also made bibliographic search techniques necessary, so, too, have electronic databases resulted in specific types of data storage, organization, and retrieval procedures to allow for retrieval of specific and pertinent data. Indeed, it will be shown that the search strategies that these electronic resources necessitate are the single greatest impetus forcing a change from ephemeral toward structural or contextual story lines.

It is tempting to make of these technologies a panacea, and it is necessary to guard against the light cliché that states cheerfully that "the medium is the message." Since Marshall McLuhan's popular work of the 1960s, it has been commonplace for academics and popular writers alike to argue that the medium by which information is transmitted determines, in great part, the content of the final transmission. Certainly, there is some truth in the formula. The printing revolution led to long-term structural changes in the way increasingly literate societies stored and processed information. It led to the creation of categories of public information impossible without both the libraries it made necessary or the profession of hack writer and journalist that it encouraged. But what McLuhan forgot, and other researchers have been at pains to point out, is that the printing revolution created a radical change not only in the way information was transmitted but also in the sources people used when writing or speaking on any issue. While the marriage of television, McLuhan's "hot" medium, and satellite transmission technology does allow for the near simultaneous presentation of audiovisual information between two or more points on earth, if the message sent around the globe is defined traditionally (what an official said at a certain time), then little, really, has changed. The oral datum has not been transformed or changed. It has merely been speeded up.

The medium is not the message if by that one means that the means by which information is transmitted defines the resulting signal. A clear distinction must be made between the medium of transmission— the specific information system's mode of data production— and the technology by which the information that constitutes the message is collected. The medium itself— the technology of transmission-exists within a social context, political environment, and economic system that will influence data— the message chosen for transmission, and determine the degree to which stories are accepted by "gatekeepers" as well as the extent of their final dissemination. It makes little difference if a news reporter with a notebook, a radio reporter with a tape recorder, or a television news crew with a video camera records a speech by President George Bush. All three will turn out stories whose messages are, at heart, identical: "Speaking from the Rose Room today, President George Bush announced he would ask Congress for billions of dollars to fund the nation's war on drugs." Whether a television announcer, radio broadcaster, or newspaper reporter crafts that introduction, the content is the same. It credits the president without analysis, affirms his insistence that the war on drugs is a necessary priority, and defines information essentially as what was said by that single— official at a single time and place. The message is constant in each medium.

What is suggested here is that the medium— any specific medium— is only one element of the structure by which the context of information, its superstructure of both data accumulation and transmission, affects the data conveyed. McLuhan focused upon the structure of the medium, the nature of a signal's transmission, irrespective of other considerations. He thus largely ignored the content of information to be transmitted. But while the specific medium of transmission may influence the reception of a datum, it is not the message in its entirety. There is encoded in any public report— irrespective of its means of transmission or its mode of production— a series of assumptions and propositions that are the root data. They are the content, and it is in the arena of content— fact and context— that these new technologies affect the superstructure of information and achieve their greatest effect.

The printing revolution made possible, in McLuhan's words, the "Gutenberg reader," who compared texts and different editions of a single text, who made historicity a possible posture by allowing not only the dissemination but the storage in libraries of vast amounts of information. It affected both dissemination, the structure of the mode of production, and the cultural superstructure of information. In the same way, the electronic data storage revolution affects the superstructure of information organization (and ideology) as well as structural aspects of data dissemination. It creates, however, what might be called the "electronic reader," who is defined by specificity and plasticity rather than by the rigidity of fixed text.

Perhaps McLuhan's dictum needs to be reversed: the message is the medium. New technologies will create fundamentally different information only to the degree that they affect the content of the information signal, whatever the medium of transmission. The base information content of the news does not change because it is broadcast instead of printed but, rather, changes to the degree a specific news outlet defines its stories in terms of different sources of information. McLuhan argued that it "is the medium that shapes and controls the scale and form of human association and action. The content or uses of such media are as diverse as they are ineffectual in shaping the form of human association." Here it has been argued that the scale of the medium is defined not simply by its range and speed of dissemination, but perhaps more importantly, by the context in which it places individual data of perceived social import. Its form is not simply a result of the medium chosen for broadcast but is a result of both the narrative form as a relay or transformation system and of any datum's source. Both of these elements are affected by technology in a way far more central than that described by McLuhan. It is not, as McLuhan suggested, that "the 'content' of any single medium blinds us to the character of the medium" but rather that concern with the medium of dissemination has blinded us to the relation between technology and the content of contemporary information.

The benefit of electronic libraries and many of the references cited in this text could have been (and, indeed, some were) culled from current magazines and newspapers readily available to any journalist or writer. But the article that finally ran in the Province was, at heart, a traditional story buttressed by some library research. It focused primarily on the work of two local psychologists and addiction researchers, P. K. Garg and S. N. Singh of Dr. B. R. Ambedkar University. Because of the skepticism of my editors, I asked the researchers for references to other articles in the field as well as reprints of their articles. I then used the local university library to obtain those references and incorporated their findings into my story. But throughout it all, I was guided by information provided by the interviewed source's perspective.

To have developed a story without reliance on that single point of view (and the research its subjects provided as substantiation) would have required hours in the library with *Index Medicus*'s yearly index of articles, searching for academic articles under the very general headings of addiction, heroin, morphine, marijuana, or cocaine. Locating articles in contemporary magazines on the efficacy of federal interdiction policies would have required further hours of research in the *Periodical Guide to Popular Literature* and, were newspaper stories to be a source, the *News Bank*. The former index lists articles published in general periodicals by subject while the latter catalogues, under general, bibliographic headings, citations based on headline information from stories in one hundred different U.S. newspapers. After these bibliographic searches, it then would have been necessary to procure the articles whose citations had been found through this research (and in areas lacking complete libraries, this work would mean writing or telephoning for copies of old news stories and applying for articles through an inter-library loan system).

This labor-intensive, time-consuming "term paper" approach is one that few reporters have the training, inclination, or resources to pursue. It requires one to be able to devote large blocks of time first to identifying the pertinent literature, then to procuring the articles or stories themselves. For this approach one needs a medical research library, a legal research library, and a decent university library if one is to complete the task without electronic assistance. Further, this approach is seen by many as "academic," an odious word in many newsrooms, and so time consuming as to be prohibitive. Certainly, it is possible in theory to create contextual or structural articles without reference to electronic libraries, but, in practice, the constraints are generally prohibitive.

Libraries and Searches

Fixed Text

There are important differences between electronic database "libraries" and their print antecedents that distinguish these information sources from their more traditional print counterparts. The most important is that print resources are fixed references stored in individual books, journals, or microfilm rolls, and electronic references are digitalized. Books and journals are closed systems, with each text a distinct entity whose information needs to be searched separately and located individually. While print made "literature objectively real and therefore subjectively conceivable as a universal fact," the immobility of the printed page and the isolation of a book or journal article on the library shelf meant that their information could be accessed only through the complex process of searching through indexes for a specific text among its millions of fellows, pursuing the whole article or book for data on a particular point, and then incorporating a recovered datum, it it was found worthy, into a new piece of lettered work.

This knowledge system created a whole series of roles based on the production of written materials (writer, journalist, editor, designer, typesetter, publisher, bookseller, reader, etc.) as well as necessitating a whole secondary class of researchers (bibliographer, librarian, cataloguer) whose job was to assist in, first, the storage and, second, the retrieval of information from those fixed information sources. It also created a two— or three-tiered system of information ranging from the general public (newspapers, mass market magazines) to the intellectual (specialty newsletters, smaller circulation magazines) to the technical (journals and newsletters written by and for members of a specific profession).

Until recently, journals and texts were mainly the exclusive intellectual property of closed, professional societies whose readers and contributors were members of specific trades or professions (physicians, lawyers, historians, economists, etc.). Writers for these journals were literary amateurs using a rarefied, professional language understood by their profession's members but not necessarily by the general public. Further, this literature was largely arcane and known only to those whose job category would argue for its perusal. Who, for example, but a pharmacologist or psychologist would know what journals to turn to for information on addiction and habituation? Few who are not members of the medical professions typically know of or use *Index Medicus*, which is usually catalogued solely in major university reference sections or specialized medical libraries. Only a lawyer or law librarian would know the journals and system of case references that make of the legal literature a potent research tool. In each of these cases and in others, the technical literature has remained isolated, like the newspaper clipping files, and accessible only to those whose job it was to know how to access it.

Fixed texts— the overwhelming mass of printed books and specialized literature— created a system, as Alexander Pope warned it might, in which there was "a lumber house of books in every head, forever reading, never to be read." Access to information has been constrained by the physical ability to search for the appropriate journal article, magazine article, newspaper story, or book that will pertain to a single topic. It moves from the broad, general background reference (general encyclopedias, specialized encyclopedias, and dictionaries) to books and then journal articles referenced in the topic's area. Books are organized by subject, author, or title, and a writer interested in a single topic must plow through library shelves of discretely stored data to find the appropriate material in which the specific information required is stored. To locate articles by topic or author in a specialized journal or magazine, one must use one of several series of references, each volume of the individual series covering only a year's worth of material. These series would include the *Reader's Guide to Periodical Literature, Index Medicus, Social Sciences Index, Business Periodicals Index,* etc.

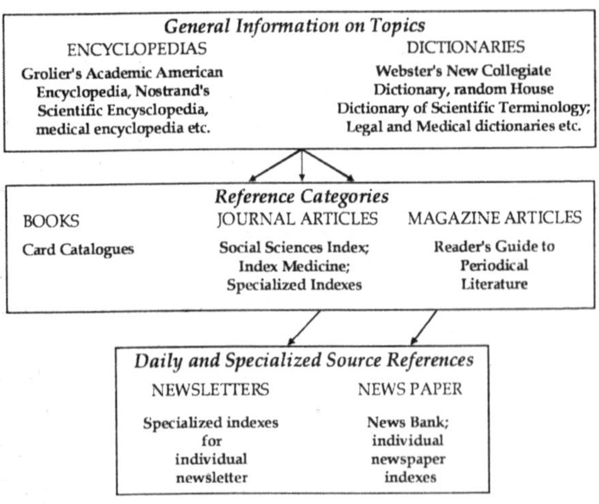

Fig. 8.1. Print Search Techniques

Thus for those interested in researching addiction to determine if the war on drugs makes any sense, one might go first to *Grolier's Encyclopedia,* whose general listing on addiction cites in its chapter notes several reference books. Even the encyclopedia's most recent edition will be several years out of date because by definition a new edition is a major undertaking requiring years of writing, editing, and production. Those books cited at the end of the article, if found in a local library, in turn cite journal articles or books by other authors and represent the thinking by experts at the time the article was written. To see if these individuals have written anything more recently, their names would be searched for in specialized indexes— *Index Medicus,* for example, and the popular literature's yearly edition of the *Reader's Guide to Periodical Literature* or perhaps another more scholarly index. Pertinent articles written since the last year's index was published or articles in a journal not indexed by the specific reference would not, of course, be found. For those using the most popular news sources, some individual newspapers (e.g., *New York Times, Los Angeles Times, Washington Post*) publish yearly indexes of their own stories, each entry catalogued with headline by general subject, and, for wider news coverage there is the newspaper story index, *News Bank.* Where articles or stories refer to other sources of information— congressional studies, presidential proclamations.

Traditional News Research Strategies

It is not surprising, given the economic constraints and general, oral perspective of the newspaper, that this classic "term paper" research method is used only infrequently by news people. If news is oral and concerned with "facts," then most of this method is not only time-consuming and expensive but, in addition, irrelevant. The general search paradigm espoused by newspaper research librarians has been geared to finding the isolated datum that can be used immediately and narrowly by the reporter or editor. As Jean Ward and Kathleen A. Hansen say in their article on news library research strategies: "Traditionally, librarians and journalists have focused on the 'fact.' A librarian usually helps [news] patrons find 'facts' much in the same way journalists seek facts on behalf of the public and for their news stories."

"Facts" are specific bits of data that have been published in the newspaper, are easily available from cumulative statistical references (state data books, for example), or are to be found in the most general reference texts. Thus in the event of a chemical spill, a librarian might use a scientific encyclopedia (e.g., *Van Nostrand's Scientific Encyclopedia*) to find pertinent "facts" on the toxcicity and chemical make-up of the leaking substance. This focus on "facts" narrows the number of references to be searched, the potential information to be retrieved, and the time required for the whole research process. Thus one would not ask a news librarian for information on the general causes of deaths in hospital. That would require searches of a technical literature not available in traditional news libraries. Nor would one be likely to ask a news librarian if a single death that has occurred in a city fits a pattern of injury that had been observed in other circulation areas or broadcast regions. Even if a news librarian attempted to search *News Bank*, for example, for stories involving a similar pattern (e.g., anesthetic-related deaths caused by machine failure), the stories themselves would be difficult to obtain and the cumulative index's headings would be too general to target the search so specifically.

So the traditional news library has focused primarily on organizing and then retrieving information first presented in its own publication. If news is primarily oral in content, then clipping files preserving stories based on what officials have said will be the critical historical resource that reporters need. Thus, at the *Province,* requests for information on anesthetic deaths drew forth a series of thick clipping files, envelopes of stories published in that newspaper and its sister publication, the *Sun*. One file was labeled "coroners" and reported on public inquests that the local coroners service had ordered. Among these stories were some involving anesthetic-related hospital deaths. Another file was the more general series of clippings labeled "doctors" and included some "coroners" stories and general, physician-related wire stories from other regions. Even more general folders, bulging with stories on "medicine" or "hospitals" might also be culled from the stacks by the diligent librarian.

Not all reporters have access to this material, of course. Those who work in distant bureaus, for example, have very limited or no access to the print resources of their employer's news library.

Reporters based in the city but away from the newsroom on an assignment cannot physically check the library's files from the courthouse, police station, or legislature news bureaus. They must call and ask a librarian to check the files for a "fact" or previous statement, a process that can take minutes or hours once that librarian is free to do nothing but address the specific reporter's research. Those who have both time and proximity may find the volume of clips to be so thick and the information cataloguing system so general as to be ultimately unusable as a viable resource. As Ted Weeger, an assistant managing editor at the *Los Angeles Times*, said: "We find that often when a reporter goes to the library and asks for clips on such-and-such a subject, he is likely to get five or six envelopes crammed full of stuff. There's no way he can read them all, unfolding every clip and then having to scan them."

If one did read those files one might find apparently relevant, past news stories whose information is presumed to be true (as was that in the *Wall Street Journal* example). But each story's fact is usually based on prior, fundamentally oral information that is itself suspect. Each clip represents a reporter's previous summation of official or expert statements, usually delivered in one or another journalistic context (press conferences, inquests, court hearings, etc.). Thus the strength of a newspaper's library files— stories based on official, oral statements delivered in journalistic context-is that they typically present as "fact" verbal observations or opinions that have been relayed through two media (oral to print or oral to broadcast) without examination. Thus traditional library research for news people is based on "facts" that can be easily searched, on isolated data or factoids originating in a specific geographic region, and on oral information, all of which, by definition, exclude broader contextual or structural issues. Ward and Hansen give the general newspaper library's "fact-oriented" search model as a five-step process in which the library's contribution occurs at stage three. It is the self-referential, closed nature of this data system that explains why "some reporters worry that the clips will prematurely establish a perspective and inhibit their independence and originality in developing the story." If the reference basis is what the subject said at a previous point, if facts are defined as what an official has said at the level of the journalistic event, then the latitude of the reporter to judge current events is going to be severely limited. Any perspective on the official's statement in a current context will reflect at best "facts" enunciated by that official in previous statements to the press. Thus some reporters surveyed by Ward and Hansen did not follow their profession's established practice and ignored library files while doing research because they recognized that past stories indeed serve as a source of orthodoxies and stereotypes provided by officials, which limit a priori the news writer's perspective.

Librarians working with clipping files and three dimensional texts have assumed that their general purpose is to support a narrowly defined search for an isolated datum usually contained in a previous newspaper or magazine story. The system supports a tautology that defines "fact" as what the official or expert said at a given place and time and bases future stories (fact checking) on what that official or expert said in the past at a journalistic event covered by a news reporter. In effect the unexamined, past statements of the source lawyer, doctor, politician, or university professor are the standard by which that individual's more recent statement is examined for accuracy. But as we have seen, officials' statements at any point are influenced by their own conflicting goals and perspectives. At best those statements are "weak facts," unsupported by other objective criteria. They cannot, by definition, be trusted as accurate outside the very limited frame of the moment. Data from other information levels (academic journals, technical journals, news reports from other, diverse circulation or broadcast regions) that would place the individual's statement into a more objective context are not typically available in this "fact"- checking, bibliographic regime. This system works best when one wants to know the mayor's middle initial, the year a senator began his first term in Congress, or a jury's findings from an inquest whose victim's name (Loewen, Marvin) is known. The whole " fact"- oriented system provides data but not, necessarily, information.

What it does not do is facilitate or encourage a systematic program for uncovering potentially appropriate information from other sources. It offers no real search strategy for broader categories of information, no method by which systemic or contextual questions could be easily addressed. The whole process affirms and supports an oral definition of news as isolated "fact," offering little impetus to those wishing to integrate bibliographic sources with the reporter's more traditional sources of information. Ward and

Hansen, attempting to enlarge the news librarian's function, defined these sources as informal and institutional. The former is data gained in conversation from other journalists, official sources, and personal contacts – what the court reporter told the medical reporter, who then talked to his contact in the local branch of the AMA. As we have seen, this information is tainted by the personal perspective and interests of those sources and their own professional agendas. The latter would include information gained from public officials, public relations releases, and official documents (court records, government records, etc.) Institutional sources are beyond the storage capability of most media libraries or, for that matter, most public libraries. Official repositories are designated as destination sources for varying types of official documentation for each level of government. Informal sources – the reporter's stock-in-trade – are dependent on personal relations, typically oral and, as the story detailing Todd's and Habash's positions made clear, biased and therefore suspect.

Electronic Library

Electronically stored information makes the discrete book, individual statement, or esoteric journal article a part of a larger, plastic whole whose sense and data can be accessed simultaneously by the generalist. Digitalized storage fundamentally alters traditional search methodologies by restructuring the lumber house of books, journals, and newspaper articles into an electronic code which can be searched for information on a narrowly defined topic at incredible speed and with previously impossible specificity. Once stored in a binary code, the text takes on whole new properties that allow not only for more efficient storage but for new means of retrieval. Tim Miller uses the following trivial example to make the difference clear:

> *Take, for example,* Who's Who in America. *In the print version each word in the two-volume set is bound to one place only on a sheet of paper; the 75,000 biographies are arranged alphabetically. Thus, we can find Caspar Weinberger in the Ws.*
>
> *In the computerized version, by way of contrast, each word swims in a digital soup, ready to be dipped out in accordance with almost*

any criterion the searcher wants to specifiy. Thus, last year, when librarians at the San Francisco Chronicle *wanted to find members of the secretive, men-only Bohemian Club, they went to the on-line version of* Who's Who *offered by Dialog Information Services, a vendor of more than 300 data bases. Within seconds the computer located the word "Bohemian" each time it appeared in an entry. Among the club members found: Secretary of Defense Caspar Weinberger.*

A search of this kind in the print version of Who's Who *would have taken a reporter approximately eight years, not counting coffee breaks.*

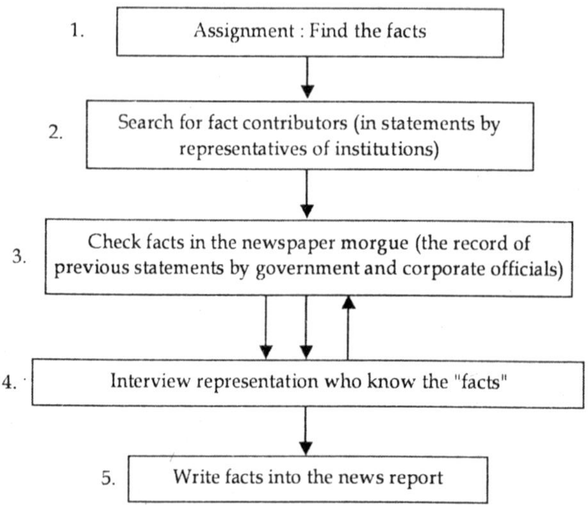

Fig. 8.2. Traditional News Librarian's Model

This is the specificity of online databases. In the print version of *Who's Who*, there is no way to find every mention of the Bohemian Club except by methodically checking each listing for a subject's possible membership in the organization. But because the electronic version of the text is, in fact, a "digital soup" in which the data's organization is unfixed, one can draw from it a directory of the club or, should one wish, determine membership in any other organization whose constituency is sufficiently important to be noted in the directory. One can, of course, be more specific. To discover whether justices of the Supreme Court or their employees belonged to the Bohemian Club, one could search the online text for "Bohemian" and "Supreme Court" simultaneously, a longer phrase that would return only those text entries describing Bohemian Club members affiliated with the Supreme Court. If there was another organization that included the word Bohemia (say, for example, "Children of Bohemian Parents") or other members of the Supreme Court staff also listed in *Who's Who* (say, the court's chief librarian) who belonged to either Bohemian group, those entries would be included in the search's answer as well.

It is this very specificity, the ability to search volumes of data with extremely narrow filters, that, interestingly, has led many to believe, in Philip Meyer's phrase, that "it's the same old journalism but with better tools." After all, the traditional news model is based on an assumption of discrete "facts" presented by individual experts or officials at a specific journalistic event, so a research tool that allows the writer to cull rapidly and precisely through masses of newspaper clippings for that "fact" should be an aid to the traditional research approach. In the late 1970s, when major newspapers first began to computerize their libraries, this move was seen as an advantage. Rather than culling through folders of news clippings catalogued in the publication's morgue, one could search with more specificity for stories that might have previously appeared on a single topic. What resulted was a chronology, a listing of pertinent stories ordered by date and defined by search phrases that cut across the boundaries of traditional newsroom divisions (business, "living," sports, news).

If all that one could search was *Who's Who* or the files of a single newspaper for a story one remembers reading six months ago, then computerized information storage would be, in fact, no revolution at all. Digitalized storage perhaps would be justified by the economies achieved in storage space and the added efficiencies that the Bohemian Club search made evident. But what is searched is not simply a single story but the whole of the digital soup. Rather than five bulging files of clippings labeled "coroner," "medical," "doctors," and, perhaps, "medicine," the reporter searching for stories on "anesthesia and death or injury" would receive a chronology of stories in which those words occurred in conjunction. Because what is being sifted through electronically is the whole story and not simply general file words (coroner, hospital, doctor, etc.), the range of newspaper data searched might retrieve stories not otherwise included in the files. Thus if there has been a story on product recalls for specific respirators or a news brief on problems elsewhere in their use, these would be retrieved by the electronic search as well. What the digitalized library yields, through search specificity, may indeed be more efficient, faster, and more complete than traditional search methods. But the computerization of, say, a single newspaper's proprietary files does not greatly expand the reporter's potential information base. "Information in clips is limited to what people at a particular paper already know about a subject. When a reporter is assigned a story unrelated to anything his or her paper has covered before, the clipping file is useless as a research source." And, of course, the information contained in those files is limited by the system of oral transmission that at present defines contemporary news writing.

Three things have happened, however, that make of this new technology a revolution. One has been that the expense of computerization has required the creation of new markets for whole classes of digitally stored materials. Just as the printing revolution made possible previously impossible economies of scale, enlarging the body of written materials readily available, so, too, has this computerization of information created its own economy of scale. The online library has become a commodity in its own right and its database is sold as a resource to any who wish to access it. Companies like Vu/Text, which computerizes newspapers, offer clients the opportunity to search the databases of all other newspapers that have chosen to participate in this system. These newspapers receive a royalty whenever their individual files are accessed, and editors have discovered they can partially recover the cost of computerization by making their digital libraries available online to the public at large and to other news organizations through a vendor like Vu/Text.

As well, popular and specialty magazines, often owned by the same corporations that control daily newspapers, have also computerized their libraries, which are being made available in the same way by one or another digital information company. What began as an efficient means of storage for an individual newspaper or periodical has become a system of increasingly communal information retrieval for all participants. So reporters or writers can search not only the database of a single newspaper company, but instead — virtually simultaneously — can search more than sixty-five newspapers and hundreds of regional and national weekly magazines as well. Reporters are thus not limited by their own library files but can access and work with the files of colleagues from around the country.

Second, computerization has made it economical and efficient to digitalize the work, research, and records of a variety of specialized publications and resources whose distribution previously was limited to individuals in specific fields. Law journal articles and court records from state and federal jurisdictions have been placed in electronic form, as has the work of academics and professionals writing in fields ranging from atomic physics to zoology. Just as the first printing revolution transformed writing from the leisure pastime of society's elites to a broadly based, print oriented system of information, so, too, has computerization made academic writing a widely available resource. This material is also available to the reporter, writer, or news librarian interested in placing news "facts" in a context. Until this development occurred, professional, "objective" research was practically available only to a limited, professional audience that read journals such as Pediatrics, *Michigan Law Review*, *Professional Geographer*, or *Demographics*.

In the same vein, the federal government, whose bureaucracy generates an enormous amount of data, discovered it was both cost-effective and efficient to store their records — and to disseminate them — through digitalized systems. Thus in 1990, for example, public releases and information updates from various federal agencies were available to any citizen with access to a computer and modem. In addition, the U.S. Supreme Court agreed to initiate Project Hermes, a system allowing the electronic distribution of the Court's opinions immediately upon completion through the Supreme Court Opinion Network to fifteen major legal and news publishing organizations that will, in turn, share those opinions with other organizations. This system will make available immediately the court's complete brief, a process that, in the past, took at the least months to sift down through traditional legal reportage systems.

In addition, the U.S. government has begun to license outside vendors to digitalize government records and sell them in their electronic form to general users. Thus much of the information that is filed with the government but is a part of the public domain can be searched electronically. Each year, for example, more than one hundred thousand corporate reports are filed with the Securities and Exchange Commission, generating over six million pages of data. In 1985, the Disclosure Information Group contracted to store the data electronically and make it available, for a fee, to the public. Until recently, these SEC filings were submitted in print form— on paper— but now the majority are filed electronically and thus available to the online researcher almost immediately. As Alfred Glossbrenner has noted, today there is virtually no significant piece of information about the finances of a public company that Disclosure does not include. Those filings can be searched with the same flexibility and specificity as *Who's Who*.

Finally, information storage occurs not as a separate part of the information process, following production of printed materials, but as an integral part of the production process itself. The newspaper Linotype operators who worked with lead type have been replaced by electronic equipment and "cold type," which makes a page plate from a computerized publishing system. Publications produced electronically code their stories or articles and information in a digital form, which can be organized bibliographically and stored electronically as soon as an editor sends the item to a page. Because searching is done by computer, stories need not be clipped and individually processed in the library but are "poured" into the digital soup. The result is that information is updated in all databases at an extremely rapid rate and that searchers need not use last year's index to find articles based on perhaps already dated work done two or more years before.

A comparison of "electronic" and traditional encyclopedia forms illustrates the difference in these two storage forms. Grolier *Academic American Encyclopedia*, which costs $800 for a set of hardcover volumes, is updated annually. Its information is stored on computer-generated, magnetic tapes, and in the 1980s was offered as an online database to both Dow Jones News Service and CompuServe customers. There is now also an electronic Grolier's, updated monthly, with two thousand more articles than its annual print cousin. The electronic version can offer those extra articles because it is freed of the space limitations its physical counterpart is constrained to accept and because articles can be easily added or subtracted to the digitalized version. Thus, during the 1988 U.S. presidential election campaign, the electronic Grolier's carried detailed articles and biographies on Democratic and Republican candidates, and then deleted the files when the election ended. In season, facts and figures on baseball's players and game statistics were also temporarily included in the encyclopedia, only to be replaced during the winter with data on hockey and basketball teams and players.

The result of all these changes has been the radical transformation of the typical news organization's library where, until recently, the resource base was largely limited to dictionaries, encyclopedias, a few magazines, and traditionally stored clipping files. Now that library is linked to a mammoth electronic information resource in which the news organization's clippings have become a single component within the millions of specific and potentially pertinent electronic files generated by a geographically diverse selection of newspapers, journals, and magazines, which may have published stories on or about any single topic. Those news files are joined by a mass of digitally stored and electronically retrievable government documentation, legal case histories, and technical reports. To search only newspapers for stories on, say, addiction and habituation would, using traditional methods, require months. To absorb the technical literature on the causes of drug abuse might require weeks. The legal issues involved would demand weeks more for those unused to the very specific bibliographic system used in traditional law libraries. The mass of potential data is overwhelming. But the fears of some that computerized information would merely overwhelm the writer with extraneous information have been balanced by the system's inherent capability to tailor information retrieval to very specific requests. It is the specificity of search technology in this digitalized information system that keeps the mass of data retrieved on any subject from becoming overwhelming.

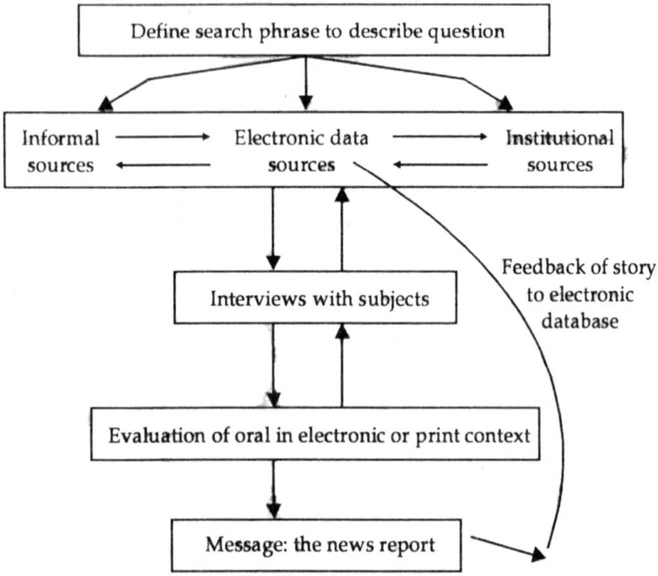

Fig. 8.3. Electronic Data Model

Electronic Model

The resulting bibliographic model that reflects these changes in the electronic news library can be seen in Figure 4.3. It is based on a tentative model of Ward and Hansen's that attempted to describe the relation of electronic databases to more traditional news library models. Their description has been modified to better reflect the position of electronic searching. In this model, the request for a specific "fact" has been replaced by the need for a search phrase that will define the question or problem area. The question may be rooted in a specific event (coroner's court, an official proclamation, a legislative budget, etc.), but what is sought now of necessity is a general perspective that will winnow the mass of data in this digital soup down to an effective base of potentially relevant information. Reports stored in electronic databases inform the reporter or editor, as does information gained from informal (colleague's or source's tips) and institutional sources (press releases and official statements). They provide a base of data by which "weak facts" can be evaluated and, simultaneously, a context broader than that of a single, biased, official source. Interviews thus become part of the information process, not the whole. What a Dr. Todd is asked-and how his answers are treated— can be based on a whole range of stories, articles, and reports selected to deal with the issues of malpractice: cause, effect, and cost. The database (legal journals, medical journals, news stories detailing previous quotes) also offers a context in which the statement of the subject is mediated and evaluated prior to writing the news report, which is then added to the electronic library and becomes available for future use by other writers or editors in any database to return the potentially crucial report, story, or journal article.

Practically, the search phrase is a strainer that allows the researcher to extract from the digital soup only those data that bear directly and specifically on the problem at hand. The trick is to assure the appropriate spaces in the strainer's mesh. If the grid is too narrow, then potentially pertinent articles will be excluded, and if it is too broad, the mass of information retrieved from a search will be too vast for careful review. As a general, operative principle, it is better to write a phrase so narrowly that a first search returns only two or three articles than to craft a phrase so broadly that one hundred citations are retrieved. It is always better, for example, to search first for recent articles, limiting the search by a six-month or one-year time frame, because this year's articles will, typically, include references to still-pertinent previous work. The narrow phrase also reflects a well-thought-out, testable hypothesis, a clear merger of events to be considered, and an aspect of that event that can be efficiently searched. What is called here the "simple search" exemplifies a narrowly defined search filter and is often a means to gather enough information to craft a full hypothesis.

Search: EAF

The traditional news model presumes there is a single "fact" that will be required by the reporter— a name, a date, a judge's ruling— and that it is the librarian's task to find that discrete datum.

Certainly, electronic data resources can provide this type of information, and this ability was emphasized in early articles on electronic resources and the news. Thus one can ask the computer to search for all references to Henry Kissinger in current news publications and report with assurance that the tally of references—10,187 in 1987— was the highest of any single reference for that year. In preparing this book, I searched an online medical database using "Bruce Beyerstein" as my search phrase because my notes did not have his middle initial (which is L.) and I wanted to include it in this book. Remembering that David Pearson had written an article in *The Nation* about the downing of Korean Airlines Flight 007 by Russian military personnel, I used his name, "Pearson, David," as the operative search phrase in a database of magazines to find the article's specific title and exact date of publication. In some databases, the family name precedes the Christian name while in others the order is reversed.

"It's great for looking up the proverbial needle in the haystack," says Dennis Rim, a librarian at the Washington Post. But the real value of the databases is in finding the haystack itself. The nature of the digital database and the language required to access it tend to lead the writer or reporter from the fact to its context. A simple example will demonstrate how this process works. In August 1989, Canadian television producer John Daly asked me to assist his station in investigating a rumor about the dumping of U.S. toxic wastes in Canada. An engineer passing through Vancouver had told BCTV news people that a company called Hawaiian Western Steel (HWS) was shipping something called electric are furnace dust (EAF) from Oahu to British Columbia. EAF was supposed to be toxic, and Daly wanted to know when and where the material was shipped, how it got to British Columbia, what exactly EAF was, how dangerous it was, and, finally, why a Hawaiian steel company would send its waste products to Canada.

To find answers to these questions, I first called Hawaiian Western Steel on Oahu, but its officials refused my request for information. I then called a local union representing Hawaiian Western members. But the union steward referred me to his supervisor, who turned out to be the company official to whom I'd first talked. He again declined comment. What was this stuff?. Who would know? Why wouldn't HWS officials discuss it? Online, I first searched the *Wall Street Journal* and *New York Times*, using "electric arc furnace dust" as my search phrase. I assumed that if

EAF was a major problem, one or the other newspaper would have had at least one article about it. No information was found. Then I repeated the search in a database of metallurgical and chemical journals and newsletters, hoping for something that would at least define the supposedly toxic substance. Six articles were returned from the search, each including source, publication date, and abstract. The following, from the September 10, 1988 issue of American Metal Market, gave me much of the information Daly and his reporters needed. The abstract is reprinted here in full:

> *The EPA has listed electric arc furnace (EAF) dust generated during steel making as a hazardous material under the Resource Conservation & Recovery Act rules, according to J. F. Collins, National Steel Producers Association (Washington, D.C.). The US generates 0.5 rail tons of EAF dust. The dusts that have reachable lead, cadmium and chromium have been prohibited from disposal in untreated landfills since August 8, 1988. It costs up to $125/ton to dispose of EAF dust in a landfill having safeguards, but the cost could increase as the number of approved sites falls. Historically 73% of EAF dust has been deposited in landfills. Basic technologies meeting the EPA's requirement of "best demonstrated available technology" for EAF dust are high-temperature thermal treatment metals recovery and chemical fixation techniques.*

The most important fact in this report seemed to be that EPA regulations had changed and now defined EAF dust as a hazardous waste because of its heavy-metal content. That change meant shipping would be regulated and storage or treatment necessitated at the waste's destination. Knowing this, I knew a great deal. I had an idea of what EAF was and an assumption-that its transportation to Canada was a result of EPA regulation changes. A call to the EPA in Hawaii confirmed the assumption, placing the whole in a regulatory context, and provided the rest of the information BCTV had requested. On file in the EPA's electronic database was the name of the company carrying the material by sea from Hawaii, its destination before the EPA regulations went into effect (a Washington-state company), and its destination following the implementation of these new regulations: Cominco, Ltd., in British Columbia. The rumor that sparked the search was both right and wrong. EAF was being shipped to Canada, but it was not being dumped. EPA regulations now required EAF to be handled as a hazardous waste and that requirement meant it now paid Hawaiian Steel to ship the material to a company large enough to treat it and extract the residual metals from the dust. Cominco is one of the world's largest mining companies and one of the few West Coast facilities with sufficient "high-temperature thermal" capacity (in short, a large and hot enough furnace) safely to extract the residual heavy metals from the dust. Daly then called Cominco, which confirmed it was handling this type of steel production by-product as a sideline and making money in the process.

The story, which began as a rumor of dumping toxic materials, became an interesting business piece detailing how a Canadian company has become a center for specialized treatment of waste products that U.S. firms can't or won't handle. An article in *Chemical Marketing Reporter*, also uncovered in the single search, listed EAF as one of thirty-nine substances that had been reclassified as hazardous and requiring either specialized landfill storage or specific extraction before normal storage would be allowed. In my final report to BCTV, I suggested they might wish to find out what other hazardous wastes were being sent to Canada for treatment and to compare Canadian and U.S. EPA hazardous waste treatment standards. Were the BCTV report to be integrated into a national story, it would have been easy to check with eastern Canadian metal companies to see if they were receiving EAF from eastern U.S. steel producers for metal extraction as well. Since Cominco is a national company with multiple plant sites, this possibility seemed likely. But BCTV, a provincial outpost for the national Canadian Television Network, was not interested in a story at that scale.

Using a traditional reporter's model, a librarian who took the time to look in a scientific or metallurgical dictionary could have discovered that electric arc furnace dust was a by-product of the steel process containing heavy metals. Such a search would not, however, have uncovered the crucial fact that new Environmental Protection Agency regulations had, in 1988, classified EAF as a hazardous waste whose storage was now subject to specific regulations. The fact of its composition took on import only within the context of the EPA regulations. This type of synergy occurs frequently in electronic data searching. Using the electronic model, I entered a search phrase that was the simplest form possible— a single noun. The electronic data sources provided information that allowed me to identify the appropriate institutional sources of information (the Environmental Protection Agency's office in Hawaii) and to ask its subjects about EAF shipments from Hawaii under the new regulations.

It is important to stress that this electronic database search did not eliminate the need for traditional, reportorial interview techniques. Sources were still called, and requests for information were made. News files were searched. But in this process, information was not limited to the oral source (denials from Hawaiian Steel, from Hawaii-based unions). Information retrieved from specialized journals and newsletters identified the individuals whose information was crucial— local EPA inspectors— and allowed for an informed interview with them. That resulted in information no newspaper or single journal database was likely to hold: names of marine shippers, dates of EPA inspection of Hawaiian Steel, destination of the furnace dust. Had a full-scale story been done, these raw data would have been the information required to set up television filming schedules. Basic reportorial techniques were empowered by the electronic storage facilities, and the "haystack" of federal regulations was found, along with the "needle" of the EAF's destination.

In the end, this was a small story. Had heavy-metal waste products been, in fact, dumped in British Columbia, it would have been a far larger issue. In that case, interviews with officials at Hawaiian Steel, Cominco, and the company that transported the materials by sea between the two sites would have been based not simply on informal rumors but on the data drawn from these electronic sources. Had BCTV wished, and had it been necessary, further searches could have been run to investigate the financial stature and business nature of Hawaiian Steel, for example, which must file reports both with the EPA and with the federal Securities and Exchange Commission.

But these things were not done. The rumor would have been great news. The actual story was pleasant news and a general business story, not what regional television stations necessarily do best. BCTV editors decided that the story of Cominco's treatment of these materials was not sufficiently newsworthy for them to invest more money in the story. The general system of priorities and perspectives that govern the news agenda was not changed. The information base which presents it with data was altered. The total cost of the database search of the metallurgical journals and newsletters, and of both the *New York Times* and *Wall Street Journal* databases was about $40.

As a footnote to this specific case study, Raul Ramirez informed me in 1990 that the Center for Investigative Reporting (CIR) was working on a television documentary that would trace the shipment of U.S. waste products to Third World countries, where storage and containment regulations were lax. The documentary was attempting to determine the degree to which products like EAF, defined as toxic or dangerous by the EPA, were being shipped to countries where regulations were less strict. When informed of the EAF search and my recommendation to BCTV that they focus on the other thirty-eight substances added in 1988 to the EPA list, Ramirez said this was the CIR documentary's approach, albeit without a Canadian focus.

Complex Search: A Medical Example

The EAF example was a simple search and used a simple search phrase. It employed a noun to locate references and information on a single and highly specific product. More typically, requests for information from electronic databases that say, in effect, "give me everything on 'X'" are too broad for efficient use of online resources. The accumulated resources of scores of newspapers and hundreds of journals provide a potential information base that requires narrower, contextual search parameters. In the early 19808, for example, *Miami Herald* news people searched electronic databases for stories about football player Joe Montana, using just Montana's name as the search phrase.

Unless the subject is as esoteric, and therefore as specific, as electric arc furnace dust, it is necessary in constructing a search phrase to use modifiers that describe more precisely both the exact subject and general context of reportorial interest. A complex search phrase addresses a factor whose examination is critical to the understanding of a boundary event with modifiers capable of narrowing potential returns to those that might bear on that event's general context. It places statements of officials at the level of the journalistic event within a context of prior research bearing on the elements of the boundary event. Creating an appropriate search phrase thus becomes the critical tool in the bibliographic search, defining not only general categories of information but their relation to other potential information parameters as well. In a real sense, it defines, by creating a hypothesis, what the final story will be.

To have asked *Vu /Text* for all articles published in its online newspaper database on the question of tort reform would have been prohibitively expensive, probably redundant, and largely uninformative. Hundreds of newspaper stories and editorials have been written on the issue. Many of them quote physicians in favor of tort reform, legal representatives against it, and the recapitulation of opinions by legislators supporting one or another entrenched position. A search for all articles on "tort reform" would not provide a context in which the issues could be examined, merely the already established positions of the very interested professional parties.

It was therefore necessary first to attempt to define the context—for the reporter to decide what it was he or she really wanted to know— and then to describe a search phrase that would bring that information forward. Institutional sources (in this case, Habash and Todd) seemed at odds over who was to blame: incompetent physicians or avaricious lawyers. Testing the venality of lawyers would be difficult (and comparing that to the avarice manifested by members of other professional groups, impossible), so the question chosen was: Why are people injured or killed in surgery? Todd's point has a certain logic— if people were not injured or killed in surgery, there would be no malpractice cases. So who is to blame in cases of surgically related misadventure? But medicine is so broad (neurology, obstetrics, orthopedics, etc.) and surgery so large a category (dental, thoracic, abdominal, etc.) within medicine that a common element in all surgical specialties, like anesthetic administration, was needed to define a context for the literature search.

To search the general newspaper, popular magazine, and specialized medical literatures for information on the relation between anesthetic administration and cases of injury or death in surgery requires a search phrase that would narrow the broad subject (anesthetic administration) to specific problems (death or injury). Anesthetic administration involves, for example, use of and problems with specific drugs (like halothane), mechanical problems with respirators and other equipment, the complex of physician interaction with both mechanical and pharmacological components, and issues of standard operating-room procedure. A search could be defined to highlight any one of these areas individually, but the first search needed to be more general. Thus, the first phrase used in this search was written: "anesth/ and (death or injury)."

The phrase includes a series of logical operations designed to limit information to be returned and define its priorities. These Boolean search operatives include conjunctions, parentheses, and a slash (/) to target the search more effectively. The slash is commonly called a "wild card" or, more technically, a "truncator." It instructs the computer to search for any word that begins with "anesth," whatever the word's suffix might be. Thus stories including, as a partial listing, anesthesia, anesthesiology, anesthesiologist, and anesthetic will all be recovered. Stories using the British spelling "anaesth/", will not, however, be brought forward, and those searching technical journals, newspapers, or newsletters that use British spelling would need to write their phrase: "(anaesth/ or anesth/) and (death or injury)."

My first search used the phrase "anesth/ and court," in an attempt to find news stories about juried cases (from civil, criminal, and coroner's courts) involving anesthetic related matters. Unfortunately, what was found instead was scores of basketball-related stories in which players were judged, by sports writers, to be anesthetized on the playing court. Even the search phrase "anesth/ and (death or injury)" brought forward a score of sports stories in which anesthetized players were dead on the court or in which those who played as if they were anesthetized were judged to have injured their team's chances in a game. These stories could be removed by including another line to the phrase directing the search to exclude either basketball or, more generally, sport or sports stories: "(anesth/ or anaesth) and (death or injury) not (/ball or sport)." Here "/ball" would remove all stories in which football, basketball, or baseball were included in the text.

There is, at present, no single, uniform search language recognized by all database services, a fact that complicates the life of any researcher who uses several different services. While at present all must use Boolean search indicators, each service has defined the truncators in a slightly different fashion. The truncation mark, for example, may be written as "/", "?", "!", "!" or "*" (anesth/, anesth?, anesth!, or anesth*), depending on the service used. Some services, *Vu / Text,* for example, allow search phrases to include instructions defining the conjunction between search words. Thus one can limit a search on *Vu / Text* by including in the search phrase a symbol limiting retrieval to only those stories in which the phrase's first element ("anesth!") appears within either the same sentence ("/s") or the same paragraph ("/p") as the second phrase ("death or injury"): "anesth! /p (death or injury)."

Dow Jones New Retrieval Service provides a similar service but in a slightly different way. It allows for the search to insist that both elements of the phrase appear either adjacent to each other (but in any order, i.e., "anesth/ and death" or "death and anesth/") or separated by any specific number of words. Thus a search for "Data adj General" would retrieve any story in which either "data general" or "general data" appeared. "Data adj7 general," on the other hand, would retrieve those stories in which the two separate words appear in any order within seven words of each other, for example: "*Data* is often found to be a *general* topic of reporters" or "In *general,* police find the issue of legally admissible *data* to be an issue."

To make this procedure even more confusing, different data services allow the user to search different categories of information. Some data sources are only bibliographic, searching and retrieving no more than author, title, source, key word, and data of publication for the materials they have stored in digital form. This form is the electronic equivalent of bibliographic index cards traditional to most libraries in which one searches by author, title, or subject. Others may search only this information and an abstract filed with its journal article. Thus one searches both the headline or title, key words, and a one-paragraph abstract that is filed electronically. But if one wants to read the whole article, one must then go to the library and look it up by conventional means. Finally, some databases— *Vu/Text* is one— include the whole text of articles online and allow the writer to search the entire database for the search phrase's conjunction.

This diversity of search languages and retrieval methods is a result of the newness of these services. At the beginning of the printing revolution, as increasingly large numbers of printed materials needed to be effectively catalogued, techniques for indexing and shelving books varied library by library and, sometimes, librarian by librarian.

Each worked according to general principles but sometimes different rules which were, in the United States, finally standardized by the Dewey decimal system. Digital information storage has evolved to the degree that, even where different symbols are used, the search characteristics are similar. Boolean truncations, use of the conjunctions *and, or,* and *not* in phrases, and general organizational principles are rapidly being standardized. Further, current explorations of new data techniques may, in the coming generation of online data facilities, allow for common language searches in which Boolean phrasing is no longer necessary. Just as, on the science fiction television show Star Trek, the science officer, Mr. Spock, cavalierly asks the computer "for information on sentient, humanoid life forms in Star System Beta Seven," data researchers will be able to ask their computer "for stories on financial mismanagement and medical problems in the Veterans' Administration hospital system." As Chapter 5 attempts to demonstrate, there are already a variety of data vendors with increasingly simple databases whose programs emphasize ease of use for the amateur researcher.

Sources

The traditional librarian's "fact"-oriented model assumes that a single datum is required by the reporter and further assumes that, in the majority of cases, it will be found in a very narrow range of sources. These include specific compendiums of data (the encyclopedia, almanac, state data books) and the files of past stories published by the newspaper or magazine. To the extent that the data are isolated and discrete, they provide no necessary links to larger structural or contextual issues, and they are trivial or ephemeral. "Facts," as we have seen, take on meaning only in a broader context, and their validity can be determined only when the information's source and quality have some impartial judge. Defining that broader perspective is made difficult, it has been argued, because of the very nature of print data storage techniques (news library files, library shelves, the broad categories of card catalogues), as well as because of the reliance by news clips on oral information that is typically presented at the level of the formalized, journalistic event. At best these are "weak facts," at best true within their own context but, without external context, anything but objective or unbiased. I do not suggest that those traces of past journalistic events are useless but, rather, that the limits of the news morgue must be recognized and placed in perspective.

The searching of the files of any single newspaper, journal, magazine, or newsletter to the exclusion of other sources will yield specific data that, if essentially a compendium of ephemeral reports, may suggest patterns and issues. In theory, journalists have always checked "the clips" in their search for information. What is suggested here is that examination of a newspaper's past stories, typically the traditional journalist's primary research method, is only a first step in which general patterns may be revealed and from which a hypothesis can then be fashioned. Consider the following example. In 1987 an Abbotsford, B.C., adolescent, Marvin Loewen, died during dental surgery in a local clinic. Following this death, the local coroner announced an inquest into Loewen's death would be held. A search of the shared library of the two local newspapers, the *Province* and the *Sun*, recovered a series of stories describing prior inquests into deaths resulting from both general and dental surgery. In many of them, an anesthestic was described as a critical element leading to the death, and most inquest juries criticized the failure of the dentist or operating physician to be prepared for emergencies. This material was suggestive but not conclusive. In eight years there had been at least ten inquests resulting from surgical misadventure, and in all of them anesthetic was a contributing or primary factor. To see if this pattern of B.C. deaths was exceptional, a reporter could then search regional newspapers in other jurisdictions (Toronto, Los Angeles, Boston, etc.). As case piled upon case, patterns in all of these stories would emerge. Time after time, death was attributed to anesthetic overdoses, failure to monitor equipment that delivered anesthesia, and equipment failure.

Because most U.S. newspapers report on court and not simply inquest cases, news copy often includes assignment of blame and an assessment of monetary damages against the physicians and dentists. These stories thus reflect a social definition of precisely who is responsible in medical misadventure and the degree of that responsibility, calculated in dollars. Coroner inquests in B.C., on the other hand, are public forums and prohibited by statute from assigning blame or assessing damages. So a search for court stories in newspapers— "anesth/ and (death and injury) and (jury or court) not/ball" would be useful. Because U.S. court cases are themselves stored electronically, those with access to an electronic database of U.S. court records (like *WestLaw*) could search there as well.

One could, of course, first do a general search of all court jurisdictions, but the newspaper search would generate case names, which can themselves more precisely and economically be accessed in the electronic court record system. Thus in the 1980s the *Los Angeles Times* reported on a number of anesthetic-related cases, including those in which a dentist was convicted of murder after injuring over thirteen patients in separate anesthetic-related incidents. His conviction was appealed and upheld at several levels, and, at each step in the legal proceeding, the court (jury and judges) made clear that legal and professional standards required physicians to adhere to specific standards of drug administration and patient monitoring, which were not followed by this doctor.

Both legal and news searches focus all deaths on physician actions: proper monitoring, properly maintained equipment, administration of appropriate levels of anesthetic drug. A judicious search of the medical and biomedical literature on a specialized national database (*Medline*) returns, then, a series of articles on anesthetic mishap in which physicians themselves acknowledge that a large percentage of surgical deaths or injuries result from failure by members of their profession to follow approved standards of patient monitoring and use of appropriate monitoring equipment in the operating theater (hospital or dental clinic).

Thematic Sources

The progression is clear. One moved in this case from the local newspaper to regional or national newspapers as indicators of recurring events. The vehicle for this exploration was a search phrase whose crafting created a context (death and injury) through which a specific action (administration of anesthetic) could best be understood. Court records and the technical literature laid bare the broad context of social and scientific judgment against which individual statements (conflicted at the institutional, instrumental, and functional levels) by boundary-event actors could be evaluated. The result was an ability to weigh the denials of boundary-event participants ("I didn't screw up") against the combined voice of the published medical professor and amateur writer. The reporter can write with authority on the basis of this type of information that, in effect, "If Dr. N didn't do x, y, and z, then everyone – judges, juries, medical researchers, and his professional colleagues – agrees he was at fault."

All this wealth of information from a variety of sources can be brought to bear on a subject as narrow as an individual inquest in which the physician says blandly, "It was just a one-in-a-million freak death" or on a subject as broad and complex as tort reform and the social cost of contemporary medicine. The whole story begins with and ends with the narrowly defined newspaper report but extends the concept of its information base from the unexamined oral statement to the written resources of legal, medical, and official authorities across North America and around the world.

Interview Land Evaluation

This material in itself can be used as research for a story but, more frequently, it arms reporters or editors with data that allows them to challenge directly, on the basis of comparable information, the official, the expert, or the academic. This possibility was made clear in the EAF search in which reports retrieved from the electronic database on new Environmental Protection Agency regulations directed the research to branch officials in Hawaii. Freed from an absolute reliance on a response from Hawaii Steel officials, (who refused comment), I could intelligently phrase issues of toxicity of the hazardous waste, and the relation between the new regulations and the Hawaiian company's change to a Canadian reclaiming site. Later questions by BCTV to Cominco, Ltd., were similarly informed. In these cases, interviews become the forum by which general information is focused on the specific case, and evaluation is a matter of placing the local or regional event within the broader context of professional standards or environmental concerns.

In the Loewen case, in which both dentist and anesthesiologist insisted they lacked any responsibility in a teenager's death, a reporter armed with electronic research could have questioned the status of the respirator prior to surgery (there were, in fact, holes in its bellows), preparedness for emergencies (the defibrillator was broken), and degree of patient monitoring during surgery (minimal, by standards described in the literature). As testimony on these points was given, the news writer would know its significance and be able to relate it to other cases, trends, and patterns. Further, when specific issues were raised in the court, the reporter would know precisely where and how to obtain information on the issue and test, in the literature, its relation to the boundary events. At the Loewen inquest, for example, the anesthesiologist suggested under oath that the teenager's death might have resulted from "carotid sinusitis syndrome," a complication so rare that a search of medical databases found no examples whatsoever resulting from procedures like the one performed on Loewen. Thus at each step the data returned provides a context in which to weigh the evidence, a means by which the oral fact is weighed against past incidence and research traditionally stored in written form but, until now, inaccessible to the public information writer.

Controlling of Search

In the late 1980s, the presence of electronic information retrieval systems has grown at U.S. newspapers and magazines, although its use is usually restricted to news librarians or, less frequently, editors who accept questions from reporters, phrase the search appropriately, and access databases on the writer's behalf. The issues seem to be education and cost. Librarians are trained in general and specific means of research, are familiar with Boolean search languages, and, as traditional custodians of resource materials, are believed to be the logical members of a publication staff to access these new resources. And if, as some believe, electronic retrieval resources are simply more efficient incarnations of traditional resources, then it is appropriate that traditional overseers of information should be in charge. On other newspapers, specific editors are charged with supervision of database use. The rationale seems to be the presumed ability of editors to assure that these potentially expensive resources are not abused (e.g., should a staffer wish to find information to assist a child in a school project) and of the perceived difficulty of using online resources. Ward and Hansen noted the importance of the territorial issues raised by these technologies when they wrote that: "Budgeting for database services, controlling costs for online searching and assigning either librarians or reporters the chief responsibility for such searches are among the practical issues now arising."

Complaints by librarians charged with the guardianship of electronic resources focused, in their study, on the failure of reporters to appropriately frame search parameters and on their desire to use the database resources in new and complex ways. Librarians both resent, in general, this incursion upon their research role and worry that the costs, usually assigned to their budget, will be excessive and without sufficient results to justify the expense. As Fredric Endres noted in 1985: "They [news librarians in charge of databases] complained that reporters were not specific enough in their request for information or that some reporters had become so reliant on the databases that they would not begin to write a story without asking for a thorough database check. Again, the librarians thought this was a waste of time, effort and money."

It is necessary to recognize that the role of the news librarian has traditionally been ill-defined. Although trained in a broad range of information storage and retrieval skills, the primary tasks of news librarians have been menial ones. Their job has been limited, in the main, to clipping and filing stories that appeared in a specific periodical or journal, and then assisting the news writer in retrieving information and answering questions based on file information. But Hansen and Ward found that 63 percent of the reporters interviewed prefer to search and evaluate traditional files themselves rather than ask for a librarian's assistance. And yet, at many newspapers today, reporters are not allowed into the physical library but must request all files (and, if there is an electronic database facility, all searches) from the librarians.

Librarians, in turn, expect the reporter to know what electronic resource is to be searched just as, previously, they expected reporters to be able to define the "fact" they were concerned with ("I want the Loewen file." as opposed to "I'm looking for a pattern of deaths related to administration of various anesthetics."). But without online experience and without sufficient training to understand the database or databases that a specific publication's library may have, reporters are unlikely to be able to frame their requests with sufficient specificity or know where that information is located in the electronic world. Finally, the focus of database searches is not on the isolated "fact" but on the context of a prior event. It is a hypothesis, with which neither public information librarians nor news writers in general have a great deal of experience.

It is the very nature of these electronic libraries that reporters must formulate their own search phrases. This skill will become as much a part of the news writer's repertoire as typing is today and shorthand was a generation or two ago. To the degree that these are new resources whose effect on the news is only beginning to be felt, one must have sympathy for librarians used to "factual" queries who are now faced with reporters whose vague questions and inclination to use electronic resources extensively might, indeed, seem like a waste of time. Because the story is no longer necessarily tied to the level of the journalistic event, questions addressed to library resources may indeed be far broader than the traditional search for a single datum-statistic, fact, or prior story. To the extent that stories are defined by the content they carry, data defined by the information news people bring to an event or interview, reporters or researchers will, increasingly, have to gain control of their electronic resources.

Growing acceptance and use of these electronic libraries will, of necessity, change relations between public information writers and the librarians who serve them. The librarian's primary, traditional function— to catalogue, store, and direct the user to potentially important files— will remain. The emphasis, however, increasingly will be on the last function, that of information directors and consultants, and not on the menial chores demanded by the maintenance of physical files. In addition, to the extent that librarians are gatekeepers of the electronic libraries, they will need to be more directly involved in the creation of a story, more aware of the relation among general information, a specific boundary event, and the means through which theories are generated and tested in the literature.

The position of librarian— the very idea of the job— was an outgrowth of the printing revolution, a result of the need for specialists who could catalogue and direct the storage of volumes of information. That role will change as electronic storage takes precedence over physical collection and data are stored not in discrete volumes but as individual bits of information connected to others in the digital soup. As this happens, the position of the news librarian will become a supervisory, editorial role and the job of story research will become a part of the whole training process for public information writers. Just as young lawyers and law clerks do research for senior partners and judges, so may young reporters eventually have, as a first assignment, the research chores of their professional seniors. But just as law clerks cannot necessarily judge the importance of a specific case, and a medical librarian cannot be sure when a seemingly ephemeral article on retro-viruses holds the crucial bit of information for a researcher, so, too, the secondary researcher or librarian cannot necessarily judge, in this context, the reporter's exact information needs on any specific story. In news as in other fields, research will become an increasingly critical part of the reporter's technique, and news librarians ever more necessary and sophisticated partners in the story process.

Current confusions and tensions between news librarians, writers, and editors are transition problems, part of the tug and pull that typically occurs when a new technology begins to replace an older, more traditional and socially entrenched system. Costs of system use are decreasing, in large part as a result of new technologies (like CD-ROM storage disks) and in part through sheer economies of scale. Large, frequently accessed systems are cheaper to use. If the thesis that pervades this book is correct and the technology is to become the primary means of accessing public information, then not only will the role of the public information writer change in the process, but the task of librarian in general will be simultaneously transformed.

Legal Paradigm

What a well-crafted search phrase does, at least in theory, is inform reporters about the characteristics of a boundary occurrence and provide them with information at least comparable to that of the speaker at a press conference or other journalistic event. The search phrase places those prior occurrences in a context of previously published academic, judicial, and periodical statements that, together, allow the newsperson to evaluate the statements of official actors on the basis of prior, printed research and previously recorded statements.

The idea that a specific current affair must be consciously and perhaps self-consciously considered as a member of some broader class of recurring event is not new, although it may be relatively new to news writers and editors. The U.S. legal system, for example, is based on a series of past judgments— legal precedents, officially promulgated regulations, legislation, the Constitution— that are the a priori context in which any current issue or event must be considered. The legal model presents an example of a system in which contemporary and often newsworthy events are framed through historical context and their relation to established social principles. Whether they search electronically or manually, first-year law students are taught in research courses "to appraise the relevant issues factually, recognize and weigh the following factors":

T - Thing or subject matter

A - Cause of Action or ground of defense

R - Relief sought

P - Persons or parties involved

"Thing" refers, simply, to place or property as a significant element in the problem or issue being considered. In the ELF example, this was the electric arc furnace dust. Defining the 'thing," as the anesthetic examples suggested, is the task of the search phrase and a crucial element in defining the context of the event.

"Cause of action" focuses the issues of a problem. In law, the cause may be a breach of contract, negligence, or some other claim. For news people, it is the structure or context that frames the whole. EPA regulations in the ELF story and medical standards for anesthetic administration in the case of tort reform were the contextual "cause" within which the "thing" or "event" was framed.

"Relief" sought in law refers to what the plaintiff may be asking for: damages, an injunction, compensation for loss of consortium, and so on. In the context of the news, it describes what the individual actors want out of the story, the frame that defines the prejudices of the subjects being interviewed. Todd, for example, wanted lower malpractice insurance rates for his organization's members. Habash wanted, for his constituency, the ability to seek high awards for their clients (which results, in contingency cases, in larger fees for the lawyer). The concept of relief allows reporters, in their evaluation of the data, to see the subject not as an unbiased information source but rather as a biased participant in the events on which the subject is speaking. Tort reform is the result of cases of alleged medical malpractice. Lawyers and physicians have vested interests in the outcome of the legislative debate. Physicians testifying in trials or coroner inquests do not want to be labeled as incompetent or ineffectual, and the relief they seek is from adverse publicity. Ideally, the database's information allows the reporter to put the subject's needs and prejudices within the wider context of impartial information and thus to judge the subject's statements accurately.

"Persons or parties involved" is not always immediately clear. In the ELF story the active and crucial role played by the EPA, which drafted new regulations in 1988, was hidden until the database turned up the changes. And yet the whole story hung on the EPA, its regulations and those who enforce them. Problems in identifying the crucial parties involved in a story— or the bias of known participants— are common in news writing wherever actors involved in an event may, for one or another reason, choose to hide their role. But there is almost always a paper trail— a document, statement, or illuminating article that is accessible to the researcher. Habash made good use of this when he quoted Todd's statements, made in an earlier context, in which the doctor blamed fellow physicians for acts of malpractice. As a lawyer, Habash understood very well that officials will take positions that may be at variance with their private views and that a good lawyer looks for the trace of that real position in previous quotes and articles. For Habash, Todd's involvement became twofold— as a physician and as a representative of his association— and Todd's views in both roles, separated by time as well as title, were not identical. The search phrase uncovers not only hidden agendas and broad context but defines the actors in terms not only of their immediate statements and postures but of their previous statements as well.

The legal research paradigm thus places any single event into a complex context with potentially broad social and historical boundaries while making over, within that context, the positions and personal interests of actors in the event. Someone is seeking "relief " or demanding "restitution" because of injuries suffered in the past. That desire is based on the argument of improper performance, failure to adhere to established guidelines, or violation of accepted statutes that define the society's notion of responsibility and establish a system in which blame can be assessed, violators identified, and damage calculated. Enforcement of a regulation, legal restriction, or prior court decision is sought in a current context. If a building collapses, what is important is not simply the testimony of its owners or builders (who may well deny all responsibility), not just what happened, but what happened within the context of the antecedent causes of that collapse and the responsibility for the structure's failure. The legal paradigm is thus a matter of matching what happened recently with what has happened before in a context in which responsibility was clearly assigned and assessed. It interprets present events in the light of past occurrences and official statements in the context of precedent, regulation, and published analysis.

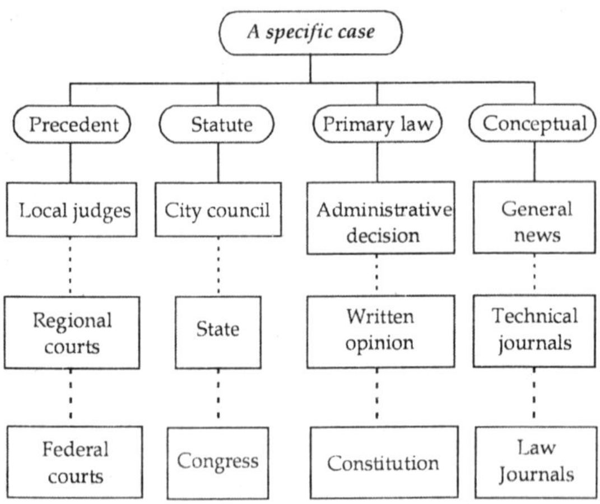

Fig. 8.4. Law Model: Sources

Figure 8.4 describes in graphic form the range of sources traditionally used by lawyers and legal researchers in placing a single case within the broader history of prior events and legal precedent. Whether one searches for precedents at the circuit, district, or supreme court levels, for example, or pursues information at the level of city, state, or federal legislation, the appropriate source will depend on the problem at hand and the precedents needed. These three general levels— local, regional, and federal-roughly correspond with the story levels defined in an earlier chapter: the ephemeral, isolated story; the structural story based on multiple cases from a wider geographic region; and the contextual story itself. The contextual story incorporates national, regional, and local information in an attempt to define the broader social context of regionally replicated events.

This issue of scale is emphasized in the U.S. legal paradigm in which primary law, those principles empowered by the Constitution, takes precedence over administrative decision (EPA regulations), legal opinion, and local court decisions. Federal law supersedes state laws which, in turn, are the context in which city and county laws are written. Using the range of available databases provides the public information writer with a similar scale of experts, authorities, and officials from all jurisdictional levels whose intelligence and weight can be brought to bear on a specific local event.

Thus reporters made aware of these levels through their use of regional and national databases can focus their queries not simply on a boundary event's participants (Dr. X, Police Chief Y) but on those who, at other information levels, are quoted as authorities on a topic or as having general responsibility in a broad legislative or legal or professional area. The degree to which information from a greater geographic scale illuminates events at the regional scale was made clear in the discussion of the CBC story on the incidence of childhood leukemia in Kamloops. There, a huge body of evidence bearing on what local officials had to say existed internationally. Its employment placed in question the official assurances, published and broadcast in the news, that no systemic or structural problem existed. "Relief," here, is defined by the broader context and not by the local statement.

The "conceptual" category describes the appropriate use, in law, of "expert opinion" by legal or other professionals concerned with and knowledgeable of the issues under dispute. Thus Todd might be called (or Habash) to give expert testimony to a legislature on the issue of tort reform or his articles may be read into the record by legislators supporting his organization's position. Those "conceptual" articles (the *Smithsonian*'s review of building collapse is one example) provide for the public information writer not only background information (the names of authorities, general chronologies of past events, generalized information) but an umbrella of theory and the general thesis of responsibility and cause, which must then be localized and applied.

Thus online electronic resources provide the public information writer with an enormous range of information at various geographic levels of occurrence. The writer has recourse to information in legal, legislative, and technical fields written at the local, regional, national, and now international levels. Court decisions, newspaper stories, magazine articles, and the work of amateur experts writing in everything from *Aviation Week* and *Space Technology* to the *Zoological Record* can be obtained with incredible specificity through the properly defined search phrase. This wealth of information brought to bear on a single boundary event creates, for almost any story, a context in which the individual occurrence is revealed as one of a recurring class, events, of legal and social decisions, for which exist impartial and expert opinion. This context makes of the statements of experts or officials in court, press conference, or press "release – whatever their title and power – no more than a single voice whose own agenda and personal or professional interests can be questioned as critically as the information they present.

Other areas like law and science have functioned in this way for years, and it is no great surprise that they have been quicker to adapt to the potential of online libraries and information storage systems. News will function increasingly in this way, as electronic information sources gain greater and greater acceptance. In the 1920s, Walter Lippmann said that the books and papers were on the desks not of his fellow journalists but of the officials. That statement is no longer necessarily true, and it is this change that is revolutionary.

There was a holier-than- thou sense about the weekly magazine's evaluation of the daily newspaper's coverage of an event that both had written about so extensively, especially since *Newsweek*'s coverage in late 1989 had not evidenced the "skepticism" it insisted the daily needed to apply. In general, one can say with authority that skepticism, like the instrumental goal of objectivity, cannot be realized until or unless the single boundary event (and its actors) is examined within a broader context of prior occurrence. It cannot happen when the primary function of daily or weekly news is the promulgation of oral information. There is no doubt that in Boston most information in the Stuart case was oral— including that of *Newsweek*'s coverage.

At least in theory, it is the function of the law to redress injustices and to place the immediate boundary event within a social context of legal precedent and social knowledge. Since these functions are similar to the institutional goals of the public information writer, it is not surprising that a paradigm of use to one profession may, with modification, be of use to the other. But lawyers have clients and, instrumentally, it is those individuals they are hired to serve. Representatives of the Fourth Estate have, in theory, no single client but rather serve a more general function in which full disclosure is seen as a social good in and of itself. News writers and editors do have agendas, however— both as individuals and as members of large, information-based corporations. The potential for progressive freedom from absolute dependence on the official press conference and statement will place in sharper relief the economic and social filters that also influence the news. Historical evidence suggests that the new technology will affect these filters, but the degree to which this effect will allow news writers to approximate their institutional goals is, at present, uncertain. No writer of Samuel Johnson's day could have accurately predicted the degree to which changes in printing technology would affect society's information base, in great part because those changes occurred within a much broader social and economic transformation. No writer in the late twentieth century can fail to acknowledge, in the description of modern technologies, that the result of their acceptance will likewise be dependent on broader sociopolitical changes in the society about which he or she writes.

Access to electronic information sources is based on a logic whose result is the search phrase. But even the best crafted search language will be of little use (and its generating hypothesis of little value) without a field of data on which to impose it. The utilization of these new resources is ultimately dependent on the organization and availability of information in a digitalized form. Since information from all these sources is now digitalized, reporters are free to draw from identical areas of data in their work. Local newspaper clips are not the only source. Regional and national newspapers are equally accessible. Decisions by courts-from the U.S. Supreme Court to the Ninth District Circuit Court— are equally accessible, as is a range of general interest and specialized journals. Where this information is stored and how it can be most effectively accessed are the next issues that must be considered in this analysis of the potential effect of electronic databases on public information in general and the news in particular.

9

Technology and Publishing in the Electronic World

Introduction

Technological change takes place in both a social and a historical context, which exist both internal and external to the organization; each context is embedded with interests, beliefs, and values about social status, the nature of meaningful work, and what problems technology can or should solve. Technology makes journalistic work more abstract in numerous ways and thus changes the nature of journalistic skill: The firsthand sentience – the sounds and sights and smells of the production of the printed word and, increasingly, human interaction as a central facet of journalists' work – are increasingly displaced by computerized interactions and electronic texts. Technology both serves as a means of rationalizing journalistic work in a way that removes, erodes, or creates opportunities for communicative and coordinative activities in the newsroom, and presents opportunities for extending old skills or creating new ones.

Increasingly, communication theorists have begun to focus on the socially constructed nature of reality, and to examine the workplace as a potential site of conflict over different interests in decisions regarding products, our culture, and our environment. Computer technologies are not neutral: They have inherent characteristics that constrain their potential in the workplace, since much of what has driven the design, development, and deployment of workplace technology is that it can be controlled more easily, and is more subject to rational principles, than humans. Machines do not tire or object to repetition or rationalized activities as do humans, and are more consistently capable of precision, thus rendering production processes more predictable, and creating a more secure environment for capital investment and profit.

Newspapers are a social construction of reality – a representation of What's important to know, and by extension, what isn't – which occurs as journalists jointly participate in the selection, framing, and presentation of events and ideas which then become The News. But this construction is also influenced by decisions and processes external to the newsroom – including decisions about labor, about profit, about technology. This chapter explores three different implementations of technology in newsrooms: electronic editing, pagination, and computer-assisted reporting, as a means for examining the ways in which newspapers are using newsroom technology to gain greater control over both the content and appearance of the newspaper, but also to gain greater control over the labor process of workers in the interest of the accumulation of capital. It concludes with an examination of new forms of work organization in the newsroom. In doing so, it links considerations of the social construction of reality by major media corporations with questions raised by labor process analysts, especially as raised by Braverman, Shaiken, and Zuboff. Labor process analysts challenge the social agreements between management and labor, which they see as resting on yet another social construction of reality, a set of practices, a discourse, a historical process: They question which work, rights, and powers accrue to owners/managers, which to labor. Among their concerns is that while the technological demands of work require greater education, training, intelligence, and mental effort, workers and society find conditions of industrial and office labor increasingly unstable, unsatisfactory, and characterized by mindlessness, bureaucratization, and alienation.

Braverman for example, challenges accounts of the organization of modern industry by modern social science to "accept all that is real as necessary, all that exists as inevitable, and thus the present mode of production as eternal" by providing a concrete and historically specific analysis of the relationship between technology and machinery on the one hand, and social relations on the other. Shaiken argues that technological development is a consequence of choice, both social and economic, and that the workplace is shaped by the interaction of workers, managers, and technology. Management, whose goals shape the design and implementation of technology in the workplace, seeks to control production as well as the activities of workers. Technology, and particularly information technology, may be designed in a way that leads to reduced skills and levels of worker input and decision making, as well as tighter control over work and workers' activities. The result is boring, stressful work.

While managers seek higher productivity from such a system, its actual costs may be lowered quality and productivity, since a system that reduces human input cannot benefit from human skill, talent, experience or creativity. In the newsroom, it isn't just journalists who lose: Newspapers lose the synergy that comes from creative and sometimes casual human interactions. The effects of management decisions, however, may be mediated by a broad range of factors, such as technology design, as well as the presence and strategies of organized labor.

Zuboff found that computerized work is more mediated than older technologies – workers must deal with an increasingly symbolic, or abstract, world, relying more heavily on their computers and less on their own sentient experience of the world. In other words, working with computers offers a new way of knowing the world. Depending on the choices made about the deployment of information technology, workers may gain communicative and coordinating skills and intellectual competence, or they may be pushed "further into the sentient but mute terrain of fatigue and nervous exhaustion".

Electronic Newsroom

Since the early 1970s, newsrooms have seen the introduction of video display terminals (VDTs), pagination, libraries, on-line and database research, remote transmission and delivery, photo desks (enhanced color capabilities and digital photo transmission and storage), and photo editing capabilities. Many newspapers, in meeting technical requirements of computer systems, have also remodeled their newsrooms so that they, in the words of more than one journalist, "look like an insurance office" more than the newsrooms of the recent past.

The capital investment decisions that result in the arrival of shiny new newsroom technology are made in complex environments. As Thomas contends, we must "conceive of the relationship between technology and organization as mediated by the exercise of power, that is, by a system of authority and domination that asserts the primacy of one understanding of the physical world, one prescription for social organization, over others". Corporate owners and managers see in these technologies a means for lowering labor costs, expanding old markets and reaching new ones – in short, a means for increasing profits. The technological choices a manager makes represent her or him symbolically within the organization; the selection of a particular technology may be a way of gaining status or influence within the organization, and influencing or sabotaging its goals. In a 1994 speech, George R. Cashau, former senior vice president/technology for the Newspaper Association of America, stated that to be useful to newspapers, technology must, in addition to positioning newspapers as key information providers, produce revenue, be faster, more efficient, economical, and easy to use. By way of contrast, George Gerbner writes that "the basic problem of journalism is... media conglomeration and the consequent reduction of staff, diversity, and *time* to do an adequate job. For journalists, newspaper technology means further loss of control to a few wholesalers and global marketers of media 'software'". Owners, managers, journalists, and technicians have different interactions with these technologies, and the technology leaves different marks on the work of each of these groups. Thus, for each group the technology has a different meaning.

Electronic Editing

Electronic editing was the first step toward a fully computer-paginated newspaper, one in which entire pages are typeset, rather than typesetting each story, headline, and caption individually and then pasting them up in the composing room, or backshop. Pagination reduces the amount of work that must be done in the backshop, and consequently the number of employees in that area. The editor's function expanded to include the remaining tasks – responsibilities such as typesetting, printing, and proofreading – which had formerly resided in the backshop. Not only were there more tasks, but they were tasks that demanded the skill to accomplish them in the abstract world of the computer, rather than the concrete activity of the backshop. Despite greater newsroom control over copy flow and improvements in mechanical accuracy, there were costs in other areas. For example, wire copy (i.e., stories transmitted by news services, such as the Associated Press, United Press International, or Reuters) began to arrive in the newsroom at 1,050 words per minute around 1976 (compared to 66 words per minute by teletype, the prior technology). By the late 1980s, wire editors who had previously received hard-copy printouts or had to feed paper tape through a reader before seeing a story, were now receiving copy electronically at nearly 10 times the speed at which it had been sent with the arrival of VDTs, roughly 10 years before. And with the increased transmission speed came an increase in the number of transmissions. Transmission speeds get faster and volume continues to increase as the technological capacity for sending, receiving, storing, and routing transmissions becomes more sophisticated and relatively more affordable: Editors in one study reported they were spending 97% of their time just pushing the buttons that released copy to other editors. In the meantime, photos were arriving 10 times faster than previously. And editors disagree over whether typographical errors were harder or easier to spot on the computer screen than on paper copy. Speed sometimes came at the cost of good editing.

This early experience with technology brought with it other concerns as well: quality of work life, editor reactions to the technology outside of actual job performance, and whether the demand for technological competence infringed on journalistic quality. Many copy editors rejected the idea that they had been turned into technicians, and strongly disclaimed the notion that VDTs had depersonalized copy editing. Others, however, found the opposite to be true – finding the work depersonalized and isolating, at times producing a newspaper of lower quality. Many missed the support of the now mostly eliminated proofreaders. There was wide disagreement over whether VDT editing required higher concentration or skill than paper editing, suggesting a demand for higher technological skill, but no increase in editing skill requirements. Most editors felt that newspapers had become more sophisticated, but that the increased sophistication related more to production process than content. They also expressed concern over the new potential for top-rank editors to read over the shoulders of reporters, city editors, wire editors, and copy editors, and about the effect of electronic editing on the quality of their work. Just as the technology brought with it an increased volume of wire copy at an increased speed, for many editors, VDTs and the higher number of tasks that came with them meant that there was less time for the more traditional tasks they saw as their primary journalistic responsibility. The demand for technological skill also took time away from editing. There was an awareness that tension was building between the concurrent demands for technological and traditional skills.

Editors who had worked through the transition from pencil editing to electronic editing were most likely to be aware of these and other effects. Many of these older employees have either reached retirement age or been "bought out" during downsizing and merger scenarios. Findings of future research will reflect the different experience of the greater number of workers who have been working with computer technology at least through college or the beginning of their journalism career. These newsroom workers are more likely to accept a workplace permeated by technology without question compared to earlier journalists – to them it is "natural," not necessarily an issue arising out of changes in economic control or ownership patterns, and subsequent choices that have led to shifting definitions of journalistic skill and quality. Both the constraints and liberating qualities built into existing technologies by a steady historical stream of social choices will influence the way new generations of journalists see their own skills, their ability to control the products of their labor, and the nature of relations of power in their workplace.

Information technology in the newsroom has had, in some ways, a reintegrative quality in the newspaper – reintegrating, in one job, tasks that had been rationalized, or specialized into many separate jobs. But the new technology brought not only new ways of doing old things, but also the capability for new ways of doing new things. Newsroom managers had to consider new ways of organizing newsroom work to accommodate the changes. The newsroom transformation showed up in a number of areas. Among them was the creation of newsroom positions to help traditional journalists manage technological change: Computer system editors/managers, usually with previous newsroom experience, provided training, advice and troubleshooting for the newsroom. The new technology provided them, and by extension, newsroom managers, with the information necessary for quantitatively assessing the performance of newsroom workers. The flow of work in the newsroom could be surveyed abstractly and symbolically. The skill to interpret that information was most often held by supervising or systems editors and technicians. It was used most frequently for settling deadline disputes with the composing room. The locus of decision making was still management-level editors, and its structure remained hierarchical.

These managers, who often had worked in several newsrooms, became increasingly accustomed to seeing and including large line item numbers on their budgets for technology as it became a more familiar feature of virtually every U.S. newsroom, as they became accustomed to greater control over the production process and demanded ever greater speed, and as newspapers gained an increasing awareness of the added value that strategic combinations of information, technology, and management can bring. One early example was the ability to put out more editions with broader geographical dispersion than before. So-called "zoned editions," with advertising and news tailored to discrete geographical areas, followed not long after.

Pagination

New data-compression technologies, plus cheaper disk storage media, have helped fuel the move toward pagination for newsrooms. But another technological shift also has contributed to the increased presence of pagination systems — the arrival of desktop publishing technology in the newsroom. With the graphical user interface, work that once involved a fairly high level of craft or systems competence can now be produced by novice users in minutes. Further, as this interface has become the primary platform for newspaper graphics, a service industry has grown to provide those graphics – either standard or customized – via dialup or automatic telecommunications transmissions. Work once done in the backshop or later, the newsroom, is often now produced by a service bureau, which distributes material for newspapers across the country and across the globe. The choices of technology for producing camera-ready materials – such as ads, typeset stories, design elements, or whole pages, which are then used to produce printing plates for the presses – for both the newsroom and the advertising department have broadened considerably. Where the decision to buy a newsroom system was once mostly one of selecting which vendor from whom to buy, increasingly it involves a choice between proprietary or off-the-shelf systems, and often requires the ability to integrate the two – always with an eye open to the need for support and new developments that might render current choices obsolete.

Often the people who make decisions about the purchase and deployment of technology come from very diverse backgrounds, ranging from data processing to typographical production (composing) to journalism, which all offer very different perspectives on how and toward what ends work should be organized. Often, there is no lost love, or respect, among these different groups. Obviously, this kind of technology has a direct impact on work organization. It provides newsrooms with the much desired ability to maintain control over their work flow. It also makes it possible to evaluate in new ways where the bottlenecks in newsroom production existed.

The decisions that drive the choice of pagination technology are usually based on recommendations from information management, managers whose background is primarily technical, in conjunction with recommendations from newsroom systems managers or mid-level managers, such as assistant managing editors. Discussions of implementation strategy are usually limited to how quickly training could be accomplished, and how much knowledge different types of workers in the newsroom need. Discussion about loss of traditional skill, job enrichment, or increased cognitive effort rarely evolve, most likely for two reasons. First, the worlds of newspaper management versus critical discussions or academic research rarely converge. When they do, they represent a collision of purpose: The broad social context in which social scientists situate the problems which newspaper managers must solve to keep their jobs and satisfy corporate shareholders provides little in the way of immediate relief to these problems. Second, the success of these managers is measured by traditional goals and understandings of efficiency and cost savings, as well as quality, rather than by the standards of a highest common good which social scientists tend to seek.

Pagination is generally acknowledged to save time in the overall page-production process since it is faster to typeset the entire page as one element than to set each story, headline and caption on a page individually and then paste them up. If however, pagination requires more time in the newsroom and more editors are not hired, then, as Russial hypothesizes, depending on the amount of time that editors spend doing electronically what was once done manually in the backshop, the quality of the paper likely will suffer.

Newsroom management wants pagination because it gives editors greater control over the appearance of the page, and because it gives them greater control over meeting deadlines. Increasingly, the digitalization of all information – graphic and text-based – that appears in the paper or is collected by the newsroom is appealing because of the possibilities for adding value through "recycling" the information through other media such as fax and electronic newspapers, and audiotext and videotex products. Pagination has improved quality control and led to *better-looking newspapers*. The tradeoff, however, is *diminished content quality,* as well as editors who are spending less time on traditional editing tasks as they spend more time on production demands – with "a majority of those surveyed spending 20% or more of their time on former backshop functions". As with electronic editing, the more time editors spend on pagination, the less time they have for traditional journalism tasks.

Russial found that the "makeup" portion of the job – that which had transferred from the backshop to the newsroom – takes about twice as long as the more traditional editor's work, which is the creative page design process. Pagination systems are, at many newspapers, contributing to what Underwood called a hybrid newspaper employee — one whose work combines the functions of copy editor, newspaper designer, and paste-up specialist. One editor estimated that 60% of the work done on his design desk had once been done in the composing room, and in that instance, because photos were paginated as well as text, the pagination process took triple the time spent on page design.

Russial suggests that paginating editors felt that their workload was increased and that it reduced the time they had for "traditional editing tasks." Pagination also appeared to increase the proportion of essential tasks, and, in particular, those that were relatively mechanical or routine. Editors on deadline may be forced to reassess their editing priorities, asking themselves whether there is time, for example, to check facts, rewrite twisted prose, write a better headline, or monitor legal concerns. An editor's decision about this is an important element in the quality of the newspaper, since the copy desk is the last stop in the newsroom before the words on the screen become the printed facts which we comfortably construe as news and reality. The guidelines for making such decisions may be changing, since, as we've seen, editors are assuming more responsibility for the production work that determines at the most basic level whether the paper gets published. In light of the changing composition of their work, the more traditional emphasis of editors' tasks on accuracy and clarity may take a backseat to their production responsibilities.

Management also expressed concern in some instances over the development of a "production mindset," noting that paginating editors seemed less eager to redraw pages between editions. "Pagination shatters a lot of the feel for journalism that editors [should] develop early on. I've seen it in action. People behave like a production department... I'm not sure what the solution is". Russial also found that moving production functions into the newsroom replicated, between paginating and non-paginating editors, tensions traditionally found between news and production. Pagination skills are increasingly a baseline requirement for hiring new editors, but editorial management may still be uncomfortable with the idea of a production functionality residing in the newsroom. Some editors see pagination as "part of a relentless march in which technological imperatives continue to drive newspapers and override the journalistic mission of the newsroom," and to express concern that news organizations have become preoccupied with "the looks and style of the newspaper at the expense of content and journalistic substance.". Again, editors with less experience seem less troubled by the changes.

Computer-Assisted Reporting

While their traditional role may not have changed as much as editors', reporters nonetheless experience pressure to learn the why and where fores of new information technology. Of course, introducing VDTs to reporters also meant reducing the need for rekey boarding stories, as well as lost jobs or retraining for the people in the backshop who had traditionally rekeyed them. And when there were computer problems, reporters found themselves frequently reliant on computer technicians who often had neither an interest in nor a clue about deadlines or journalism and its nobler pursuits in the interests of humankind. By the early 1980s, reporters were being drawn into a new level of computer use as newspapers increasingly turned the burgeoning stacks of clips, which tend to decay or become lost in various newsroom shuffles, into electronic libraries, or morgues.

As off-the-shelf personal computers (PC) clones began to replace proprietary VDTs in newsrooms, breakthroughs in networking technologies and computer architecture made it possible to connect PCs to mainframes, and in many instances to replace them. In a 1984 survey, more than half of the 600 newspapers responding were making use of PCs somewhere in their operation. Along with PC capabilities came the capability to put modems in the newsroom and allow reporters to dial up the burgeoning number of commercial and government databases available on line, and eventually through Internet connections. Koch argues that the primary tension involved in introducing electronic databases into newsrooms is between the apparent costs of the database systems' introduction and its benefit to the news gathering effort. But he also predicts changes in the content and narrative form of the news, as well as new forms of relations between "public information writers and their subjects." Journalists will gain greater flexibility, no longer bounded by "beats," leading, if you will, to more interdisciplinary coverage. This new organization of reporting will also change relations between news people, "who, in the past were divided by their respective responsibilities for a specific, topical specialty rather than united in their ability to focus on a story or issue". He questions whether these "electronic resources" will "enhance or impede what might be called the 'minimal completeness and objectivity' criterion by which news people judge their own performance," but concludes that the derivative new form will finally allow "daily news writers" to approach the standards they have "long asserted". He also predicts that newsroom managers should see improved productivity "as reporters are empowered to cover with increased criticality progressively broader classes of events".

Reporter use of electronic databases affords several potential benefits. It can make reporters less reliant on traditional sources; widen the considerations of their research; make more information available to them, more conveniently, in less time. It provides an opportunity to enrich reporters', and by extension, readers' understandings of issues. On the other hand, it is also expensive, and may draw resources from other, equally or more important, needs in the newsroom. As reporters spend more time with on-line research, they are likely to spend less time with other types, such as interviews and observations. Research shows that reporters have tendencies to become dependent on database sources, just as they have with official and expert sources. However, research does not extend to considerations of what social, economic or internal political pressures may contribute to this dependence. For example, do chain newspapers encourage or discourage reporters to rely on databases more often than newspapers with different ownership structures? And while interdisciplinary news may present greater flexibility, it may also represent the loss of specialized knowledge which arises from intimate and regular contact with a subject. The best possibility is that these and other computer-assisted reporting techniques are used to enhance rather than replace traditional news-gathering techniques.

There are additional possibilities, of course. For example, print journalists already conduct an increasing number of interviews by phone. Greater reliance on database reporting is likely to further reduce the face-to-face contact they have with sources. Reporters acknowledge covering a growing number of major events without going to the scene. In increasing newsroom use of computer-assisted reporting, managers will need to look closely at the tacit knowledge that successful reporters bring to their work. Interviewing may be a form of professional knowledge that is essential, a skill that will be destroyed or lost to the extent both that it is less practiced, and that newsrooms rationalize the work of reporters. Print reporters already compete with increasing numbers of media outlets, and are having increasing difficulty gaining access to public figures. Speculatively, if interviewing skills declined, access would become even more difficult. Reporters may find that although they approach interviews with greater in-depth knowledge and better questions, they have less of the tacit knowledge that makes them able to persuade sources to talk openly with them. Journalist William Greider claims that, already, "Most reporters aren't interested in finding out what happened. Most journalists are interested in finding out about news, which is another commodity, one interested in what's the angle today, or this week or tomorrow. They want to plug a hole in their story or give their pieces a voice to make their point".

Because of the costs of and the need for technical skills demanded by electronic research, reporters may have less control over what information is available to them than before. Research shows that they typically perform narrow searches that offer them information rather than understanding. The training they receive, in most instances, is designed to teach them basic commands, not the more complex skills needed to use the new technology as a means of developing a broader and more deeply contextualized news account. In other words, this kind of practice is likely to exacerbate the trend of treating events as discrete rather than linked, despite the potential that would allow opportunities for what many critics would see as "better" journalism, although Koch shows more optimism in his predictions for interdisciplinary beats and "empowered" reporters capable of greater productivity. The set of characteristics that can make a news product "better" is enormous. To date, conclusions about better newspapers through better technology have often accepted unchallenged the link between technical improvements in speed, accuracy, productivity and better news products. As applied to the latter, that link is highly suspect. As Weaver and Wilhoit point out, "Even though the bulk of U.S. journalists perceive new technological devices as improving the quality of their work and saving time, it may be that in the long run such devices will change the nature of the messages created by these journalists in ways that do not benefit the society at large".

Depending on the balance between on-line database and royalty costs versus labor costs, managers also may find that, just as it is often less expensive to publish syndicated columns and features than to pay staff to write, it may be less expensive to draw research from on-line sources than it is to send reporters out to cover all but the most high-profile local stories. Although editors argued that "good reporting habits as traditionally taught" would overcome the downside of database use, it is clear from the experience of both copy and pagination editors that journalists do not always have discretion over their use of traditional skills. Journalism schools are also under increasing pressure to ensure that graduates have adequate technical skills by the time they enter the newsroom. Unless students are required to take more courses, students may come to newsrooms with less knowledge of traditional skills and practices. As in other jobs in the newsroom, there may be a tension between the demand for technical versus communicative skills.

It seems unlikely that databases will provide greater objectivity, since although information will be stored, retrieved and reproduced in a different form than before, it will continue to be gathered by humans. But increasing reliance on a narrower range of sources could lead to declining quality and standards of reporting and an increasing appearance of news stories which are little more than continually redigested and reinterpreted pieces of assembled data.

New Forms of Electronic Publishing

Newsrooms — and society generally — have gained more experience with technology, as well as a greater sense of its unexpected, or "unintended," effects. A new generation of newsroom managers includes former reporters and editors who underwent many of those changes. At the same time, newspapers are calling themselves information companies or information providers, and newsrooms are colliding with marketing departments and learning to think about how they can "add value" to the traditional news product. In this process of self-reconceptualization, newspaper companies have begun to reorganize the newsroom into teams, a form of work organization first linked to the flexible manufacturing processes in computerized industrial plants.

Newsroom work teams take several forms, often called design desks: Some focus primarily on pagination and design, while others stress the creation of a "better packaged story." Whether in newsrooms or manufacturing facilities, cross-training, so that employees are "interchangeable," is implemented either as a part of, or in conjunction with, the team structure. Russial's study of newsroom pagination and work organization found that newspapers are still experimenting with new forms of staff organization and job design. Technological deployment may be creating new organizational problems, for example, lack of leadership, skilled staff or other resources, and possibly limiting a newspaper's ability to change in other ways.

Many newsroom design desks handle layout and pagination almost exclusively, and are implemented to "control the look of the paper, speed and cost". Design desks often lead to better looking pages and greater uniformity throughout the paper, as well as improved coordination among editors, designers, and reporters. Editors sometimes report feeling more creative. Often, papers with design desks have created new job classifications to handle the reorganization of work. Page designers, who have more newspaper experience and may be paid comparably to other editors, laid out pages and sections, while design assistants, who function as technicians and for whom newspaper experience may be considered unnecessary, may be paid substantially lower wages. One news executive was quoted as saying, "We don't want to pay someone $900 a week to 'design' those holes. We want to get someone who can mass produce".

Some other papers organize work so that more technically adept editors handle pagination, leaving other, perhaps less adept editors to more traditional tasks. Russial found that many editors acknowledged that it may be important for pagination to be done by editors, despite its technical nature, since "most editors felt more comfortable with other editors" making decisions about necessary adjustments such as trimming a story or photo or adjusting the layout. One newspaper based its decision about which pagination system to buy on the belief of editorial management that "it would allow the production function to be shifted to news professionals with the least degradation of their job and with the greatest opportunity to preserve editorial control over the many little decisions that must be made to implement the larger decision of drawing the page". Russial's study indicates that newsrooms feel some tension between, on the one hand, rationalizing design desk activities so that editors handle tasks which require high-level skills while technicians are assigned more routinized work, and on the other, recognizing the value of professional judgment and retaining maximum levels of editorial control.

Work team strategies also allow management to construct a newsroom more responsive to marketing needs by moving the newsroom away from its traditional assembly line structure in which "stories are passed from reporter to editor to production with little communication in between. This structure facilitates the need to meet daily deadlines, not necessarily what works best for readers". For example, the "maestro approach" is, from its inception, a means of understanding what stories are important to readers and then matching the skills of the newsroom to the challenge at hand. It is intended to promote stories that evolve out of a process that focuses on readers' questions. The maestro, or team leader, directs, orchestrates, and referees, as well as reserves space and color, or "whatever it takes to tell the story in the most meaningful way for readers". Auman also found that newspapers implement team strategies to create a management tool that make newsroom employees and machines more effective in the overall activity of telling stories by creating teams of copy editors, photographers, page designers, and reporters. Underlying this need is increasingly stagnant circulation which drives newspapers to seek new ways to attract readers, with many deciding that better organization and presentation of information are key.

Under ideal circumstances, teams can, as Auman suggests, restructure the newsroom production process in a way that brings together the issues of organization and presentation – integrating writing, editing and design; but she also questions whether, in the process, content is subverted to art and presentation. At their best, teams reorganize traditional tasks to take advantage of new information technology potential as well as human creative potential. Yet depending on their makeup, they may emphasize design over content and cede control of the news to the design desk, and thus may represent a threat to traditional standards of quality based more on content than appearance.

In some newsrooms, design desk employees are cross-trained on a variety of tasks, so that "word people acquire visual skills, and visual people acquire word skills". To fill these positions, editors seek journalists with layout and design skills first, and news judgment second. Large papers rank Macintosh computer graphics skills third, but papers with circulation under 100,000 placed a priority on more traditional journalistic skills, although many of those papers plan to use Mac-based pagination systems. The successful design desk editor, concludes Auman, "is perhaps a new breed of journalist who has an integrated editing mind – who is a word person but who can integrate words with visuals". It is also clear, however, that technical skill continues to rank high.

Auman's study found that editors on design desks spent about half their time on page design and layout, 15% on pagination, and the remainder on tasks such as headline or cut line writing, creating infographics, photo editing, and coordinating people and elements in a story or project on a page – with some variation in task depending on the size of the paper. Among these tasks, the more time a design desk spent on creating graphics, page design, and pagination, and the less spent on headline writing, the more likely editors were to rate the desk a success. This is reflective of the hiring priorities that newspapers have established: Editors whose primary skills are in design and layout seem more likely to focus on presentation over content. This type of value system would have been nearly inconceivable prior to newsroom implementation of desktop publishing technologies which provide flexibility in manipulating page elements and executing more complicated design concepts.

Applebaum and Batt found that in industrial work sites, systems of work organization similar to the above often include only a few select workers; the number of participants in workplace teams who have actual authority to make decisions is often limited to an upper echelon, already more empowered than most workers. The structure of the newsroom teams replicates this by choosing primarily newsroom leaders with seniority as the team leaders. While other workers may have input, it seems likely that they ultimately have less influence than the leader.

One aspect of the logic behind design desks, however, seems to be to continue a trend toward automated production work that has been moved to the newsroom, which has already created a production mentality among some editors. By separating out the less skill-intensive work, managers are creating new entry-level work in the newsroom, sometimes and sometimes not an opportunity to develop skills or to find a stepping stone into better paid and more skill-intensive positions. Managers recognize the importance of professional judgment and have designed the desks, in many instances, in ways that leave the traditional hierarchical aspects of organizational decision-making intact. Newsroom teams, in some incarnations, may provide an environment that allows workers to broaden their skills and to contribute more creatively to projects, but these types of newsroom variations on teamwork remain nascent.

Conclusion

News is a social construction rooted in journalistic routines and practices, and newspapers are central tools we use to construct our own individual and collective senses of reality. Decisions about how to design and deploy information technology have changed some routines and practices of journalists at U.S. newspapers, and transformed understandings of what basic journalistic skills are. Journalists' work has traditionally required communicative and coordinative skills and the manipulation of symbols. Social choice about technological deployment and design have led some workplaces to replicate the 19th-century logic of automation, in which work is alienating, meaningless to workers, and gutted of opportunities to show any but operational skill. Other choices have led to workplaces that encourage workers to develop new intellective skills and creativity in dealing with technological change.

Technological change occurs in both social and historical contexts which exist both in and outside the newsroom. Issues as diverse as concern over social status, and interests, beliefs, and values about what constitutes meaningful work and even the extent to which work should be meaningful, as well as what problems technology can or should solve, all influence whether a workplace takes one direction or the other. Often the people who make decisions about the purchase and deployment of technology come from very different backgrounds ranging from data processing to composing to journalism, which all offer very different perspectives on how and toward what ends work should be organized.

During the last 20 years, computers and computer skills have become integral to getting the news out, and editors, relatedly, have acquired increasing responsibility for production processes. In doing so, the emphasis on traditional journalism skills has shifted to share predominance with computer skills, which often reorients the nature of work from sentient toward abstract, sometimes shifting emphasis from subtle features of journalistic accuracy to the more immediate allure of technical precision. Editors' work is often more stressful than it was previously. They frequently need more skills, have a broader range of duties, less backup support, and earlier deadlines for more stories and more products – whether those products are zoned editions or Internet editions. The shift from sentient to abstract work, increases in the pace and quantity of information flow into and within the newsroom, and the additional responsibility of producing divergent products also have increased the pressure of this work in many contexts. Often, additions to staff have not been commensurate to increases in breadth and quantity of work.

Many workers, unable to affect the process of change, have responded by leaving the newspaper or the industry, taking with them their skill and experience, or by becoming demoralized and halfhearted in their work. They felt that the procedures of "techno-journalism" were robbing them of the ability to produce a newspaper that met their expectations of quality, and leaving them with a technical skill that had little coincidence with their primary interest in the profession. Recent downsizing trends in the industry are likely to intensify and widen this response. Clearly, in such instances, it isn't only journalists who lose: Newspapers lose the contributions of motivated and engaged journalists, and they lose the synergy that comes from creative and sometimes casual human interactions. However, research into the effects of both team production and older methods of work organization indicate that unions have been an important factor in retaining quality production standards and protecting worker rights. Weaker union structures present less threat to management control of the labor process in the newsroom than the strong printers unions whose power was diminished with changes in production technology. As research into these questions continues, it will be important to evaluate the extent to which the same holds true in newsrooms.

Research into the deployment of information technology into U.S. newsrooms in forms of electronic editing and pagination shows that goals have been to reduce staff and increase profit and efficiency – to replace human bodies with machines, to speed processes, and to gain greater control over the labor process. The unintended consequences have reduced opportunities to utilize existing skills, and left work meaningless and workers without control over their work; worker demoralization and loss of product quality often accompany these consequences. This is not inherent in the technology, but is a result of the social choices that surround its design and deployment.

As computerization of newsrooms proceeds, it will be important to investigate whether new forms of work organization in the newsroom will provide journalists with the opportunities necessary to develop critical judgment and analysis skills that have traditionally been a primary requirement of journalistic practices. To date, available research shows that editors report a loss of traditional skill, and a more depersonalized and abstract environment. The direction of computer-assisted reporting remains ambiguous. Journalism schools are under increasing pressure to ensure that graduates have adequate technical skills by the time they enter the newsroom. Unless students are required to take more courses, students may come to newsrooms with less knowledge of traditional skills and practices.

Will these newsrooms attract or keep people to whom the use and development of high-level versus operational skills is important? Are high-level skills fundamentally at odds with the prevailing logic governing the deployment of information technology in newsrooms? Among the consequences of the logic of automation is that employees are eliminated rather than challenged to participate as full members of the organization with equal stakes in improving quality and imagining new production possibilities. Despite the creation of derivative products and the need for new employees to produce them, the number of people required to produce *any given item* continues to decline with automation. Often, experienced workers are seen as liabilities rather than assets. Those who remain in the newsroom may receive the training, education, opportunities, and structure that will help them develop the intellective skills that will enrich their jobs and add value, but the specter of unemployment will remain a destabilizing and corrosive undercurrent in the newsroom and in the news industry.

This has implications for society, of course, regardless of the product. But it matters more if the product is a newspaper, if the number of voices who participate in constructing this particular "symbolic consumer product" declines, whether through departure from industry or because the work itself begins to quiet and dull journalists' curiosity and passion. While new opportunities for participation arise out of new technological and media forms such as the Internet, even here it is likely that the logic of capital and accumulation will influence, if not shape, social choices in a manner that constrain the liberating potential of these new forms. The set of characteristics that can make a news product "better" is enormous. To date, conclusions about better newspapers through better technology have often accepted unchallenged the link between technical improvements in speed, precision, productivity and better news products.

Ultimately perhaps, the most central issues that these explorations will help to illuminate is what impact the reshaping of news work and the reorganizing of American newsrooms will have on the final product — the information by which a community knows itself, and on which it bases its judgments. Since news is a social construction that reflects not only society, but newsroom practices, it seems unlikely that a largely automated newsroom will be able to respond with spirit to the challenge thrown out to it in 1861 — "It is a newspaper's duty to print the news and raise hell."

10

ELECTRONIC LIBRARIES

Introduction

To understand fully the practical potential of online information, one must consider the organization and retrieval system of these electronic libraries. It is not enough simply to urge the use of appropriate search phrases because each phrase must be applied to one or another storage archive. Just as it is of little use to know that a book or article is germane if it cannot be retrieved from a traditional library, so, too, must each search phrase be applied to a specific section of the electronic library, from which it can be "downloaded" and later read. Here, unfortunately, is a problem because there is at present little consistency among the multitude of databases currently available online. The enormous volume of data now stored in digital form and the unique problems this system of organization and retrieval presents have given rise to a whole range of somewhat different solutions to the bibliographic problems that this new technology has created. In 1990, for example, there were over four thousand different databases available online and more were being added, virtually month by month, to the digitalized reference system.

Most of those databases are not accessed directly but, rather, through distributors— Dialog, Lexis, Dow Jones, and CompuServe are the best known— that package and offer a series of electronic information services to their clients.

None offers the complete range of stored online information (the most any one service may carry is perhaps one-third of the total number of databases stored digitally at any one time), and each uses a slightly different search language and system of user retrieval in its operation. Some databases offer the full text of articles while others supply only the bibliographic information required to locate an article or book in conventional libraries; some of the former allow the user to search the whole, digitally stored article while other databases or vendor systems can be searched only through key words stored online with the article; in the case of newspapers, some systems will apply search phrases to the whole of a digitally stored article, which can then be retrieved in full, while others search and can retrieve only a story's headline, date, and page location. Further, there is an astounding redundancy within this disarray. A few critical databases are offered online by all major vendors, while some specialized vendors simultaneously offer the same information in several different databases. Thus *Medline*, a major medical database published by the U.S. National Library of Medicine, catalogues and permits retrieval of references to individual articles published in 3,070 different journals. But the database *Medline* is itself composed of three separate databases– *Index Medicus, International Nursing [Literature] Index*, and the *Index to Dental Literature*. Each of these is, in turn, carried individually by some, but not all, data vendors that offer *Medline* as an online resource. To complicate matters further, some of the individual journals that appear in these databases, and thus in *Medline*, are themselves indexed on large data services. Thus one can search for information on *Medline* as a whole, its component databases like *Index Medicus*, or the electronic files of digitally stored, individual journals like the *New England Journal of Medicine* or Britain *Lancet*. Further, much of the information that can be retrieved from *Medline* is duplicated in the electronic files of *Excerpta Medica*, catalogued in Amsterdam, Holland, which abstracts 3,500 separate journals dealing with medicine and biological sciences.

To increase the confusion (and the specificity), this biomedical material is also catalogued and retrievable by general topic through specialized, subject-oriented databases like *Biosis*, *Ageline*, or *CancerLit*, which individually pull from the general medical, pharmacological, and medical engineering literature information on, respectively, bioengineering, gerontology, and cancer. Finally, specialized vendors have cropped up to facilitate access to all this literature, wherever it is stored, through simplified access language systems that dedicated users can subscribe to alone. Thus physicians may choose to access the available medical literature neither through *Excerpta Medica* nor directly from *Medline* but, rather, through PaperChase, a service designed to facilitate online research by medical personnel unfamiliar with the use of other, more general data suppliers.

At the beginning of the printing revolution, when cataloguing was a new science and the idea of the right of public information was a new concept, similar inconsistencies existed. The very idea of the consistent, logically ordered array of knowledge that the encyclopedia presented was a radical attempt during the Enlightenment, not only to catalogue information as it poured in, but to organize that information in a systematic and uniform fashion. Ordering of texts concerned with biological science, for example, occurred only as that science grew and the varying categories that librarians may recognize today (pharmacology, zoology, internal medicine, genetics, etc.) were needed to systematize and store what was once a single, simple grouping of materials on "natural science."

Electronic databases, which began as a more cost-effective means to store certain types of static data— court records, government records, scientific records, and business company data— have matured to cover interactively a range of technical, scientific, and governmental literatures. The technology for digitalized mass storage is barely a generation old, and today's means of access— the personal computer coupled with a modern— has been readily accessible to most users for at most only a decade. That the consistency and efficiency that typically result from maturity in an industry have not occurred in so short a time is not, perhaps, surprising.

There are at present some indications that even newer technologies may eliminate some of the worst problems of redundancy and facilitate a universal search language across varying storage systems. CD-ROM storage technology, for example, makes it possible for individuals to access enormous bodies of information (like a year's records from *Index Medicus*) at home and at their leisure. Advances in fiber optics technology are creating systems that will increase both the amount of information that can be carried by any one data line and the speed of its transmission between host and home computers. The linking of serial computers to simultaneously search large databases with. simpler search phrases is a technical advance so new at the time of this writing that its potential effect cannot yet be evaluated. The history of technological innovation suggests that, as the industry matures, redundancies will decrease and ease of use will increase. But in an industry barely a decade old, what is needed today is an understanding of the data storage system's general organization and its viability for general researchers at present.

The contemporary anarchy of storage retrieval systems and search languages is, strangely, a boon to the writer or researcher seeking inexpensive access to complex electronic databases. A general understanding of both the storage systems currently in use and of the very redundancy which seems so inefficient allows one to find the least expensive but most comprehensive source for any single information bit. It is the purpose of this chapter to describe current storage systems of digitalized information and to suggest ways in which search phrases can be applied to varying, easily available systems in an inexpensive and yet cost-effective manner.

Vocabulary

To make sense of this situation, one needs to adopt a specific vocabulary. Because there is as yet no single accepted lexicon describing the interlocking hierarchy composed of specific files, at one level, and large digital service companies at the other, the following descriptors will be used in this book:

- **File:** A single article, bibliographic citation, or abstract retrieved from an electronic search.
- **Database:** A single collection of articles or citations stored by one company, which may or may not be the vendor. Thus newspaper articles are stored on the Vu/Text database, medical files may be stored on Medline or CancerLit, etcetera.
- **Supplier:** Companies that make one or more databases available by providing the combination of telephone lines and electronic technology necessary for the accessing of digitally

stored databases. PaperChase supplies the database Medline, for example. Vu/Text is both creator and supplier of the Vu/Text database, which may also be accessed through other vendors.

- **Packager:** Some suppliers, Vu/Text, for example, package and sell their own database product. These are the equivalent of specialty retailers in the general commercial world. Other companies, like Dialog or BRS, package and sell a number of databases created by individual suppliers. Most users access the electronic library at the level of the packager.
- **Gateway distributors:** Vendors that make available the services of one or more packagers on a one-time, fee-for-use basis.
- **Wholesale Distributors:** General service distributors that offer a variety of services, including "gateways," in a general service system. CompuServe is perhaps the best example.

To see how this works, consider the results of the online search that obtained citations and information on articles by David Pearson which appeared in *The Nation* about the destruction of Korean Airlines Flight 007 by a Russian military fighter in 1983.

Heading #1

TI: K.A.L. ?007;? questions that won't go away. (Korean Air Lines jet shot down in Soviet air space).
AU: ?Pearson-David.?
SO: The ?Nation? (NATNB), volume 245, Sept 5, 1987, p. 181(6)
PD: 870905.

Heading #2

TI: New pieces in the puzzle of Flight ?007:? journey into doubt.
AU: ?Pearson-David.? Keppel-John.
SO: The ?Nation? (NATNB), volume 241, Aug 17, 1985, p. 104(7)
PD: 850817.

Heading #3

TI: K.A.L. ?007:? what the U.S. knew and when we knew it.
AU: ?Pearson-David.?

SO: The ?Nation? (NATNB), volume 239, Aug 18, 1984, p. 105 (19)

PD: 840818.

These three "files" were retrieved with the search phrase: "Pearson and Nation and 007" from Magazine Index, a database that contains references ("bibcites") to several hundred magazines published since 1959. It contains neither abstracts nor an article's full text, and thus all searches of this database must focus on article titles, authors, and specific Journal names. The asterisks around Pearson's name, that of the magazine, and 007 indicate that these words or phrases were elements of the search phrase that has been retrieved. The search returned three story citations with the information necessary to locate the article electronically or in a traditional library. The subheads of each "file" are clear: TI indicates the full title of the piece as it appeared in the magazine. AU is short for author or writer. SO is the original source of the article, including publication date, volume number, the page the story started on, and the total number of pages in the article itself. Finally, the PD number is an electronic locator in the digital soup through which the article or citation can be retrieved.

Had I wished, I could have applied the same search phrase to *Magazine ASAP*, another database whose files contain and will return the full text of approximately one-quarter of the articles referenced in *Magazine Index*. Both magazine databases are products of a single supplier, Information Access Company, a subsidiary of Ziff-Davis Publishing, whose business since 1978 has been both to store magazines in a digital form and to make them accessible (as citations or in full text) to electronic searchers. Dialog Information Services is a primary packager of Information Access Company's product. To access these databases, I also could have linked electronically with Dialog to find these citations on *Magazine Index* or, through *Magazine ASAP*, to locate the stories in full.

But I subscribe neither to Dialog or Information Access Company. To access this information, I dialed a gateway distributor whose purpose is to make available online the services of a number of packagers, including Dialog, for those who need occasional access to a number of different services but have neither the training in their use nor the sufficient need of service to justify a personal subscription. This gateway, a product of Telebase Systems, Inc., is called EasyNet, and it is available either as an independent service or, under the name IQuest, on the CompuServe system. CompuServe is a wholesale distributor of the products of other distributors, packagers, and suppliers. CompuServe provides a gateway to Telebase Systems computers, which in turn rent time from Dialog's computer system. Dialog stores and sells a series of specific databases, like *Magazine Index*, whose specific files (individual stories or articles) are what one wishes to find. This electronic wholesaler is the world's largest, a huge electronic information system with, in 1990, more than half a million subscribers. It offers access to an incredible array of digitally stored information through an interlocking system of gateways and direct services. Thus the series of system levels accessed to retrieve these three citations were, as follows:

1. CompuServe (Wholesale Distributor)
2. EasyNet (Gateway Distributor)
3. Dialog (Packager)
4. Information Access Company (Producer)
5. Magazine Index (Database)
6. Pearson David and 007 and Nation (Specific Files)

In my search for references to the articles by Pearson, I could have entered this system at any level. For example, were I interested in accessing only these files— and had I known where they were— I could have gone directly to Information Access Company for permission to use their system. For a price, one can sign up with almost any distributor or producer, and, in return for a monthly or yearly fee (in addition to charges for each minute of online use), subscription to the service provides access to the data that producer or distributor supplies. If all a researcher is going to use is files from popular magazines catalogued in these databases, then signing up directly with Information Access would be a cost-effective way to go.

If, however, I frequently needed to search for a wide range of information— from articles on medical affairs to business reports and, perhaps, some federal documents as well— Information Access would not answer more than perhaps one-third of my research needs.

Packagers like Dialog (BRS, Lexis, etc.) make available hundreds of different databases covering a number of subject areas, and, for frequent users of a wide range of digitalized information, they are a better alternative. On Dialog, access to the *Magazine Index* is billed at $75 an hour, but for those familiar with the system's search language and organization, finding the appropriate file holding Pearson's articles from *The Nation* would take less than five minutes and be more cost-effective than the gateway route.

Direct subscription to a specific packager is also the most efficient way to use electronic databases when the supplier has specialized in an area of highly technical data with an eccentric system of organization. For example, WestLaw, the digitalized compiler of court records, is perhaps the best example of a producer individuals almost always sign up with directly. Legal researchers and law librarians seeking information from the volumes of previous legal judgment use such a system on a daily, sometimes hourly, basis. In addition, those needing WestLaw's services with enough frequency to justify its cost will almost certainly be familiar with the specialized techniques of legal research. These techniques have been required because of the eccentric system of information storage traditionally used by the U.S. legal system and the specialized needs of the legal profession.

Cases are stored and retrieved — electronically or manually — not simply by subject and case name but, as importantly, by jurisdiction and court location. Those seeking precedents from New York State courts, for example, must use a specific Court Reporter — case compilations for a single jurisdiction — to review the pattern of judicial decisions on any topic. But because the U.S. legal system is national, researchers must simultaneously seek for judgments or decisions rendered in all other jurisdictions. Finally, because federal judgments supersede state-level decisions or local precedents, lawyers must also look for pertinent case law at the federal level when researching a legal problem.

In addition, there are highly specific tasks unique to the legal field but critical to legal research. It is, for example, often necessary to take a legal citation and "shepherdize" it, to look through all court records occurring after but based on a single decision (like *Roe v. Wade*) to determine if that decision has been challenged, modified, affirmed, or overturned by any U.S. court (at any level). This type of specific search is facilitated and simplified by electronic searching but is so unusual that even the general reference librarian may be ignorant of its need or use. Thus WestLaw represents a producer whose services and search system are designed to fulfill the specific needs of a highly specialized type of research. Because of the individualized search needs of legalists and the volume of data this database holds— two hundred years of court records generated at federal and district levels, as well as state and federal statutes— WestLaw's customers typically sign up directly with the provider for its service. Thus those who seek legal databases will find few gateways leading into such a service, although WestLaw customers are offered more general access, through different links, to general information services.

To search for files from a magazine like *The Nation*, on the other hand, presents no unique problems of storage or retrieval. Magazines in general provide thousands of stories which can be catalogued in a consistent and simple fashion by publication name, subject, and author. Thus the file for any one magazine story is part of a broad class of publicly presented information compiled by a single packager or producer and simultaneously made available through a distributor like Dialog Information Services. If I subscribed to Dialog, I could have entered the system at that level and, using its printed and online directories, found the file for *Magazine Index* and retrieved these citations in that way. The advantage of using EasyNet is that, had Dialog not contained the necessary databases to successfully conclude this search, EasyNet's gateway would have accessed the products of other major packagers and producers that might contain the necessary information. For more specialized subjects or periodicals less frequently accessed, the possibility to simultaneously search the products of two or more packagers can be an enormous help. Further, as a general, introductory service geared to the occasional user and neophyte, EasyNet offers free online assistance to clients having trouble locating the appropriate database and crafting a satisfactory search phrase.

CompuServe is the supra organization, offering access to EasyNet (and through it to Dialog) under the name of IQuest, much as Sears used to sell major brands of appliances manufactured for the wholesaler under its own house name. I used it because I do not need either EasyNet's or Dialog's proprietary databases with sufficient frequency to justify the expense of a full subscription to either company. Since I use the services of any one producer (Vu/Text, BRS, PRS, etc.) only occasionally, it is cheaper and more efficient for me to be able to rent time on all of their services through a gateway like CompuServe's. Another benefit is that by using either EasyNet alone or CompuServe's IQuest, I do not have to worry about the fact that each of the major producers uses a slightly different search language. The EasyNet/IQuest gateway provides a translation filter that allows the subscriber to employ a single search language, whatever the packager or producer may use as a stand-alone service.

Certainly, CompuServe charges for this convenience., I spent $12.60 an hour for "connect" telephone-line charges and $9 for the successful search of the EasyNet gateway to Dialog, Information Access's primary vendor. The basic pricing system for access through the gateway is a unit price of $9 for the first ten citations received. If one wants more information, one has to pay an additional $9 for the next ten "hits" and then pay again for the next series, and so on. Since my online search took only five minutes and I received fewer than ten "hits" in this search, the whole cost was only $1.05 connect time plus $9 for the references, which were available at the library down the street from my office. Through Dialog, on the other hand, one is charged a flat fee per hour, which varies depending on the database accessed through its lines. *Magazine Index*, for example, costs $75 an hour on Dialog, while *Medline* costs only $30. But because a good researcher is online only briefly, it may still be cheaper for a skilled librarian to use a service like Dialog rather than a gateway service. The search for references to Pearson's articles, for example, took about three minutes, and thus would cost only $3.75 on Dialog (presuming familiarity with the location of the files and the system's search language and retrieval mechanism) while, through IQuest, the charge was $9.

Those doing frequent, long searches through a gateway system like CompuServe's IQuest may find the unit charging system prohibitively expensive. To retrieve one hundred citations from a variety of sources, with a price of $9 for every ten units of retrieved citation, becomes costly. The number of citations returned can be limited by appropriate search phrases (limiting articles by date, by seeking only "review" articles, etc.), but those who need frequent access to a wide range of subject categories find that direct subscription to individual database producers (Vu/Text, WestLaw, Information Access, etc.) or packagers (Dialog, BRS, Lexis, etcetera) is more cost-effective. For those with only a sporadic need of access, however, gateways provide a relatively simple, convenient, and inexpensive data access system. In addition, for the purposes of this book, focusing on access through the gateways (and wholesale distributors) makes the general digital system's organization clearer and allows the examination of several packagers and suppliers.

Compuserve

Few people, excepting perhaps those professional data brokers whose business is to carry out online searches for clients, use even a portion of the total range of databases available from any producer. Users quickly find there is a small core of databases that they access repeatedly and a smaller number that may be needed only on occasion. Physicians and medical personnel typically focus on one of a score of biomedical, medical, or medical-economic databases, while ignoring files like *Magazine Index*, where Pearson's story citations were found. News reporters will use medical files infrequently but may make constant use of newspaper records, including their own publication's, made available by the producer Vu/Text. Business writers and investment brokers have frequent recourse to specific files describing the financial health of regional industries, important markets, exchanges, and specific businesses but may rarely, if ever, use medical files.

For the generalist or the individual who uses electronic resources infrequently, a gateway distributor like EasyNet or a wholesaler like CompuServe provides perhaps the beat opportunity to access a variety of digital information services and categories. For the novice, this type of general information service also offers perhaps the best and most cost-effective introduction to online services. Not only is the range of potential services unusually broad, but the amount of online assistance provided is far greater than what is offered by more specialized electronic data storage systems. Experienced librarians and researchers may sneer at this "hand-holding," but ease of access and online help in everything from honing a search phrase to information on where one can look for appropriate materials allow the neophyte to learn easily what it may have taken the professional researcher years to master.

In addition, focusing on CompuServe's information storage and retrieval system reveals much about the world of electronic information and its accessibility to public information writers. As it is the largest and most diverse online system currently available, a description of its components provides the opportunity to examine the full range of online library and data service resources. In addition, because CompuServe does provide gateway access to a number of producers and packagers like Dialog, BRS, Paper Chase and EasyNet, it is an excellent vehicle through which to examine the range and type of files currently stored electronically. It is not the purpose of this chapter to advocate one service over another because those choices will depend, ultimately, on the individual user's ability, specific data needs, and financial resources. Nor is it the intention of this text to duplicate the work of those who have written tutorials for specific gateway services, for producers, or for the use of online resources in general. Rather, the intent is to make clear the general organization of online "libraries" so that the effect of these resources on public information can be better evaluated and discussed.

Informal Sources

The news librarian's model of the news search included both informal sources — the statements of friends, colleagues, and topical advisers in any subject area — and formal news source's — previous story clips, articles, official statements made at the information level of the journalistic event, and attributed quotes — as sources of news information. Most electronic information vendors and distributors focus only on the formal sources, but CompuServe, through its "Special Interest Groups (SIGs)," commonly called "forums," provides a whole range of informal information sources that allow the news writer to communicate directly with specialists in most major fields.

SIGs are systems of data storage and communication in which individuals sharing interest in or concern about a specific subject area can exchange information or question others with expertise in that area, hold "online conferences," and store files of stories, programs, or graphics for use by the forum's membership. They began in the early 1980s as technically oriented groups who largely traded computer programs, programming tips, and general information on the use of the then newly available personal computer and its software. While computer-and software-oriented programs remain popular, they are now matched by interest groups representing aviators, physicians, lawyers, investors, news people, educators, travelers, public relations professionals, and space technology enthusiasts. Each interest group has a specific electronic area on the service and a specific area within the CompuServe computers that includes a "library" for longer files a member may wish to have stored in digital form for future communal use. There is also a "message board" on which members post comments or statements for others to read and comment on at some future time and a Citizens' Band radio-like electronic area available for real-time discussion should two or more members wish to use their computer terminals to communicate directly with other members of the group. Finally, any SIG may host a" conference" in which a guest (usually an authority in the field) will be available to answer questions as forum members plug into the system on their computer keyboards.

These services can provide informal but potentially critical background information to the public information writer. Membership in any professional forum is dominated by, but not limited to, members of a specific profession— all CompuServe subscribers are welcomed in any interest group or forum. Thus a reporter interested in tort or tort reform could leave a message with both the physicians' forum and the lawyers' forum asking for information on how members of each group view the issue. In addition, when a news event breaks, forums whose members are involved or interested in that occurrence will typically carry a large amount of information on the specific event itself. Thus, when Pacific Southwest Airlines Flight 1771 crashed in California in December 1987, reporter Tony Russomano of KGO-TV, San Francisco, accessed the Aviation Forum (AVSIG) to see if its members had information not otherwise available from police, airport, and crash-investigation officials.

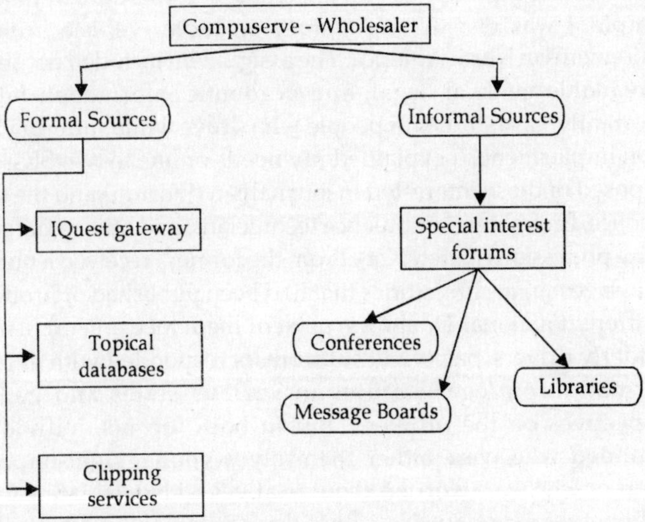

Fig. 10.1. CompuServe Organization: General

AVSIG participants, which include many professional pilots and airport employees, discussed online rumors that a man had smuggled a gun on board the plane at takeoff and complained about lax airport security procedures that allowed easy access to any plane by airline and airport employees in general. Russomano thus arrived at the scene of the crash with information from airline and airport personnel alleging not only the presence of a gunman but blaming generally lax airport security throughout the United States for the ability of hijackers to smuggle weapons aboard commercial airplanes. He therefore had from the beginning a hypothesis related to the immediate event and based on information given informally by airline personnel. Further, that information provided a context greater than the immediate disaster, a perspective based on airline and airport employee concerns over lax security for airport personnel as a contributing factor to the immediate *and* previous air disasters.

Of equal and perhaps greater long-term value is the availability of individuals who may be interested in a subject but may not have professional expertise in the topic being investigated. The huge membership of CompuServe SIGs virtually guarantees news writers a wide base of experiential and anecdotal information. In 1990, for example, I was researching a story on motor-vehicle licensing requirements in North America. The assignment included not simply all available medical, legal, and academic information but, as importantly, case studies of people who drove while suffering from vision impairments. I explained my needs online to two SIGs, one composed of those interested in journalism (JForum) and the other for police, firefighters, ambulance technicians, and other emergency service professions (SafetyNet). From the former I received a number of messages suggesting stories that had been published or produced on different national TV shows, most of them focusing exclusively on elderly drivers. SafetyNet subscribers responded with detailed information on legal statutes in various states and general perspectives on the problem. But in both forums, individuals responded who were either themselves young, sight-impaired drivers or who were worried about relatives with debilitating visual conditions who continued legally to drive automobiles despite those infirmities. Several agreed to discuss their concerns and personal problems on camera.

It is difficult to assess the value of this type of resource precisely because it is "informal." These two anecdotal examples suggest a utility that remains, at present, largely untapped and certainly unstudied in any meaningful way. But then, the impact of traditional, informal sources on news reports— the unattributed information and tips provided by colleagues, editors, and sources— is similarly difficult to evaluate. What seems to be clear is that news reporters and editors have traditionally relied on a variety of sources professionally based and community-generated— to gain background information on topics of potential interest. Both broad information categories are represented online and can be focused on both breaking news and more general, longer-term, "investigative" and public affairs stories.

Formal Sources

If the efficacy of these informal sources is difficult to evaluate, the value of more formal electronic resources is not. The previous chapters' analysis of published articles and public issues (e.g., the shooting down of KAL 007, tort reform, deaths resulting from the improper administration of anesthetic) has been largely dependent on information gained from these formal resources. Most of the research for this book was carried out in the electronic equivalent of traditional, print libraries, in the files of specific journals, magazines, and newsletters organized for use by professional researchers or specialists in specific fields. But in the late 1980s a series of specialty databases were introduced which attempted to assure that the layperson would have access to the broad base of information through simplified search procedures. Illustration 5.2 shows in greater detail than Illustration 5.1 could the range of formal resources currently available online and the interrelation of the system's three major formal components: specialty databases, clipping services, and the IQuest gateways.

Specialty Databases

Increasingly, CompuServe offers not only a gateway service to major vendors like Dialog but, simultaneously, a series of specialized databases that provide journal and newsletter information on specific topics. These databases typically consist of fewer total files than those accessible through specialized vendors, provide a search system with "menus" that guide the novice through their use, and, finally, are less expensive to use than their more detailed and encyclopedic counterparts.

These databases are sometimes called "unbundled" because they provide a core of information from a smaller base of journals and newsletters than the "bundled" databases offered by full-scale packagers or specialty producers like PaperChase. They thus promise a simpler search procedure and language of file materials on a specific topic. The trade-off for this simplicity is that the search is carried out on a small, less technical database. By 1990, one or more of them on CompuServe covered these major fields: health, law, marketing and management, media news (through newsletter coverage), data processing, and a general business database drawn from the financial sections of a selection of North American newspapers.

An example of both the utility and the limits of this type of database can be seen in the following example. In February 1990,

Health Database Plus, consisting of electronically stored articles from a select number of specialty journals and popular magazines on medicine, was searched for information on the relation of anesthetic or anesthesia and death or injury occurring from anesthetic use. The following text records that search, with minor editing to remove redundancy and increase legibility. It utilized the search phrase "anesth/ and (injury or death)," which is, in the course of the search, narrowed only to those articles dealing with dental injury or death in an anesthetic setting. Figures or words in bold were entered by the author. Information in italics explains, where necessary, the progression of stages in the search. The series of prompts and responses is that of the interactive system:

- HEALTH DATABASE PLUSHealth Database Plus
- Copyright 1990 Information Access Company
- Copyright 1990 Ziff Communications Company

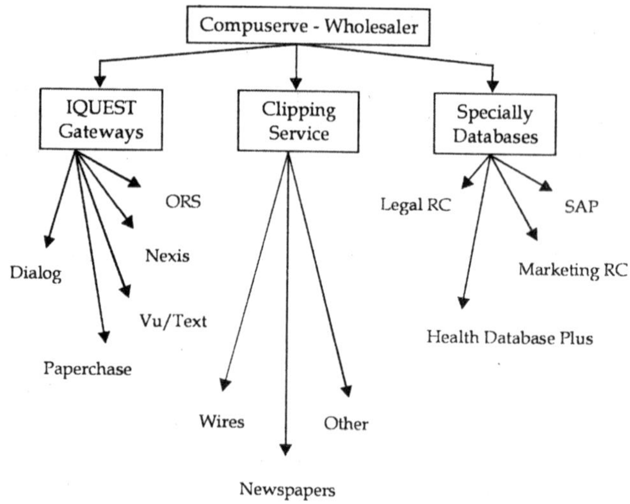

Fig. 10.2. CompuServe: Formal Sources

(Health Database Plus's producer is Information Access Company, which is owned by Ziff Communications Company.)Enter choice («CR» for more)!

1. Search Health Database Plus
2. Quick Reference
3. Exit

Last page, enter choice !-> 1(This choice indicates a desire to begin a search.)START a Search for Articles by Specifying:

1. Key Words (words occurring in article titles, subject headings, company names, or product names)
2. Any Words (words occurring anywhere in articles)
3. Subject Headings
4. Publication Names

Enter choice («CR» for more) !

->1

(To limit the potential data retrieved, one asks the search phrase (here called key words) to be applied only to the article's title or general bibliographic heading. By choosing option 2, a larger field in which the issue might be only a passing or secondary reference, all references would be chosen.)

Enter key word or phrase (? for help):

(Keying in a "?" brings assistance to the neophyte uncertain of how to phrase the search.)

(anesthetic or anesthesia) and (death or injury)

Words Anywhere: [anesthetic I anesthesia] & [death] injury] 254

(Only) Full-text articles matching ALL search methods: 250

(The total response to this search is a large and unmanageable 254 articles or citations. Even when those citations that are only abstracts or bibliographic references are eliminated, the number returned is still large.)(Further) CHOICES:

1. Display a Menu of Matching Articles
2. Match Full-text or Abstracted Articles
3. Narrow the Search
4. Replace (Erase) an Existing Search Method

5. Widen the Search Using an Existing Search Method

Enter choice ->3NARROW the Search for Articles by Specifying:

1. Key Words (words occurring in article titles, subject headings, company names, or product names)
2. Any Words (words occurring anywhere in articles)
3. Subject Headings
4. Publication Names

Enter choice (CR for more) ->2

Narrowing the Search. Enter word or phrase (CR no change, ? for help): ->dental

(Only cases involving injury or death resulting from application of anesthesia during dental procedures will now be returned. One could also have added the word "review" to the 250 citations first returned, to narrow the whole to review articles, or similarly narrowed the search by asking for only those citations published in the last one or two or three years.)

Words Anywhere: [anesthetic or anesthesia] & [death or injury] & dental

Full-text articles matching ALL search methods: 23

Having narrowed the file to twenty-three articles, I was again offered the choice of displaying the retrieved articles in either full text or only as an abstract, further narrowing the search, or creating a new search. By choosing to review only abstracts, the cost of the system's use is reduced and a general idea of both the information that can be retrieved and its journal location is gained. Since each full-text article downloaded carries a surcharge of $1.25 in addition to the database's $ an hour user fee (and CompuServe's $12.50 an hour access charges), those on research budgets will use the full-text service sparingly. Even with faster baud (transmission) rates currently available on modern modems, the cost of downloading even twelve articles can become prohibitive. I find it is cost-effective only when there are fewer than five review articles whose references can then be checked at a local library.

Further, if abstracts are available, they sometimes provide enough information for the public information writer seeking general background on a specific topic. Consider the following example returned by Index Medicus, *logged through PaperChase for information on review articles in the medical literature on the relation between anesthesia and injury or death:*

TI: Anesthetic Mishaps and the Cost of Monitoring: A Proposed Standard for Monitoring Equipment.

AU: Whitcher C., Ream, A.K., Parsons, D. et al.

SO: J. Clin. Monit. 1988; 4: 5-15

ABSTRACT: Review of insurance data indicates that approximately 1.5 claims are paid per 10,000 anesthetic procedures, a conservative estimate of the incidence of preventable serious injury associated with anesthesia. Insurance data permit estimation of the premium cost for the anesthesiologist and hospital, per operating room per year, of $69,429.00.

We propose the use of an enhanced monitoring standard requiring a pulse oximeter, capnograph, spirometer, halometer, automatic sphygmomanometer, breathing circuit oxygen analyzer, stethoscope, electrocardiographic monitor and temperature monitor. We suggest that this premium cost, together with the estimate that 50% of incidents would be avoided, predicts a resultant saving of over $27,000/ operating room/year, a saving equal to the entire cost of the enhanced monitoring system in approximately 8 months, or a yearly saving of over five times the annualized expense of the monitoring system. Thus, in addition to the moral imperative to monitor a patient during anesthesia to avoid injury and death, there is an economic incentive to monitor efficiently.15

KEY WORDS: Monitoring: standards, Injury. Risk. Anesthetic mishaps.

The value of both returning abstracts in a search and including "review" in the search phrase is evident here. The article as a whole reviews a specific data collection or literature and thus, if retrieved in full, provides a wealth of sources that can be manually searched in the library. For the public information writer interested in the issue of anesthetic administration (or tort reform or medical performance), the abstract itself is a gold mine. Here is hard clinical evidence, presented by physicians and phrased in economic terms, that failure to use widely available, cost effective monitoring equipment contributes to 50 percent of the operating room, anesthetic-related incidents. It equates monitoring (a moral imperative) with prevention of death or injury and, further, argues that the cost of appropriate monitoring equipment would pay for itself in less than a year.

The full text of the article, later retrieved from the library, is even more complete, but, were one checking for information the day before a court hearing or inquest, even the abstract alone would empower the reporter (or lawyer) intent on finding out precisely why a healthy person died during anesthestic administration. In cases in which anesthetic death has occurred and an attending physician who did not appropriately monitor the patient disclaims all responsibility, Whitcher et al. give the lie to the physician's assurances that" everything that should have been done was done." The article lists equipment that could and, according to the authors, should be in an operating room, while eliminating the possible rejoinder by doctor or hospital administrator that monitoring equipment is prohibitively expensive. It suggests that half of the incidents of anesthetic mishap would not occur if a full complement of monitoring equipment was in place (and in use), while suggesting there is a "moral imperative to monitor a patient during anesthesia to avoid injury and death."

For a story on tort and tort reform, this article also is an important piece of information. If the deaths that lead to litigation are preventable and if by not using appropriate equipment, physicians violate a "moral imperative," then perhaps the issue is not the size of awards made by juries. After all, one-half of all "incidents" would not occur if proper monitoring techniques and equipment were used. The articles insist that the real cause of these accidents is the failure of hospitals and their anesthesiologists to assure proper monitoring equipment is available. To decrease malpractice claims, the article states, increase monitoring of patients.

The use of serial menus that, at each step, direct the user to specific options is a key attraction of both unbundled services and those, like EasyNet/IQuest, designed to facilitate electronic research for the generalist or occasional electronic researcher. At each step the options offered— of narrowing a search phrase (by year, date, subject, or key word), defining the amount of information to be returned (full text or abstract), previewing the number of articles returned, accessing online "help" functions where the user can seek assistance— as sure that the best possible search is conducted while keeping costs at a minimum. By charging only for stories or abstracts retrieved and keeping to a relatively low hourly charge, both unbundled and gateway accessed services provide a cost-effective alternative to the more expensive and more complex, if more complete, full scale bibliographic products available through dedicated packagers like Dialog, which charges $30 an hour for access to *Index Medicus*.

In addition to the $12.50 hourly charge for CompuServe, the unbundled *Health DataBase Plus* charges users an additional $15 an hour and $1.50 per article retrieved. PaperChase charges a flat $15 an hour connect time (in addition to CompuServe's charges), and *Index Medicus* on Dialog costs $30 an hour. Retrieving 250 articles (which, downloaded, would probably take more than an hour) would be expensive on all systems. The menu system of unbundled and gateway services is designed to assist the inexperienced researcher in narrowing potentially large data fields to as few critical references as possible. For a reporter covering a medical inquest into the death of an individual during dental surgery, a bill of over $400 (230 reprints at $1.50 per reprint, additional charges for use of *Health DataBase Plus* and $12.50 an hour for access to CompuServe) would be, at most newspapers and broadcast stations where I have worked, considered prohibitively expensive. By limiting the retrieval costs to the abstracts of 23 articles (or less), the bill is kept under $50 for current references in the field.

For reporters and other public information writers who often need only general background in a field like medicine, unbundled systems may provide sufficient information to allow for intelligent questioning of a coroner, physican, or other medical official. Further, the magazines indexed here, unlike those in *Index Medicus* and PaperChase, include popular publications like *Hippocrates*, as well as more technical publications like the *Harvard Medical School Health Letter*. Unbundled services thus provide a bridge between the popular magazine field, catalogued in *Magazine Index* or *Magazine ASAP*, and the technical literature of a database like *Index Medicus*. If the results are not sufficient or if the topic requires a more detailed examination of the biomedical, pharmacological, or another specialized literature, then the occasional researcher might wish to use a gateway service like IQuest (or the CompuServe gateway to PaperChase), where more complete databases can be accessed.

This simple example underlines, again, both the importance of the search phrase and its absolute relation to the ability to access materials from the digitalized library. Like the traditional library card catalogue, understanding the digitalized storage system is the key to finding the appropriate information and receiving it in the desired form (full text, abstract, or citation). It is also the means by which these libraries can be used cost-effectively. One could retrieve all 250 full-text articles, but it is doubtful that most would be of interest or of use to the layperson. Typically, scientific articles on any subject are narrowly focused and often redundant, replicating and commenting on the work of previous researchers. Appropriate search phrases that progressively narrow potential files to the clearly pertinent, topical story (with references to past works) allow for highly specific and cost-effective research. When applied to specialty databases, which include popular summaries of academic research, the advantages for the layperson or generalist are clear.

IQuest: Screens

Sometimes information offered by the unbundled services is not enough. They did not, for example, contain information on electric arc furnace dust, or law journal references to tort reform, and may not cover the critical technical articles like Whitcher's. For this type of information one may need the resources of a full-scale packager like Dialog, in which the sheer volume of available sources can be daunting. If one were to search all the medically related databases on Dialog, which includes not only medical journals but those related to chemical, biomedical, and bioengineering fields, the results of a search for relevant articles on anesthesia and death or injury would be unmanageably large. A skilled medical researcher could probably pare the thousands of potential articles to a manageable size, but those unfamiliar with medical issues, uncertain which databases would be critical, and perhaps less than expert in the system's use might simply resign the search in despair.

In its gateway service, IQuest provides a service called "screens," which allows the user to see both the number of citations that will be retrieved for any single search phrase employed and the specific databases in which those articles or citations can be found. The importance of the latter cannot be overstated because full-service packagers require searchers to direct their queries not to the system at large but, rather, to a specific database in particular. One cannot simply say, "Find me review articles on anesthesia and death or injury" and expect the computer to do the work. The search phrase, at this point in the development of these technologies, first must be directed at a single database (*Biosis*, *Embase*, *Index Medicus*, and so on). Thus honing the search phrase to define the context of a problem is only half the task. The second and no less critical part of full-service online research is to apply the phrase to the appropriate database.

Much the same thing happens in contemporary print libraries. In a typical city library, one can search in vain for references to specific problems in biomedical engineering, anesthesiology, or any other specialized area of knowledge. For those, one must go to a specialized or university library where medical texts (or law journals, engineering newsletters, or marketing guides— whatever the specialty sought) are stored. The same division of storage is replicated in the electronic world, although access is facilitated by the computer network itself. But one still must know where the information is and go to it, electronically, before it can be retrieved.

These screens, in effect, apply the remedial assistance of the unbundled service's menus to the power of full-service packagers, whose very wealth of bibliographic resources is often an impediment to their use. Since these screens cost only $5 per search, they provide an enormously cost-effective arena in which a search phrase can be tested against the full complex of available databases. Simply, they allow a person to test a hypothesis, framed as a search phrase, against the multiplicity of available online resources. To see how this system works, consider the following examples. The first uses IQuest's menu and screen system to locate information on injuries or death occurring from anesthetic application in general. The second is specific to anesthesia in dental surgery.

PRESS TO SELECT ?Main Menu?

1. IQuest-I System helps select the database
2. IQuest-II Search a database of your choice
3. SmartSCAN Search multiple databases
4. Instructions

H for Help, C for Commands

-> 3(This is the command to begin a scan and narrows the parameter of searches through a series of questions and screens.)PRESS TO SELECT

1. Business
2. Science & Technology
3. Medicine & Allied Health
4. Law, Patents, Trade names
5. Social Sciences & Education
6. Arts, Literature, Religion
7. People
8. News
9. General Reference

H for Help, C for Commands

-> 3(Clearly, the general subject area is databases storing information on Medicine and Allied Health. The other categories would be important were a different search to be instituted.)PRESS TO SELECT

1. Medical Research
2. Pharmacology
3. Nursing and Allied Services
4. Consumer Health

H for Help, C for Commands

-> 1 (Medicine has been subdivided as a general topic into the subspecialties. If one were interested in a case involving a nurse anesthetist, number 3 might be preferable.)

Enter your medical topic

Type H for Search Guidelines.

-> (anesth/ or anaes/) and (death or injury)

(Since many journals do use the British spelling, anaes/ is included as an alternate to the U.S. spelling.)

Is: (ANESTH/ OR ANAESTH/) AND (DEATH OR INJURY)

Correct? (Yes/No)-> y

(If the answer is no, one is prompted to write a new search phrase.)

Scanning, please wait...

Scan completed.

Medical Research scan results for: (ANESTHETIC OR ANESTHESIA) AND (DEATH OR... PRESS TO SEARCH

Title	*Format*	*Source/Type*
Ageline	2 abstract	journals
AIDS Database	0 reference	journals
AIDS Knowledge Base	0 full text	journals
Books in Print	1 reference	books
Cancerlit	168 reference	journals
Combined Health Information	5 abstract	multiple sources
Embase	2486 reference	journals
Health Instruments File	0 abstract	multiple sources
? Medline (1982 to date)	1271 reference	journals
Rehabdata	2 reference	journals
Sport Database	23 reference	journals

? Good choice for professional literature.

A ADDITIONAL CHOICES

(Choices listed include beginning a new search, narrowing these results by adding additional qualifiers to the current phrase, etc.)

H Database descriptions

(Retrieves a description of all databases named in the search.)

SOS Online assistance

(This brings research assistants online at no charge to assist those having trouble in the search.)

Total Charges thus far: $5.00

What has happened is that a second, selective process similar to that employed in the search phrase has been used to identify specific databases to which that search can be applied. The total number of potentially relevant articles returned is far larger than that of the unbundled service, and the journal categories in which they occur indicate the type of information that will result. By entering "H," a description of the individual databases is provided. *Embase,* for example, where 2,486 references answer the query's parameters, is described by the command "Database Descriptions" as: "*Embase* – From January 1974; updated weekly. Includes extensive abstracts of articles related to biomedicine from medical journals worldwide. About 60% of the records contain abstracts." *Embase*'s packager is BRS and was surveyed, here, through the Telebase Systems gateway, called IQuest by wholesaler CompuServe. Its research base begins with articles published in 1974 and new articles are added to the database each week.

Medline, on the other hand, where the next largest number of returns is found, is carried by Dialog, is updated every month, and its oldest online files are from the year 1982. The description included from the screen is as follows: *Medline* (1982 to date)– Updated monthly. Indexes articles from medical journals published worldwide. Corresponds to *Index Medicus, International.*" Thus the database *Medline* is an electronic version of the traditional print reference, *Index Medicus, International.* Clearly, these two databases (*Embase and Medline*), which cover the issues of medical equipment and procedure, are where the required information will be, but, equally clearly, the search phrase needs to be honed further. This information is just too much even to begin to sift through it. One could add *Review* to the search phrase, which would limit results solely to review articles or, if any of the phrases can be more narrowly defined, that step will also limit the returns to a manageable size. Using the word "dental" in the search phrase to modify "anesth/" is one example of a modifier limiting a search's returns.

The following screen represents a second search using the phrase "(anesthetic or anesthesia) and (death or injury)":

Title		*Format*	*Source/Type*
Ageline	0	abstract	journals
AIDS Database	0	reference	journals
AIDS Knowledge Base	0	full text	journals
Books in Print	0	reference	books
Cancerlit	0	reference	journals
Combined Health Information	0	abstract	multiple sources
Embase	30	reference	journals
Health Instruments File	0	abstract	multiple sources
Medline (1982 to date)	19	reference	journals
Rehabdata	0	reference	journals
Sport Database	0	reference	journals

While the use of two such screens, each costing five dollars, may seem somewhat extravagant, the advantage of this system for one unfamiliar with the databases covering any one field is evident. Accessing *Medline*, one of the least expensive databases available on Dialog, costs $30 an hour. *Embase* is more expensive on an hourly basis. To download over one thousand (or even one hundred) references on a fishing expedition for information would quickly run up a data search bill of several hundred dollars and require days of reading before one could find the truly pertinent articles. The screens, by identifying individual databases and their general subject boundaries (and there is, in fact, some overlap between *Embase and Medline*, which, for example, both catalogue the *Journal of the American Medical Association*) and allowing one to preview a search before it is run, show the writer or researcher how to narrow the parameters of a search. Further, because these screens list the format of materials in each database, those who wish not only the bibcite but also a formal abstract (or the full text) can choose their databases accordingly. Finally, the whole allows one to avoid duplication by showing overlap of the subject areas of major databases (*Embase and Medline*, for example). It has been my experience that, when the search can be narrowed (especially through the use of the search qualifier "review") to under fifteen citations, retrieval of abstracts along with standard locational information provides sufficient direction and, sometimes, enough general information to warrant the time and expense.

IQuest: Simple Searches

Gateways also provide menu-driven services that choose the appropriate databases from the array of packager services they carry and automatically retrieve pertinent citations. The advantage of this system is that, if one has no clue at all about where to address a highly specific search phrase, the system goes into "automatic" and does the work itself. Unlike the screens, which identify databases where appropriate information may reside, this menu-driven system retrieves targeted articles themselves. When BCTV asked for information on electric arc furnace dust, for example, I had no idea what database would have information on so esoteric a subject. It was a topic quite beyond my experience. Rather than search through a catalogue of databases to find one that dealt with environmental issues or metals or metallurgy, I used the gateway distributor's screens, which assist in defining a subject and automatically find the appropriate supplier, database, and file. After logging onto the Telebase Systems network via CompuServe, I recorded the following session. Again, numbers or phrases in bold were entered by me, and information in italics is a commentary on choices made through this system:

1. IQuest-I System helps select the database
2. IQuest-II You name the database
3. SmartSCAN Scan a group of databases
4. Instructions

-» **1** *(Had I known where to look, I could have named the database and gone directly to the subject. Were this a contextual search, like that in the anesthetic example, I might have chosen a screen. As it was, I needed to* *know, first, what electric arc furnace dust was. So I allowed the system to find the most appropriate database for me.)*PRESS TO SELECT

1. **Business**
2. Science & Technology
3. Medicine & Allied Health
4. Law, Patents, Trade Names
5. Social Sciences & Education
6. Arts, Literature, Religion
7. Entertainment & Travel
8. Persons
9. News

H for Help, C for Commands

-» 1 PRESS TO SELECT

1. Accounting
2. Banking & Finance
3. Companies
4. Economics
5. **Industries**
6. Insurance
7. Management
8. Marketing
9. Taxation

H for Help, C for Commands

-» **5** *(Because I was interested in the steel industry's relation to EAF)*PRESS TO SELECT

1. Agriculture & Food Science
2. Construction
3. Energy
4. Finance, Insurance, Real Estate
5. Government & Defense (U.S.)
6. **Manufacturing**
7. Retail Trade
8. Services

9. Transportation, Utilities, Communication
10. Wholesale Trade

H for Help, C for Commands

-» 6

Enter Search Phrase:

-» **Electric Arc Furnace Dust**

Is: ELECTRIC ARC FURNACE DUST Correct? (Yes/No)-» y

Ten citations with pertinent abstracts were returned in this search. All came from a database whose files were composed of articles from the following magazines or trade newsletters, none of which I previously had heard of: *Chemical Marketing Reporter, Journal of Metals,* and *American Metal Market*. The stories and abstracts included reports on the announcement and later implementation of Environmental Protection Agency regulations concerning EAF, defined its metal content, and announced creation of a special high temperature furnace in France designed to reconvert European EAF to usable metals. These files were drawn from *Trade and Industry ASAP*

Industry ASAP, a database covering approximately four hundred publications. Its supplier was Information Access Company, and the distributor was Dialog. Had I examined a dictionary of databases for an appropriate place to address this query, I would probably not have thought to access *Trade and Industry,* and, although technical information on EAF would certainly have been available elsewhere (perhaps in a database of federal regulations), this means was sufficient to find all the data I needed. The abstracts provided the technical information I lacked (on both the heavy-metal content in EAF and requirements for removing those metals) and placed it in the social context (new EPA regulations) that the story required.

The whole cost $9 for the IQuest search (a flat rate for the first ten responses) and $12.50 per hour for CompuServe online charges. Since the search took at most ten minutes, final cost was $9 + $2.08, or $11.08.

Gateway versus Packager-Based Services

Experienced reference librarians and trained data researchers may dismiss gateway services and their menus as time-consuming and unnecessary. Those users familiar with Dialog, BRS, or other full-service specialty packaged services like Dow Jones News Service, PaperChase, or Vu/Text, can and do bypass the steps of screen and menu search. Familiarity and practice have given them the experience to know either what databases will be most useful in any search or how to find quickly, on any system, the appropriate database to address when searching for information on a new topic. A trained researcher interested in EAF but uncertain where to look for information could have logged onto Dialog's electronic *Database of Databases* or, on BRS, the *Database Directory*. On IQuest, the electronic database directory is the *Directory of Online Databases*, although it seems to me the menu or screen systems do the same on this service and costs less to use. Each of these electronic directories provides general card-catalogue-style information on the databases carried and could be best searched by asking the computer to match "metals" or "steel processing" with the appropriate database. Experienced researchers would more likely have used the general *Trade and Industry ASAP* database in the past, and experience might therefore have told them to try there first. But most news professionals are not trained researchers. They are not familiar with the thousands of online sources (or traditional library resources) through which arcane information can be both located and accessed.

For the free-lance writer, periodical reporter with limited resources, or advocate on a budget, screens and menu driven searches are a cost-effective way to define a search phrase and limit a search before hundreds of dollars are spent browsing through the electronic library. Screens are basic tools that allow writers new to electronic researching to limit and define the areas they wish to examine. If the search phrase is so narrow that no "hits" are returned, there is no charge. If the phrasing is too broad and thousands of possible matches are returned, the search language can be tightened at minimal cost. Gateway services assure the widest possible mix of providers at the least potential cost, and these search aids assure that lack of familiarity with those services will not prevent their broadest possible use.

Librarians versus Writers

For neophytes with the means to both hone their search phrase and identify potential sources for that information, these unbundled resources, screens, and directed search systems offer one possible resolution to the practical conflict between writers and librarians over control of electronic databases. As the previous chapter noted, librarians are often exasperated by the failure of reporters to phrase their searches appropriately or to know precisely where the data sought may be located. They dislike badly framed questions, and demands for general, unfocused searches can, indeed, be expensive, time-consuming, and wasteful. Furthermore, many reporters want to conduct their own searches. They do not want librarians to decide for them what information is most pertinent to a specific topic. These unbundled resources— screens and menus— provide an economical means by which both reporters and librarians can share the work of focusing not only on traditional "fact" at the level of journalistic event- what was said by an individual to a fellow reporter at a previous time— but rather, as in this case, on the context of the boundary event itself.

Reporters need to know the general parameters of available information and, while creating a theory to fit the general facts of boundary event and official statement, need some access to the electronic resources currently available in the newsroom. Librarians who are charged by their employers with supervision of all resource materials and placed under budgetary restraints need to be able to exercise some authority over the use of these potentially costly electronic resources. A logical compromise might be to delegate screen searches to the reporter while reserving control of the full and still expensive databases to the librarian. Reporters then can hone their phrase, develop a knowledge of potential databases, and, in this "pre-search," define the parameters of information sought. Full searches of whatever service is subscribed to by the publication would be the librarian's job, and decisions on limiting those searches would remain the resource specialist's prerogative.

When, on occasion, I've had the opportunity to access directly a large packager like Dialog or needed the services of a specialty supplier like Vu/Text or PaperChase, I've first done an IQuest-style screen search to learn exactly which databases had the largest number of files pertinent to my subject area. A similar system may be equally effective if institutionalized in a periodical news office where budget restraints imposed by corporate home offices continue to create shortages in specific editorial departments. Even though most news organizations subscribe to one or more major services (Dialog, BRS, Lexis, etc.), this type of gateway or wholesaler's screen may still be efficient and economical. Because of the duplication among services, it is often the case that sources identified by the screen search as available on one service will also be available through another. For those times when that duplication is not the case, a tightly written, menu-driven search through the gateway wholesaler would allow the public information reporter to access the truly critical datum on a one-time and cost effective basis.

Specialty Services

It is necessary at this point to enter a caution concerning the use of databases and to correct the impression that all sources are equally and easily available through distributors and wholesalers. At least at present, availability is a more complex issue. While there is considerable overlap among the information bases of major packagers like BRS, Dow Jones News Service, and Dialog, each will maintain databases to which the other does not have access. Further, some sources can be accessed in only a limited fashion through gateway services when compared to the full range of services offered by the supplier to individual subscribers. Thus Vu/Text's files of more than 65 regional newspapers are available to users of EasyNet (IQuest), but no global search system is offered to these gateway fee-for-service clients. Through these secondary distributors, one can search only individual newspapers, not the accumulated information of all files simultaneously. Corporations or individuals who subscribe directly to the Vu/Text service, however, can use a global search system that applies any single search phrase to the combined databases of all its member newspapers. WestLaw, the supplier that stores U.S. court cases, offers its subscribers access to other data storage systems, but users of most other packagers and distributors cannot access the court files on an occasional basis.

Thus, choice of vendor is in reality the first step in an electronic search because it determines the type and form of the data that will be retrieved. I subscribe to CompuServe as a general wholesaler whose greater access to a number of systems promises the widest possible range of occasionally used information. In addition, I have at various times subscribed to one or more packagers or suppliers—

like WestLaw or Vu/Text, whose more specialized databases were critical to a specific project or job.

One can predict with some confidence that the disparity between producers' and distributors' systems is a temporary phenomenon. Links between individual suppliers will increase as the technology matures, and the ability to access disparate files stored by a variety of producers and distributors will become increasingly common. The gateway linkages are only one example of the growing interconnection among all these services. The increasing purchase of electronically stored services by university libraries also suggests that, in the future, online information services may be generally available as an adjunct to the traditional print storage system.

Clipping Services and Business News

One final category of CompuServe's news system needs at least brief description. The clipping service is a system that will automatically identify and electronically store articles or stories from the electronic versions of various news services. The service matches a user's search phrase— stored online— with the electronic version of specific newswires, updated daily or hourly. Any stories that match the search phrase are retrieved and stored electronically for the reader or researcher. At present, the services monitored and to which search phrases can be applied on CompuServe include: the Associated Press (AP) national newswires (i.e., *AP US & World, AP Sports, AP Financial*), United Press International (UPI) news wires, *Reuters Financial Report, McGraw-Hill News* (another business newswire), *Over the Counter NewsAlert*, and the electronic edition of the *Washington Post*.

If one subscribes to this service, whose use carries a surcharge, one places a search phrase online and directs that it be applied to one or more of the newswires the service covers. After the search phrase has been logged in, any story carried on a monitored news system will be identified and automatically stored online until the user calls up that personal file for review. Thus if the search phrase logged for clipping were "anesth/ and (death or injury)," stories about anesthetic-related deaths carried on the AP or UPI wires or in the *Washington Post* would be captured auotomatically, as would stories relating to manufacturers of anesthetic related equipment if an individual was reported killed or injured by that product. Unfortunately, the service is at present heavily weighted to business-related information.

Regional wires and general newspaper coverage are not yet as available on this service, although it is likely that, as the technology advances, what can be continually searched automatically and the number of sources that any individual can thus access, will increase.

Dow Jones News Service

CompuServe's clipping service competes with that of Dow Jones News Service (DJNS), which offers another business-oriented news tracking system keyed to stock and industry symbols of potential interest to the investor or business writer. That system is called *Track* and is designed to allow investors to follow both the prices and general news concerning the fortunes of specific companies. Each *Track* folder – called a "profile" by DJNS – can contain up to twenty five stock symbols (i.e., IBM, CNS, S, TL, etc.) or codes for a specific area of production (computers, news, automobile manufacturing, retail, etc.). After filing the symbols online, the user can automatically log onto the system and call up the "profile," and the value of each stock so listed will be returned immediately. In addition, those symbols function as individual search phrases for stories appearing in publications monitored by the Dow Jones News Service. In retrieving the folder, one also simultaneously receives notice of any articles in which the company name or industry at large was mentioned. Citations so stored are displayed by title and date and can be read in full through Dow Jones News Service's full-text news database package, *Text*.

Those not using the clipping service can, of course, search the digitally stored business library independently. Its holdings are a good example of how the broad spectrum of any one field – in this case newspapers, wire services, and periodicals – is tailored by an individual packager to provide a focused electronic service. *Text*'s databases include the full text files of the weekly *Barrons* (1987 to present), *Business Week* (1985 to present), the *Wall Street Journal* (1984 to present), Dow Jones News Service (1979 to present), the *Washington Post* (1984 to present), McGraw Hill's online database of twenty-five business publications, and *DataTimes*, a database of 150 regional and specialized business magazines. Also on this service is a press release newswire that digitalizes and makes available corporate statements by company public relations departments.

In addition, DJNS offers an almost overwhelming array of databases from a variety of suppliers concerned with almost every aspect of business and industry. These range from *Disclosure,* an online library of mandatory Securities and Exchange Commission filings (10-K and 10-Q) submitted to the government by companies operating in the United States, through corporate reports by Dunn and Bradstreet or Standard & Poor's, to a database listing mandated filings for ownership of 5 percent of any company.

The service's business orientation and corporate affiliation have earned the computerized library a large following among corporate research divisions, although for the general reporter, writer, or researcher its deficits, at present, may outweigh its advantages. The prestige of the Dow Jones cachet and the size of the system's database offerings made Dow Jones News Service the premier distributor of computerized corporate information in the early to mid-1980s. By 1990, however, many of its databases were simultaneously offered by other wholesale or gateway distributors (like CompuServe) and packagers (like Dialog). Its higher yearly membership charges and connect fees, coupled with an unusually complex online search and command language, make it a frustrating resource for all but those specialty researchers concerned primarily with financial and business news who took the time to become familiar with its eccentricities.

Just as medicine was used, earlier, as a topical example to describe the means by which pertinent information on a specific scientific area could be accessed, Dow Jones News serves as an example of an online research tool that focuses a number of computerized resources to provide information services for those interested in financial issues. Where PaperChase was conceived as a specialized tool for the medical professional, so DJNS was conceived as a broad array of finance-related, computerized suppliers that would be of interest to the corporate official or business writer. The increasing availability of its various component services elsewhere diminishes the researchers' necessary reliance on the individual service itself, however. A number of alternate, more general information services now offer similar databases and the products of the same packagers, making it possible to report on business affairs by using the services of independent distributors.

Subscribers accessing daily stock prices on DJNS, for example, were until recently unique in their ability then to immediately access published news reports on the company whose stock price per share had just been electronically searched. This ability to key news stories to changes in the price of an individual stock was one of the great advantages of the *Track* program. Now CompuServe offers a similar service. Subscribers accessing a specific stock price are informed when a news story has been run by one of the news services included in the clipping service. Those wishing to read these stories can then immediately access the news stories. Thus, after typing "AAPL," the exchange symbol for Apple computer, and the command "Go Stocks," the online service provided me this morning with the price of the company's stock. A bulletin simultaneously informed me there were news stories about the company and, by typing the command "CoNews" (surcharged at $15 an hour), I was given a menu of current stories about Apple computer from both Reuters and AP newswires.

Business Example

Whichever the wholesaler or distributor chosen, the effects of this technology on business reportage are evident in the following example. In 1987, the Akron, Ohio, *Beacon Journal* won a Pulitzer prize for its 1986 coverage of the takeover of Akron-based Goodyear Tire and Rubber Company. When, in October 1986, general wire stories stated that Goodyear was among the New York Stock Exchange's most actively traded stocks, it was perceived by both the media and financial traders as a possible takeover target. To track the rumors, analyze potential buyers, and follow the attempt, *Journal* reporters used several computerized resources. These included specialized databases like *Disclosure,* composed of information submitted by U.S. businesses to the government, whose detailed financial information on possible buyers allowed news reporters to determine with some degree of certainty whether those companies would be able to command sufficient capital to take over so large a corporate target. *Disclosure* is available on DJNS, Dialog, and, among other gateways, Information Access Company's EasyNet.

In addition, *Journal* reporters made good use of stories filed by colleagues for other hometown newspapers in the cities where Goodyear's potential suitors were located. "If a rumor came up on deadline, in a matter of a few minutes, several of us could access a lot of information on Vu/Text." It is likely that, had the *Journal* used only DJNS, which does not provide a gateway to Vu/Text files, it could have accessed similar information from the regional business services of DataTimes's database. Whether it used *Disclosure*-based information through DJNS's or CompuServe's gateway is irrelevant. It is probable that other databases, like those tracking insider trading, were also used, and the information recovered from these regional news services and the Securities and Exchange filings was sufficient.

The critical point is that an array of databases covering federal filings by private corporations and general news files from around the country allowed local reporters to analyze actively and monitor the possible sale of a major hometown employer. Rather than accepting the word of involved corporate parties, *Journal* reporters were able to determine, step by-step, the actions taken by Goodyear's suitors and also to make informed guesses at the potential effects for their city of those possible changes in the corporate structure of their principal employer. Newspapers in those cities where bidders for Goodyear had home or branch offices could be searched for indications of corporate health (and therefore if there was sufficient capital to justify the bid) and for the bidder's degree of participation in community affairs. Where suitors had taken over other corporations in the past, newspapers in the target cities (as well as corporate reports) provided information on the effects of those previous mergers or acquisitions. Was the target company broken up to pay for the takeover? Were wholesale layoffs at the target company instigated? Was the original management left in place? Did the suitor keep, after the fact, promises made during the period of bid, counter bid, and negotiations?

Here again we see the degree to which conflicts among the institutional, instrumental, and functional goals of the subjects must be judged within a broader context than statements delivered at a press conference. Corporate officials are charged, institutionally, with protection of the shareholder's investment, the care of their company, and (hopefully) its improvement. Instrumentally, these goals become a pledge to produce a product or provide a service so unique, valuable, and necessary that the public will not only accept it but choose that product or service over others. Functionally, those officials earn their living through employment in the company and their ability to advance in the corporate world is defined by the success of the parent corporation under their stewardship.

Those pursuing the successful purchase or merger of one company by another must insist on the long-term benefits of that action for both company s' products or services as well. CEOs must state that this change will benefit all shareholders. They must assure the public at large and investors in particular that a board's decision to make or accept a merger is in everyone's interest. But these assertions are uniformly suspect because the corporate executive's primary obligation is to the firm's financial condition, not the greater community's benefit. The company officials' careers, incomes, egos, and reputations are bound up in the takeover or merger move. Successful financial marriages, like the 1989 merger of Warner Communications and Time-Life, made multimillionaires of corporation executives who, before the deal, may have been only wealthy millionaires. Those who spoke most forcefully and publicly for the merger were often individuals who stood to gain the most and whose views on the deal should have been most suspect.

Thus to weigh the future effect of any deal whose value is trumpeted by participants (the sale of a local newspaper to an information conglomerate, the choice of a public transit system for a city, or the courting of a specific industry for a depressed region), one must examine the uniformly rosy statements of corporate leaders through an analysis of the past actions of their companies and, perhaps, a good look at the potential benefits any successful negotiation will bring to them as individuals. By using these databases and receiving an accurate and complete picture of a company's financial structure (from federal filings), one can predict the possibility that a successful merger will overextend the purchaser, with disastrous results for employees and stockholders. Where a company has, in the past, swallowed and dismembered smaller rivals, firing longtime workers and decimating the symbiotic relations between company town and local residents, it is likely that local newspapers have written about those actions.

If skepticism is an important component of objective journalism, as *Newsweek* suggested in its analysis of the Stuart murder case in Boston, it is critical when the future of a town's primary employer is at stake. To wait passively for the public announcement by suitor or target board members is to accept without either thought or skepticism the statements of individuals whose objectivity (as participants and financially interested parties) is clearly open to question. By using federal documents and the reports of colleagues in a dozen different cities, however, one can put together an actual picture of the financial effects for both suitor and target.

Critical Databases

In the mid- 1980s, those interested in buying a first computer but bewildered by the array of products then on the market were sometimes advised to choose their hardware only after deciding what software would be used. Whether one bought an Apple Macintosh, whose graphics system was superior, or an IBM-compatible computer with extremely limited graphics capability, depended, in large part, on the type of work for which one needed the computer. Drawing and painting programs were, at one time, available for the former but not the latter system. If, on the other hand, one needed to analyze large amounts of almost any type of data, the clear choice was an IBM-compatible system. At that time, Apple vendors offered nothing as powerful as the sophisticated database, mathematics, and computational software marketed for the IBM-compatible computer. By 1990, however, the software bases of the two systems were similar and the potential of both had become, for the average

user, virtually identical. Both computer systems now offered software and hardware to facilitate graphics, data analysis, telecommunications, and page-layout functions. Both provided large storage systems and a variety of accessories (i.e., scanners, modems, laser printers, plotters, and so on) that made it possible to customize, through software and hardware choice, the system chosen.

In the early 1990s, the choice of digital information supplier depends not on the power of any one vendor's computers but on the availability of databases that can be accessed through any single online distributor. It makes no sense to subscribe, for example, to

Dow Jones News Service if the files that will be most constantly accessed are from past issues of popular magazines, scientific reports, or non-business sections of regional newspapers. Dialog, on the other hand, would be a needless expense for those whose primary information requirement was to gain informal information from members of a professional community like the forums that are CompuServe's stock-in-trade. To use CompuServe primarily for its IQuest gateway when the writer needs daily access to highly technical or academic databases would be similarly inefficient. The choice of distributor depends, then, first on the availability of databases from primary suppliers and, second, the cost-effectiveness of the system for any user.

Business and Financial

Disclosure

Files from: *Eighteen months* Supplier: *Bechtel Corporation* Provides: *Detailed financial information contained in federally mandated filings to the Securities and Exchange Commission by public and private corporations (10-K and 10Q filings). On Dialog it is* Dis-closure Spectrum Ownership *closure Spectrum Ownership, a database updated quarterly with summaries from all SEC filings. On BRS it is updated weekly under the name* Disclosure *and contains slightly different information. Both are available through EasyNet gateway.*

ABI/Inform

Files from: *January 1971* Supplier: *Data Courier, Inc.* Provides: *Lengthy abstracts from business and management magazines, stressing general business management and, secondarily, product information.*

Business Periodicals Index

Files from: *June 1982* Supplier: *H.W. Wilson Company* Provides: *An electronic version of the standard Business Periodicals Index with references from most major English-language business magazines concerned with marketing, economics, industry, and finance.*

Dun's Market Identifiers

Files from: *Yearly reports* Supplier: *Dun's Marketing Services* Provides: *Basic information from public records on virtually every U.S. business with more than ten employees. A variety of services, including* Standard & Poor's, *provides a wealth of information in varying degrees of detail on U.S. companies, private and public.*

PTS databases

Files from: *1972* Supplier: *Predicasts* Provides: *A family of databases whose individual files index information on worldwide business literature. Individual databases include:* PTS U.S. Forecast; PTS New Product Announcements; PTS Mars *(advertising and marketing);* PTS International Forecasts; PTS F&S Indexes *(company, product, and industry information including information on mergers and acquisitions worldwide).*

General Information

Magazine Index

Files from: *1976* Supplier: *Information Access Company* Provides: *Files covering 370 magazines with a wide range of subject matter. Also see* Magazine ASAP, *a holding file for recent articles that are then stored in* Magazine Index.

National Newspaper Index

Files from: *1979* Supplier: *Information Access Company* Provides: *Full coverage of the* New York Times, *the* Wall Street Journal, *and the* Christian Science Monitor.

News Search

Files from: *Updated monthly* Supplier: *Information Access Company* Provides: *A short-term index of stories, articles, and reviews from more than fifteen hundred magazines, journals, and newspapers. Files are placed, at the end of a month, in databases like Magazine ASAP. Holds on a temporary basis files that will be transferred at the end of each month to the* Legal Resource

Index, Management Contents, *and* Trade and Industry Index *databases.*

Government Cendata

Provides: *Demographic and economic information from both the 1980 census and more recent, inter census surveys. Also included is the text of Census Bureau press releases.*

Congressional Record Abstracts

Available from: *1976* Supplier: *Capital Services International* Provides: *Abstracts of the proceedings of the Congressional Record, which is the record of debates and actions by the U.S. Congress. Includes coverage of committee and subcommittee reports, laws, executive communications, speeches, floor debates (including inserted material), data on bills, roll-call votes.*

Federal Register Abstracts

Available from: *1977* Supplier: *Capital Services International* Provides: *Coverage of federal regulatory agency action published in the* Federal Register. *Includes presidential proclamations, executive orders, text of proposed regulations, and compliance requirements and legal notices issued by federal agencies.*

Medicine and Science

Enviroline

Available from: *1971*

Supplier: *Environmental Information Center Provides: Digital version of printed indexes:* Environmental Abstracts *and* Environmental Issues. *Provides abstracts of articles on environmental issues published in government documents, industry reports, conference reports, newspapers, and magazines.*

Medline

Available from: *1966*

Supplier: *U.S. National Library of Medicine*

Provides: *Indexes articles in medical and biomedical sciences from three sources: "Index Medicus", "Index to Dental Literature", and "International Nursing Index". Also offered in a simplified search version with some full-text services through PaperChase (Beth Israel Hospital).*

SciSearch

Available from: *1970*

Supplier: *Institute for Scientific Information*

Provides: *A multidisciplinary database whose references are expanded from those printed in* Science Citation Index. *It covers virtually every journal of both pure and applied sciences.*

Private versus Public Access

The writer, reporter, or researcher needs to be able to describe not only the context of information pertinent to a specific event but also its likely location by database. Then the question arises whether that database's supplier is available either through a gateway subscription or a full service distributor to which the writer or reporter— individually or as a corporate employee— has access. This search is not dissimilar to the print researcher's search through various library systems for a book, journal, or document whose temporary acquisition requires a trek through the hierarchies of library storage.

Contemporary print libraries exist within a hierarchy that provides a rough parallel to the computerized complex of files, databases, suppliers, and distributors. There is the neighborhood library, for example, which carries very general reference materials and popular fiction. It is linked to and can draw on the resources of a city's major library, whose holdings include a far greater number of technical and popular resources. In some systems, the city facility is a subset of the state library system, which links its urban members through a program of interlibrary loans to facilitate the efficient sharing of resources among all members. In addition, state (and sometimes city) libraries may be repositories for official state or federal documents. Use of the system is time-consuming, as all who have waited weeks for an interlibrary loan to be dispatched must know, but addresses the essential issue of allocating, information resources through a huge network.

Parallel to this general public system may be one or more specialized library networks, of which the state or provincial university library is the most important. In both Canada and the United States, university libraries house extensive collections that, in many areas, far exceed the state system's resources. These include specialized collections in law, medicine, engineering, and the sciences, whose holdings may be part of individual colleges or schools within the greater university system. In the United States, private libraries serving specialized needs also exist, often duplicating the holdings of state or university libraries. Thus, in Columbus, Ohio, the federal court's law library largely duplicates, in its holdings, those of Ohio State University's law library. The latter is reserved for the exclusive use of members of the OSU faculty and community while the former is available to the public. In Honolulu, a special medical library is available for the exclusive use of state physicians while the University of Hawaii's library holdings on medical topics (textbook and journal) are available to all state residents.

Today most people take for granted the rather hard-won notion of general access through this interlocking library system to a range of public information. Both the right to and the necessity for citizen access to these print storage resources are assumed, in terms of both public documents and general research tools. Private libraries are no longer a critical part of the printed information storage system, although in Sam Johnson's day they were the critical repository, especially when the private library belonged to the royal family. In contrast, in this early phase of development, electronically stored information is at present squarely in private hands. The history of the printing revolution suggests that this may be a transient phase in the development of digitalized information resources. Just as books stored in public libraries became part of the communal knowledge system at no direct cost to the user, so, too, electronic databases will eventually enter the public domain. The increasing availability through university libraries of computer data stored on disk, the subsidization of interactive databases by specialty libraries, and, finally, the increasing use of computerized storage as a primary means of information access in academia, are all indications of this trend. Experiments in the late 1970s and early 1980s by the French government, which has made computer terminals available at no charge to citizens interested in accessing official information stored digitally, also suggest one way in which this revolution will progress.

Private versus Public Information: United States

In the early 1980s a number of barriers existed that denied the majority of citizens access to computerized information. Chief among these was a lack of the physical equipment (computer and modem) required to go online and an inability to use the equipment appropriately where it was available. Of perhaps equal importance and greater long term importance were the trend to privatization of information by the U.S. government and its insistence that all computerized information, even public records, should be sold-preferably through private corporations. In the 1980s the U.S. government under President Ronald Reagan acted to assure that federal information stored in a digital fashion would be "privatized" and that citizens seeking to access this data could do so only through private vendors. This action, in effect, created the specter of private corporations controlling the dissemination of public information. In addition, federal officials in the 1980s attempted to draw a distinction between the right of public access to printed information and its right to digitalized information. Where citizens had a right under law to the former, the latter, according to officials supervising compliance with the Freedom of Information Act of 1966, was not to be covered by similar guarantees. Public records stored in digitalized form were thus officially removed, despite previous accessibility to their printed form, from the public domain.

The debate over these decisions, which first became public in late 1989, centered around the more than four hundred computerized databases then maintained by the federal government, many of them covering research and general information that, traditionally, had been considered in the public domain. Federal databases cost, at present, between $15 and $30 an hour to use, while privately controlled databases, often based on that same public information, cost between $50 and $100 an hour to access. Examples of the former include the Environmental Protection Agency's *Toxic Release Inventory* (TRI), mandated by the 1986 Super fund law; the

Department of Education's *ERIC* educational resources database; and the National Library of Medicine's *Medlars*, costing, at present, $20 an hour. Examples of private databases of federal information include *Disclosure*'s summaries of SEC 10-K filings, which retail for at least $70 an hour from private suppliers, packagers, and distributors, and the proposed *Edgar* database of other SEC documents, whose projected cost to the public is between $50 and $125 an hour.

The debate on access and the rationale behind this privatization are complicated by the role played by large information and news-oriented corporations – Knight-Ridder is perhaps the most prominent example – that have entered the increasingly lucrative digital information field. As news corporations, they are institutionally committed to the best and most economical systems of information dispersal possible. Their institutional goal (and the basis of their First Amendment protection) is based on public access to information. The news professional's institutional role as guardian of the public's right to information would be meaningless were the professionals and their employers also dedicated to the limited access of data in any form.

But as providers of those privatized records through their digitalized information services, companies like Knight Ridder (which owns both Dialog and Vu/Text) have a vested interested in maintaining and increasing private corporate control of digitalized information – whatever the source. Their agents – the reporters and editors who supposedly prepare the news while free of restraints – are thus in an unenviable position of having to question the corporate position and uphold their institutional goals (and perhaps thus jeopardizing their functional goals) or refrain from entering the debate. While the debate is, at this writing, focused on the storage and retrieval of public documents, the issue will probably become one of general public access to all digitalized records and the degree of accessibility that will be guaranteed to the public.

As governments and private corporations both move to computerized filing and storage of documents, public records and documents in general will be increasingly accessible only to those with the ability to access required data by computer. Experiments have already begun at various levels in North America to assure public access to official records and information. Thus, in the province of British Columbia, officials in 1989 were making available on an experimental basis many computerized, digitalized records to news organizations and concerned citizens with computer and modem. In 1990 citizens of Hawaii with access to computers were being urged to use a local number to access the state legislature's daily calendar to check on the status of bills coming to the floor or committee. In addition, the U.S. Supreme Court's Project Hermes and electronic bulletin boards run by various federal departments provide another indication of the degree to which access to information-either at cost or at a premium— will increasingly be defined by the individual's access to computer technologies.

Just as public libraries were born to assure general public access to books, journals, and magazines printed and sold for profit by private companies, one suspects that the resolution of issues concerning access to digitalized information will require an equal assertion of the right of the public to both its own records and to official files in general. Public libraries grew out of a need not only to address the storage needs of a progressively massive volume of printed information, but to guarantee that access to information was not limited by privilege or class. It has been noted that some university libraries have begun to allocate some of their resources to assure that faculty and students have access to computerized data in a variety of fields. In this way, the library retains its role as purveyor of information irrespective of the mode of storage, and the concept of public access is asserted. One may assume that, although currently unusual, this policy will become generally accepted and that with public access, attempts will be made to lower the cost of electronic services through reassertion of the public nature of federal records (and thus the necessity of their dissemination at cost) and through market forces that assure that individual databases may be offered by a variety of distributors. In the short term, issues of control may create a conflict among corporate officials serving information companies that simultaneously act as suppliers of a variety of information types and as public representatives of the Fourth Estate, which, at least in theory, is a guardian of public information. In the long run, such a system (as production increases and the market becomes saturated) would retrace the steps that have brought about the print-oriented public information system many now take for granted.

Conclusion

Digital information storage systems provide an interlocking and to some degree hierarchical resource whose data can be used by popular writers (whatever the medium) to consider critically the statements of traditional news sources. The organization of this data matches, in some ways, the search phrases used to address the data in toto. Just as the online researcher must define a problem or topic in such a way that appropriate references will be retrieved, so, too, must that search phrase be addressed to an appropriate information packager or producer.

Within the current division of newsroom labor among librarian, reporter, and editor, there is disagreement about what information is pertinent and about control of available online libraries. An issue of "how much" should be searched, "where" information should be sought, and "what" is appropriate is a function of both appropriate phrasing of any particular problem and knowing the general resources available through online subscription services. At present there are three levels of data vendors offering a wide array of information, much of which may also be accessed in printed form. Individual suppliers, like WestLaw, offer specific services directly to the subscriber; packagers make available the products of a number of suppliers for the researcher whose information product needs are both consistent and broad. Finally, gateway distributors make available on a fee for-use basis the services of more specific packagers as well as informal information sources.

These categories are not hard and fast. A supplier may offer subscribers a link to the resources of one or more packagers, and it is possible that a packager may have links to specific services also provided by the gateway distributor. By describing menu and screen systems on a gateway distributor, available systems accessing the widest array of packagers have been discussed. These "user friendly" mechanisms allow even neophytes to gain control of their own data search and offer one way in which the control of information can be shared between the electronic resource's librarian gatekeeper and the client writer or researcher.

The overlap and repetition of service of current vendors are a result of the youth of the industry and disjunction created by the rapidly changing nature of a new, swiftly advancing technology controlled by private corporations in an evolving market. Because of the rapid changes in this industry and the almost certain assumption that new vendors will emerge as older ones disappear, change, or merge, the emphasis in this chapter has been on the broadest possible classifications and not on the currently available services of any single company. While it is clear that the digital storage of information will become increasingly common during the 1990s, the structure of corporate access is not yet defined. Indeed, the public's right to information stored in digital form will be as critical an issue in the coming years as the potential these resources may provide to writers or researchers in any specific segment of society.

Because digitally stored information is not yet free to the public through a system of government-supported libraries, issues of cost are as critical today as those of technical ability to access electronically stored information. Understanding the potential of an online database to provide critical information is of no value if the writer or researcher cannot afford to access the data. Thus the argument returns full circle to the relation between economic priorities in society and the institutional goal of news and public information corporations to provide appropriate information to its clients and society at large.

Bibliography

Altschull Herbert, *J. From Milton to McLuhan: The Ideas Behind American Journalism* . White Plains, N.Y.: Longman, 1990.

Barthes Roland. *The Eiffel Tower and Other Mythologies* . New York: Hill and Wang, 1979.

Bate W. Jackson. *Samuel Johnson* . New York: Harcourt, Brace, Jovanovich, 1975.

Brodeur Paul. *Currents of Death: Power Lines, Computer Terminals and the Attempt to Cover Up Their Threat to Your Health* . New York: Simon and Schuster, 1989.

Brooks Brian S., Kennedy; George, Moen; Daryl R., Ranly, Don; *News Reporting and Writing* , 3d ed. New York: St. Martin's Press, 1988.

Chomsky Noam. *Necessary Illusions* . Toronto: CBC Enterprises, 1988.

Crosby Harry H., and Bond George R. *The McLuhan Explosion: A Casebook on Marshall McLuhan and Understanding Media* . New York: American Book Co., 1968.

Cuadra-Elser Staff. *Online Databases in the Medical and Life Sciences* . Santa Monica, Cal.: Cuadra Publications, 1987.

Davis N. M., and Cohen M. R. *Medication Errors: Cause and Prevention.* Philadelphia: George F. Stickley, 1981.

Diamond, Edwin. *The Last Days of Television.* Cambridge, Mass: MIT Press, 1982.

Dranton Robert. *The Business of Enlightenment: A Publishing History of the "Encyclopedie"* 1775- 1800. Cambridge, Mass.: Harvard University Press, 1979.

Eisenstein Elizabeth. *The Printing Press as an Agent of Change*. 2 vols. Cambridge: Cambridge University Press, 1979.

Epstein Edward J. *Between Fact and Fiction: The Problem of Journalism*. New York: Vintage Books, 1974.

Financial Sourcebooks Staff. *Online Sources: A Step-by-Step Guide to Access and Using Business and Financial Databases*. New York: Financial Sourcebooks, 1988.

Garfinkel H. *Studies in Ethnomethodology*. Englewood Cliffs, N.J.: Prentice Hall, 1967.

Glossbrenner Alfred. *The Complete Handbook of Personal Computer Communications*. New York: Brody, 1985.

Hage Per, and Harary Frank. *Structural Models in Anthropology*. Cambridge: Cambridge University Press, 1983.

Herman Edward S., and Chomsky Noam. *Manufacturing Consent: The Political Economy of the Mass Media*. New York: Pantheon, 1988.

Hill George Birkeck. *Boswell's Life of Johnson*. 6 vols. New York: Harper and Brothers, 1891.

Inlander Charles B.; Levin Lowell S.; and Weiner E. *Medicine on Trial: The Appalling Story of Medical Ineptitude and the Arrogance That Overlooks It*. New York: Pantheon Books: 1988.

Jacobstein Myron J. *Legal Research Illustrated*. Mineola, N.Y.: Foundation Press, 1987.

Johnston R. J. *Philosophy and Human Geography: An Introduction to Contemporary Approaches*. 2d ed. London: Edward Arnold, 1986.

Keane John. *Public Life and Late Capitalism*. New York: Cambridge University Press, 1984.

Kernan Alvin. *Printing Technology, Letters, and Samuel Johnson*. Princeton: Princeton University Press, 1987.

Koch Tom. *The News as Myth: Fact and Context in Journalism*. Westport, Conn.: Greenwood Press, 1990.

Lapham Lewis P. *Money and Class in America*. New York: Ballantine Books, 1988.

Leighton Joseph. *The Individual and the Social Order*. New York: Appleton, 1926.

Ley David. *The Black Inner City as Frontier Outpost: Images and Behavior of a Philadelphia Neighborhood*, Washington D.C., : American Association of Geographers, 1974.

Liebling A. J. *The Press*. New York: Pantheon Books, 1981.

Lippmann Walter. *Public Opinion*. New York: Free Press, 1965

Lyons Louis, ed. *Reporting the News*. Cambridge, Mass.: Belknap Press, 1965.

Manoff Robert Karl, and Schudson Michael, eds. *Reading the News*. New York: Pantheon, 1986.

McLuhan Marshall. *The Gutenberg Galaxy: The Making of Typographic Man*. Toronto: University of Toronto Press, 1962.

Prichard Peter S. *The Making of McPaper: The Inside Story of USA Today*. New York: St. Martin's Press, 1987.

Rachline Allan. *News as Hegemonic Reality*. New York: Praeger, 1988.

Ross Steven S. *Construction Disasters: Design Failures, Causes, and Prevention*. New York: McGraw-Hill, 1984.

Sontag Susan, ed. *A Barthes Reader*. New York: Hill and Wang, 1982.

Ullmann John, and Honeyman Steve, eds. *The Reporter's Handbook*. New York: St. Martin's Press, 1983.

Wain John. *Samuel Johnson: A Biography*. New York: Viking Press, 1974.

White Alan. *Truth*. New York: Anchor/Doubleday, 1970.

Wosik John F. *The Electronic Business Information Sourcebook*. New York: John F. Wiley and Sons, 1987.

INDEX